ART OF
//MAKING MARKS

25 years of Wacom pen/tablet technology. The past, present and future of the pressure sensitive pen based computer input device, its adaptive and creative uses in the arts and design industry, and its wider range of application beyond.

Author: Ric Holland

| Sponsored by:
Wacom

Art of Making Marks
ISBN: 978-988-99591-7-3
Sponsored by
Wacom Company Limited

2009 First Edition
Published by Systems Design Limited
The Publisher of IdN Magazine
4/F Jonsim Place, 228 Queen's Road East
Wanchai, Hong Kong
T: +852 2528 5744
F: +852 2529 1296
E: info@idnworld.com
W: www.idnworld.com

© 2009 Ric Holland/Systems Design Limited. All rights reserved. No part of this book may be reproduced or transmitted in any form or by any means, electronically or mechanical, without the prior written consent of the publisher. All artworks are copyright 2009 by the credited artists, their representative or copyright holders. Every effort has been made to ensure the credits and contact details listed are correct, however, if any errors have occurred the editors and publisher disclaim any liability and respectfully direct people to the website www.artofwa.com for any updated information or corrections.

Author/Editor: Ric Holland
Publisher: Systems Design Limited
Editorial Assistance: Sabine Mende
Production Assistance: Izumi Tosa, Heidi Thurner and Mig Holland

Contact information:
www.wacom.com
artofwa@wacom.com

This book is sponsored by:

wacom

Special thanks to: Laurence Ng, John Derry, Dr Phillip George, Masahiko Yamada, Shigeki Komiyama, Noboru Fujisaki, David Spencer, Stefan Kirmse, Han Stoffels, Scott Rawlings and many more people throughout Wacom, you know who you are, thanks for your support and encouragement.

Technical and Web Support:
Brendan Holland, Ryan Farrow - Coconut Graphics

Transcription Services:
Su Pollard -Smart Docs Pty Ltd

Cover images by the following artists –
Ron Cobb, John Derry, Nick Pill,
Steve Stamatiadis, Matt Taylor, Man Qin,
David Davidson, Fernanda Cohen,
Evan Shipard, Lok Jansen,
Raziman Baharudin, Robin Preston,
Saul Zanolari, Yongkiat Karnchanapayap & Onuma Chintanasathit, Jean-Luc Touillon,
Waheed Nasir.

//MAKING
DIGITAL
MARKS...→

IT CAN START WITH JUST A DOT

THEN THE DOT BECOMES A LINE
A Line can be considered in two ways. The linear marks made with a pen or brush or the edge created when two shapes meet.

ALL LINES HAVE DIRECTION
Horizontal, Vertical or Oblique. Horizontal suggests calmness, stability and tranquillity. Vertical gives a feeling of balance, formality and alertness. Oblique suggests movement and action.

LINES CAN BE EXPRESSIVE
Movement and action can be expressed by using pressure and tilt to control the variation of width, shade and character of a line.

JOIN SEVERAL LINES, AND WE HAVE A SHAPE
A shape is a self contained defined area of geometric or organic form. A positive shape in a painting automatically creates a negative shape.

THEN WE THINK ABOUT THE SIZE WE GIVE TO THE SHAPE
Size is simply the relationship of the area occupied by one shape to that of another.

AND WE GIVE IT SOME COLOUR
Colour, Hue, Value, Tone, Texture....

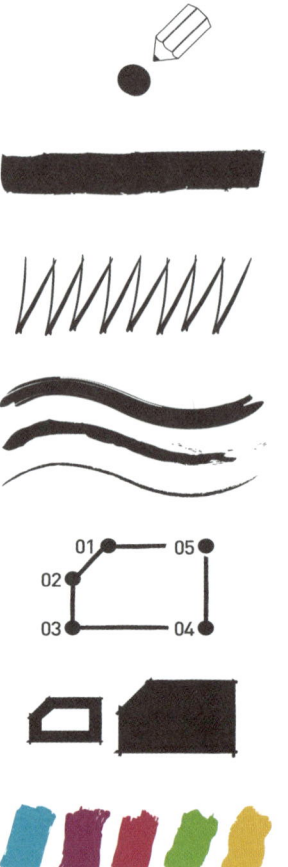

SO THERE WE HAVE SOME BASICS OF MAKING DIGITAL MARKS.

But then there is still... the Art of Making Marks.
A topic that has been explored, refined and perfected by many in this book and yet maybe we all have only just begun if we look to the future of digital mark making.

With a global explosion in the production and consumption of digital images, photos, music, interactive games and video content we have become immersed in our digital lifestyles.

Amongst a host of devices such as mobile phones, MP3 players, digital cameras and computers of all shapes and sizes, sits a range of tools from Wacom called pressure sensitive pen/tablets and screen tablets.

These humble digital tools enable millions of people all around the world to write, draw, paint, create and interact with computer devices, creatively and intuitively.

This book endeavours to showcase some of the world's foremost digital pioneers and creative innovators who use these digital tools to make their expressive marks. It will inform you about the history of digital mark making and provide some useful insights and inspiration from the close up and personal perspective of people who are passionate about creativity and love what they do.

Whether or not you are a creative professional, a dedicated enthusiast, a student or you have never even heard of making expressive use of Wacom pressure sensitive pen/tablets, this book will open your mind to the creative professional's best-kept secret.

// INTRODUCTION
author Ric Holland

Welcome to Art of Making Marks, a comprehensive history of expressive digital mark making, told through many conversations I have had with Industry Pioneers and Creative Innovators - people who I believe have made significant contributions to the development of technologies and creative techniques, and have helped form the digital creative industries we recognise today. Read about the early introductions of pen/tablets from Wacom's President and CEO **Masahiko Yamada**, and early partner technologies like Quantel's Paintbox systems and the introduction of PC based image manipulation software that got it all started back then and also take away rare insights on possible future computing technologies. Journey with pioneers **John Derry**, **Mark Zimmer** and **Tom Hedge** who developed Fractal Design Painter. John Derry weaves a story of art and technology development in a way that only John can. **Russell Brown** the Creative Director of Adobe since it's early beginnings shows his humorous side and serious depth of knowledge to bring us up to the present state of play. Be taken behind the scenes through my interviews with **Keshen Teo**, designer of Wacom's new branding while at Wolff Olins agency and **Jeremy Sutton,** who gives us his views as a portrait painter crossing back and forth between traditional painting and digital tools. Be inspired and excited by some future visions from **Bill Buxton** who pioneered the concept of multi-touch user interfaces and was chief scientist at Alias. Now with Microsoft, he is behind exciting developments with Surface technology and Tablet PCs. **Duncan Brinsmead** a chief scientist at Autodesk, developed 'Brushes' in Maya and he continues to push the creative boundaries in CG (Computer Graphics) for the benefit of movie audiences around the globe.

The chapter on Creative Innovators presents a series of interviews I have had with people like **Ron Cobb** to name just one more amazing person to read about in this book, representative of his creative professional field 'Concept Art'. The diagram on the contents page might help to illustrate the creative professional world. Note the lines are blurred as everything now is connected digitally and people cross over from one field to the other in their everyday job tasks.

So my gratitude goes out to all those Industry Pioneers and Creative Innovators who made this book possible with their unique and insightful interviews. It surely is my great pleasure indeed to know them all. Many of the beautiful images in this book come from top professionals in their fields. However I would like to point out that creativity is for everyone and a Wacom pen/tablet is just a device to help break down any creative barriers to self expression, letting loose a primal human urge to make expressive marks to illustrate emotion, communicate ideas or just as often as not to have fun. Wacom pen/tablets for me have always been the link between man and machine for all creative disciplines and now even for not so creative industries like medicine, finance, geology, construction, etc, and so the list has actually become endless. Maybe that's my next book! Don't take my word for it though - please read on and let these stories inspire you to pursue your creative dreams, thus creating your own digital style in life. The Showcase towards the back of this book highlights my point by mixing up Professional, Semi Professional and Amateur art works done by artists and designers from different parts of the world and diverse cultural backgrounds. You can find extended content and interviews at my blog site www.artofwa.com - look for the URL addresses throughout the book.

Just so you have a little background knowledge about me, most recently I have been working as a full time employee with Wacom but have spent many more years working as an Artist/Illustrator, Graphic Designer, Art Director and Creative Director using Wacom pen/tablets along with a host of technologies. I was traditionally trained in commercial art and graphic design in the late 70s and then as the tide of digital technologies rolled in through the 80s and 90s I just kept soaking it all up and pushed the technology to achieve the results that fuelled my 25 year long design career. I ran my own design business Extreme Digital through most of the 80s and 90s. Joined MetaCreations Corporation before their melt down and then was hired as Creative Director for IBM's e-Business Innovation Centres in Asia Pacific before the Dot Com bubble burst. Since then I've continued to enjoy a rich and diverse career in digital media consulting and teaching but with always more to learn. Drawing and painting is still in my blood and so working at Wacom has been satisfying my desire to get back to those roots. Art of Making Marks is also the title of my PhD Thesis I intend to complete over the next couple of years. Email me at artofwa@wacom.com if you would like to comment or contribute. My intention is to delve even deeper into the concept of expressive mark making, starting from the early cave paintings and progressing through time to show how expressive mark making techniques have evolved with the way humans communicate and illustrate concepts. I will document the refinement of various tools to capture expressive hand motions from people with highly developed motor skills and how that has then been translated into the digital tools of today. I pose the question, have we reached the point where it's just as natural to be expressive with digital tools as it is with physical art tools and techniques? My goal with this particular book, Art of Making Marks is to lay down some foundations on which you can draw your own conclusions, opening up your senses to many new creative possibilities.

RIC HOLLAND
Wacom
web: www.wacom.com
blog: www.artofwa.com

this page + previous page:

**Yongkiat Karnchanapayap &
Onuma Chintanasathit** //Bangkok
http://www.PictoVerse.com

* view more information and content from this artist on www.artofwa.com

 Art Of Making Marks

// CONTENTS

- ○ 25 years of Wacom: Time Line — p.010
- ● About how it all started: Masahiko Yamada - Wacom President and CEO — p.016
- ● The story behind Wacom's branding: Keshen Teo - Creative Director at Pajama/Wolff Olins — p.020
- ● From the eye of a portrait painter: Jeremy Sutton — p.026

- ● Industry Pioneers
  - John Derry — p.033
  - Russell Brown — p.049
  - Douglas Olson — p.056
  - Bill Buxton — p.058
  - Duncan Brinsmead — p.063

- ● Creative Innovators — p.066

  design
  - p.087 Ken Lambert
  - p.089 Gerry Haggerty
  - p.091 Allan Macdonald
  - p.095 Tin&Ed

  photography
  - p.098 Julieanne Kost
  - p.102 Dr. Phillip George
  - p.104 Richard Luxton
  - p.111 Ted Blore

  video/audio productions
  - p.117 Bryn Farrelly
  - p.120 Craig Calhoun

  visual effects
  - p.125 Steve Rosewell
  - p.130 Julian Tytney Taylor
  - p.133 Nigel Allen

  animation
  - p.135 Matt Taylor
  - p.138 Cindy Bower

  art
  - p.067 Ron Cobb
  - p.073 Nick Pill
  - p.077 Marco Nero
  - p.081 Jake Hempson
  - p.086 Steve Stamatiadis

- ● Wacom showcase — p.139

25 YEARS OF WACOM

1984
- WT series, first commerial graphics tablet with cordless input device

1983   1984   1985   198

25 years of Wacom

1983
- Foundation Wacom Co. Ltd., Japan

---

technology elsewhere & other advances

1975
- First "real" digital camera (Eastman Kodak) using CCD image sensor (Fairchild), took 23 seconds to save an image, weighted app. 4KG

1981
- Quantel Paintbox creates the market for video graphics and later the industry standard

1983
- Microsoft Word 1.0 released for MS-DOS

1984
- Apple Macintosh launched - first micro computer with graphics user interface (GUI)

1985
- DTP introduced - key players Apple, Adobe, Aldus, Linotype

---

in the film industry

- The Last Starfighter - one of cinema's earliest films to use extensive Computer-generated imagery (CGI) for special effects.

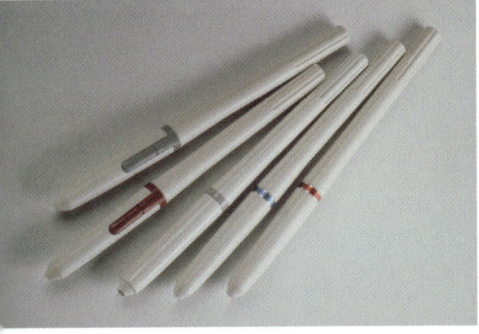
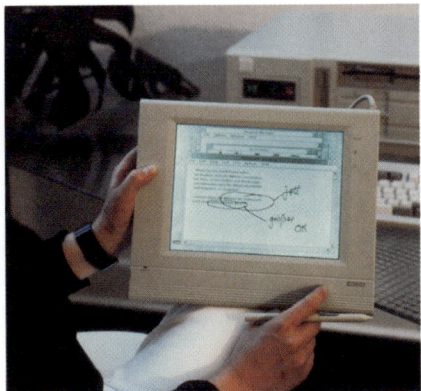

1992
• First large LCD Tablet (PL-100V) for direct pen-on-screen input launched, 9.4" inch display with 640x480 pixel resolution, VGA, 16 gray shades
• PenTop, pen computer launched
• UD-series, first multi-mode tablet for two handed-input

1991
• First Wacom tablet driver for Macintosh supporting pressure sensitivity

1987
• SD series, first graphics tablet with cordless, battery-free, pressure sensitive pen

1988
• Meeting Staff - electronic blackboard launched

1987   1988   1989   1990   1991   1992

1988
• Foundation Wacom Computer Systems GmbH, now Wacom Europe GmbH (EHQ)

1991
• Foundation Wacom Technology Corporation in Vancouver (HQ America)

1987
• Adobe Illustrator 1.1 shipped for Macintosh

1988
• QuarkXPress debuts for Macintosh

1989
• First Color Post Script Printer
• Corel Draw for Windows debuts
• Intel 486 Chip released
• Nintendo Game Boy - handheld video game console

1991
• Adobe Photoshop 1.0 launched - professional industry standard for digital image editing and creation
• AOL launched - internet service provider for consumers
• Apple introduces Quicktime

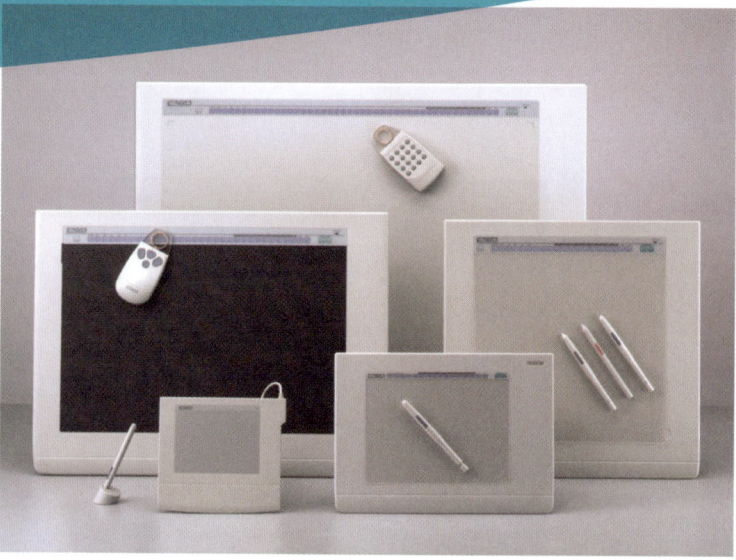

1993
• PL-200 TFT colour LCD display (9.4inch) for direct pen input, VGA resolution 640x480 pixels, VGA, 256 colours

1994
• ArtPad, world's smallest pressure sensitive pen tablet

1995
• ArtPad II/UltraPad series (with added eraser)

1996
• PL-300 interactive pen display with colour LCD (10.4 inch) with SVGA resolution with 800 x 600 pixel and 18 bit colour

1993   1994   1995   1996

1995
• Established tie-up with Autodesk to develop next generation of PC CAD software

• Ninteio handwritten hanji recognition software launched

1996
• US President Clinton signs communications reform bill using Wacom electronic pen

• Internet home page set up (http://www.wacom.co.jp)

1993
• Fractal Design Painter v 1.0
• World Wide Web is launched
• Portable Document Format (PDF) launched
• Adobe After Effects 1.0 release
• Adobe Photoshop 7.0 includes a new brush engine with extensive support for Wacom pen tablets.

1994
• Microsoft releases Windows NT.
• Internet has 25M users
• First Playstation (Sony) for video games launched in Japan
• Bluetooth research begins
• Microsoft acquires Softimage

1995
• Adobe aquires Aldus
• Microsoft releases Windows 1995
• Yahoo domain was created

1996
• WWW has 18Mio pages
• Macromedia Flash
• Maxon Cinema 4D v.4 released for Windows, Alpha NT and Macintosh
• Autodesk 3ds max (formerly 3D Studio Max) a modeling, animation and rendering programme - v 1.0 released

• Jurassic Park (Universal Studios) – Landmark in the use of computer-generated imagery

• The Lion King (Disney)

• Toy Story (Disney/Pixar) – The first feature-length film created completely using computer-generated imagery.

 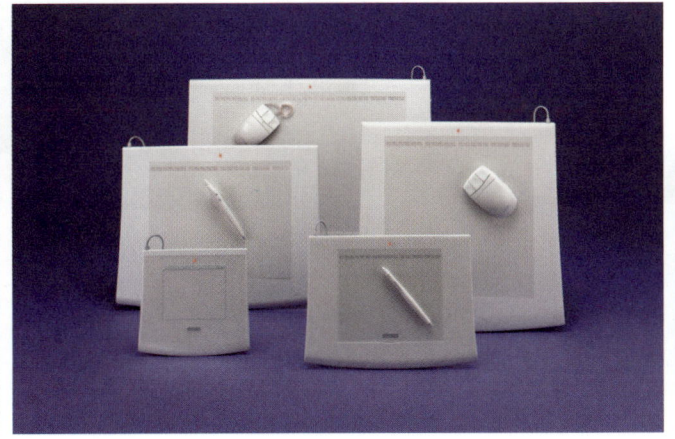  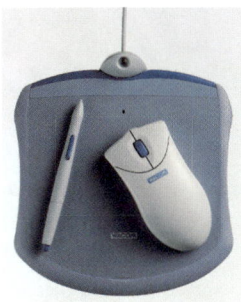

1998
- PL-400 interactive pen display (13.3 inch) with XGA resolution, 1024x768 pixels and 24 bit colour
- Intuos Graphics Tablet System, series for professional users Airbrush, 4D Mouse, Tool ID

1999
- Graphire Mouse & Pen Set (FAVO) - consumer tablet launched;
- Intuos comes with USB connection

1997   1998   1999   2000

1997
- Pen-Tools tilt-and pressure sensitive Adobe Photoshop compatible plug-ins

2000
- Wacom China Corporation established (now subsidary)

10-year history of developing pressure-sensitive pen technology; over 60 applications across PC, Mac and SGI platforms supporting the Wacom pen standard

1997
- Steve Jobs returns to Apple
- Macromedia Flash 1.0
- Windows overtakes Macintosh
- MetaCreations - merger of MetaTools and Fractal Design (Ray Dream)
- Google.com was registered

1998
- DVDs became the new standard for consumer video, replacing VHS tapes
- Apple iMac (in bondi Blue) - all-in-one-Macintosh
- Alias|Wavefront ships Maya 1.0 for Windows; a high-end 3D computer graphics and 3D modeling software package

2000
- Dot-com bubble burst
- Corel buys MetaCreations
- Apple introduces OSX
- Maxon BodyPaint 3D as an integrated version for CINEMA 4D and standalone version for other 3D packages.

- Titanic (Fox/Paramount)
- A Bug's Life (Disney/ Pixar)
- Star Wars Episode I (Fox) – First film of a trilogy including special effects

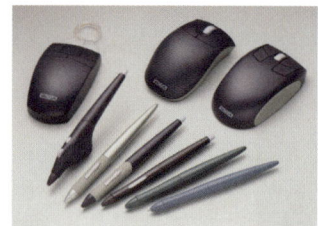

2001
- Cintiq 15X Interactive Pen Display with XGA resolution, 1024 x 768 pixel, 24 bit colour, USB connection
- Graphire2 Mouse & Pen Set in Steel Blue aimed at the digital world of home computing
- Intuos2 comes in new 'midnite' colour scheme - 8 input devices on option

2002
Wacom tablets with USB connection (PenPartner, Graphire/Graphire2, Intuos/Intuos2, PL-500 and Cintiq range) will run under Mac OS 10.2 and support Inkwell's handwriting recognition.
- Cintiq 18SX interactive pen display - 18.1 inch format LCD with continuously adjustable angle and rotation

2003
- Graphire3 consumer product line for photo and video editing

2004
- Intuos3 - avanced technology and ground-breaking design

2001   2002   2003   2004

2001
- Wacom displays pressure-sensitive pen sensor for Tablet PCs; low-cost, low-power embedded sensor technology will bring handwriting capabilities to next generation PCs (W8001)

2002
- The new Fujitsu Siemens Computer Tablet PC with Wacom's Penabled™ technology will be officially launched on 7 November 2002, simultaneously with the announcement of Microsoft's XP Tablet PC Edition.

2003
- Listed on Japan Securities Dealers Association (JASDAQ)

2004
- Wacom® Penabled™ technology features in HP Compaq Tablet PC 1100
- launches single chip Solution "W8002" to improve mobile phone usability and speed new application adoption

2001
- Apple iPod launched
- Apple iTunes launched

2002
- Intel ships 3GhZ Pentium4 Chip
- CD-ROM

2003
- Mobile Phone users reach 1.52 billion

- Shrek (DreamWorks) – Computer animated film
- Monster, Inc. (Disney/Pixar)
- Harry Potter and the Philoshoper's Stone (Warner Bros.)
- The Lord of the Rings trilogy starts (New Line) - huge amount of special effects included

- Ice Age (Fox)

- Finding Nemo (Disney/Pixar)
- The Matrix (Warner Bros.) – First live-action film to be released simultaneously in regular and IMAX theatres

2005
- Cintiq 21UX interactive pen display launched, setting new standards for digital pen-based imaging
- Graphire Bluetooth - Wacom first wireless pen tablet for Mac and PC
- Intuos3 A5 Wide - trend of wide screen monitors and laptops
- Graphire4 consumer pen tablets for digital photography, features ExpressKeys and scroll wheel

2006
- Favo "Hello Kitty Editon" limited ediotion launched in Japan

2007
- Prototype of Signature LCD tablet presented at CeBIT
- Bamboo range of consumer tablets launched, Bamboo provides an enhanced and creative way of using computers at home or work.
- Cintiq 12WX - first hybrid product combining the advantages of a Cintiq interactive pen display with the portability and compact size of an Intuos3 pen tablet.

2005 | 2006 | 2007 | 2008

2005
- Listed on the first section of the Tokyo Stock Exchange

2007
- Wacom launches new brand to express a new strategic direction for the business, developing new tools for creative professionals and expanding the offer to a wider consumer audience.

2008
- New interface technology called RRFC touch technology launched - enabling operations using both pressure sensitive electronic pen and finger directly on the screen
- Wacom enhances the Bamboo experience; Additional opportunities for communication, personalisation and creativity plus increased Web 2.0 interaction
- IKEA Germany chooses Wacom's Signature Tablet STU-500 to reduce costs and paperwork
- Intuos3 launches into outer space; and is used for Research in the International Space Station

2005
- Adobe aquires Macromedia

2006
- Autodesk acquires Alias

2007
- Microsoft launches Windows Vista
- Autodesk released version 1.07 of Mudbox (before Skymatter), a 3D sculpting tool
- Apple iPhones - entry in the cellular mobile phone market

- Ratatouille (Disney/Pixar)

- Wall-E (Pixar) – Computer-animated-science fiction-romance film

About How It All Started
Masahiko Yamada
Wacom's President & CEO

Back in 1983 we were just a very small company. The IT industry was at an embryotic stage and within a year or so the PC came to be a potential platform for the future, but no one knew what it could do. So we started with the micro processor as the basis for pen/tablets to work on. Then we began to realise that eventually people would see pen/tablets as an expressive device like traditional pen and paper. This was a very far out vision, but we already saw the pen as a very important element. Looking at it in those days the only interface devices were the keyboard and the mouse, which was still only just about to be announced. We thought that these devices were probably not good enough for people to express themselves with, so that's how we started with the computer pen from a very early stage.

So the idea of using a computer as if it's not just a computing device was very fundamental to our thinking. If technology is presented as only just hardware that forces people to learn how to use it then that defeats the real purpose, because a tool is just a tool and shouldn't limit or over-shadow the creativity of people. That's why we basically focused everything on developing the pen.

We had started producing the first cordless pen/tablet but with a battery powered pen in 1984. It hit a performance limit pretty soon due to its technology limitations. This brings us up to the 1987/88 time frame. Two or three years after we had started the company, we realised that our EMR® (Electro-Magnetic Resonance) technology enabled higher performance, battery free pens and multiple levels of pressure reporting. We put that into a product and announced it in 1987. Right after that Quantel saw it and they approached us to see if we could provide them with an OEM product. Quantel was our first corporate customer and soon after that or almost at the same time in parallel Shimaseiki a company in Japan known for textile design systems also wanted to use our pen/tablet technology. Those two companies were large customers for us in the early days.

ARTIST JEREMY SUTTON WORKING ON A PORTRAIT FOR WACOM'S PRESIDENT AND CEO, MASAHIKO YAMADA

In 1987 we started to see if we could use pressure technology in 'off the shelf' PC based computer graphics applications. In 1988 we took the product to the US and showed our technology in a very small trade show booth. We also saw that there was no one actually writing any applications for pen pressure input technology and we decided to do something to promote the idea. We found a very small Macintosh based black and white application called Pressure Paint which was probably the first one of its type ever sold. The pressure capability worked 100% for us and we took it around to various US software companies.

That's when we met Mark Zimmer right after he had finished working at Letraset on ColorStudio. He got the idea very quickly and began to use our first pen/tablet as a basis for writing Fractal Design Painter. So what he brought to the market was revolutionary and very much in line with the notion of simulating natural media. People could now work in a way that was natural and intuitive for them. And so Painter became a big hit, also the packaging was great, being an actual paint can and because it was very simple and said what it did. Everyone enjoyed using it and so it was a great success.

Now the market had split into a vertical market for the high end professional, with systems like Quantel and then there was a horizontal market for products like Photoshop and Painter and all the follow up products since. Between the early to mid 90s those two products really drove the market and were the launching pad for our business.

"THIS IS THE DIRECTION WE ARE TAKING NOW AND WE WILL SEE HOW THAT PLAYS OUT IN THE WAY THE COMPUTER INDUSTRY DOES BUSINESS IN THE FUTURE..."

In the mid to late 90s as well as 2D graphics applications, more and more 3D applications were introduced into the market and this is when Bill Buxton at Alias began to really show his muscle. Bill was at Alias for a long time as chief scientist and interface researcher whose concepts had begun to impact the industry. I think it started from Maya in a real sense. Before that Bill had done a lot of study papers and presented at many conferences, and really is a guru in new interface concepts and products, but until Maya came about all those concepts in my opinion were a little bit like a dream. This is when Alias started to understand his ideas and began to put them into their applications.

Alias Studio Paint came before Maya and is really a very powerful engine itself and the interface was very nicely done, so Maya I think took some part of that heritage. Of course Maya itself is not used for the auto design industry but some of the concepts behind it made a very interesting link between 3D and simple 2D painting. That's what I believe was another breakthrough for our market.

It takes a long time to really incorporate new user interface concepts and improvements into software products because they have already covered the market and have to provide many features for the industry such as ease of use and intuitiveness, combined with powerful computing capabilities and all nicely packed into a seamless product. Probably there is another generation of product line that Autodesk now have to develop. So today they have their legacy human interface, but in the future who knows what they're going to come up with for the next generation human interface experience in their product lines.

MASAHIKO YAMADA

..if we continue to provide innovative solutions for our customers in professional and general markets, then our company will have been worthy of doing business for 25 years and worthy to continue doing business for yet another 25 years.

From the mid 90s the internet began to change the way people did business and that's how we have expanded beyond the professional high end market to design agencies and professionals at home such as freelance artists and web designers. From 2000 we began to see the internet changing into broadband so that it's now almost free to send high resolution images and collaborate remotely. Also the digital camera appeared and that expanded vastly the way people do imaging work. Digital printers became available for low cost and with very fine resolution output.

Those things also began to impact the way people do computing at home, so when you are riding that type of trend, starting from very high end industrialised niche into the wider agencies, freelance and individual user markets of today, you have to look at the entire user base. While we are providing for the professional users, at the same time we are addressing the huge end user demand and expansion coming from the general end user community. And that also impacts the way people see computing, people don't care about what technology is inside the product anymore. Instead they want to see things done simply and more intuitively and that's where they see our value. So Wacom is now taking the challenge of how to get out of this 'technology only' type of company culture to move into more of a 'user interface solutions' culture.

That means we have to understand people first and what they need. No matter if it's for professionals or just general end users, you need to understand people first. We want to assemble or develop technology elements for any situation so our value will shift from a technology provider to a solution provider. That's where we see pen, touch and display products and technologies including optics and colours becoming much more important in coming years than what we have seen before. Wacom we believe will continue to provide very advanced solutions to the professional artist and designer communities, however also in addition to that we want to expand the business base, solution base and technology base to a broader market so that eventually people don't even notice what they're using is a computer. We want to make it so intuitive that people carry it around as if they are carrying pen and paper.

This is the direction we are taking now and we will see how that plays out in the way the computer industry does business in the future. I'm really quite happy that we had a very lucky situation in the past and what we provided as products changed the way people do their work. So if we continue to provide innovative solutions for our customers in professional and general markets, then our company will have been worthy of doing business for 25 years and worthy to continue doing business for yet another 25 years.

Looking 25 years out into the future I think computer products and computer technology will become really just like air conditioners and general appliances of today and so people won't notice the information flowing. All communication will be in real time anywhere you go, whatever you do you can be connected at all times and not disrupt your privacy or efficiency. Computers and technology will become real life supporting tools, but not in a way to control or disrupt the way people live and enjoy life. So we don't know if we are making pens in 25 years and we don't even know if there will be any big name companies still out there at that time when hardware has become just navigation devices or interactive tools and software has becomes just services. So we are seeing huge changes in the industry coming and it will continue on through. Eventually people wouldn't talk about computers anymore. I don't really know what lies up ahead, who knows, but I do know it's likely to be very exciting for all of us.

ARTIST JEREMY SUTTON WORKING ON A PORTRAIT OF WACOM'S PRESIDENT AND CEO, MASAHIKO YAMADA

Art of Making Marks

THE STORY BEHIND WACOM'S BRANDING FROM THE BRAND DESIGNER HIMSELF
Interview with **KESHEN TEO**
Creative Director and Founder: PAJAMA
Creative Director: Wolff Olins (while on Wacom re-branding project)

Ric Welcome to the art of making marks and thank you for joining us. Could you please introduce yourself and tell us some of your thoughts about developing great brands and how you developed the new Wacom mark?

Keshen I'm Keshen Teo, founder of the business Pajama. When asked to look at the branding for Wacom, I was deeply excited because I had always used Wacom products. Wacom came to me by accident some years earlier because I was playing with the software application called Painter as I was always interested in painting. When I tried using a Wacom pen/tablet I thought that it was just an amazing product. Suddenly I was able to paint on the computer and I was able to make changes that I couldn't do when I was using real paint and so I was very excited. When looking at the issues that Wacom face now and in the future I could see that clearly their technology is moving into all sorts of new areas, and possibly even beyond the pen. Therefore I thought that it's important for Wacom to think about future technologies in terms of the five senses. How will people enjoy technology in the future and create things using their five senses? So that was the starting point and because of the pleasure that I got from using my Wacom pen/tablet. It almost felt to me as though I could smell the paint while creating the sensation of making something real. I decided that the notion of embracing the five senses is important. When it came to actually creating the symbol I didn't want it to be about paint technology necessarily but something that encompasses that notion of using the five senses and also of breaking boundaries. Allowing people to break boundaries and for the organisation to do the same as well, reaching out to different kinds of experiences, so be it touch or even smell and taste. But that's maybe just looking way ahead.

So the symbol I thought wants to express the excitement one gets from the product. It's almost a child like excitement from using a Wacom pen/tablet. You just have to say wow, I really want to do something amazing with this. So that kind of child like excitement is part of it and there's also a little history about being in Japan that inspired me. I spent about seven or eight years working in Japan on and off, and I was inspired by the use of images that looked a bit child like. Perhaps in the Western world, people want things to look quite clean and professional looking but I was very keen to make something that may even be viewed as slightly jarring and not quite so clean cut. So in a way it's not like the Apple symbol, and I wasn't trying to create a smart looking 'swoosh' but something jarring, breaking through and looking a bit like a human being saying 'Wow it's an amazing day!' kind of thing.

I wanted something that had a certain raw energy that could live in different worlds. I think that this brand has to live in different worlds, whether it's sci-fi or painted worlds, or the world of just writing love letters, or the world of enjoying different kinds of experiences. So it's about reaching out through all your senses so that you can feel more through this, you can see more through this, and you will want to make your special moments through this.

Ric The mark you came up with can tell many stories. It bounces around, it's noisy, it's friendly. When I saw it for the first time, and having been very closely connected to the original Wacom logo, took me a little while to embrace. However it came to life for me when I saw it animated. The character in it you describe, expressing itself in various worlds, caught in a frozen moment brought it to life for me as being fluid and alive.

Keshen It has a certain kind of 'Manga' DNA in it, although it doesn't need to have eyes and a nose and a face on it. I think sublimely I was inspired by some of the things I've seen in Japan. I'm just so fascinated by how people in Japan like whimsical, silly things that often mock life. The Salary Man for instance, where the Salary Man does push-ups, and it mocks the traditional stereotype. I don't know who buys the toys and for whom, but it just looks very funny to me. The 'Lazy Panda' which kind of stacks up together and it can just flop down. I like the way people think of forms as tactile and interactive, as if these things have real gravity, you didn't just draw them like they are perfect Disney toys, but these things have real emotions, whether it's sloppy, whether it's lazy, angry, etc.

Ric So the world can have an effect on them just as it does with us.

Keshen Yes, and these toys have all those full emotions, it's like we don't have to make toys anymore which are just perfect and sweet and just for children. So that in a way kind of inspired me to make something that had some rawness, and encompasses emotions. I was quite keen that there was a Japanese feel to it, which actually forms a lot of my inspiration. I knew that if I drew from that inspiration I would make something that at least you're going to say what is this and be slightly uncomfortable with it at first. In a way it's a good thing to make something that people will sit up and notice and not say well that's just another nice clean corporate logo which looks like it fits in with all the other technology brands, a clean and smart looking 'swoosh'.

Ric Please explain your views on branding and describe to us your process in arriving at this mark?

I think a successful brand needs to start with a strong idea. I think the idea then needs to impact on the internal culture of the organisation. It should impact on the way you communicate, it should impact on the way you think about your products, and it should impact on the way you think about your environments. So I think in a sense a brand is holistic, and if you have a strong idea, then your idea will inspire change in the organisation.

Brands have to be simple for people to get it, and it has to be true. It has to be true in a sense that it needs to inspire real actions. It has to inspire people internally to do what feels right and good for the company. Equally it has to be true for the people using it, to feel that it wasn't just marketing and that they deliver on the promise. The product IS actually amazing. So what you project is this exciting image. The exciting world of Bamboo needs to be real to the person using it and that you don't get a kind of disconnect to say 'But actually it's not what it says on the tin!' So I think it's important to be truthful, and to focus on the quality of a product. And I think what's good about the Wacom product is that I think it's always delivered on its promise. So the brand carries the excitement and the promise of quality and the actual product needs to deliver that excitement and the promise of quality as well.

Part of the challenge for many brands is to work with good partners and the right partners. Sometimes partners may not help you to deliver, and may actually affect the way people see your brand. A classic example is Apple Computer. Occasionally it blames Sony for overheating problems or something but I think Apple is a strong brand in that even with technical glitches it gets through it fine. It builds a very strong relationship and loyalty with its customers. That loyalty is on so many fronts, it's just the whole aura of the brand and the philosophy of the brand and that is so deep. I think everybody gets it that there 'is' an Apple philosophy. That brand essence is what people understand and I think that people will forgive you occasionally. Brands, companies are like human beings, we make mistakes. So I think that when it comes down to partnerships, and partnerships actually not delivering for you, it's even more important therefore that you have a brand that's rooted in meaning and philosophy that people understand and really like to engage with. So that when you make mistakes, because there will be times where there are some technical glitches, people forgive you. You then say sorry and here's a little something back. That's why I think it's important to build a brand holistically, to think in terms of its values and its meaning, and that you build a strong relationship with your customers, and so they stick with you.

So brand isn't just for the sake of tarting-up or updating yourself, although a lot of companies do think in terms of that. They might think they are slightly out of date and need to upgrade their look. I think if a brand is really true and strong, it will inspire people to change. What I feel about Wacom is that there is a lot of appetite for change and there is a lot of appetite to embrace the holistic concept of pushing the boundaries of interface, so that people can make better use of technology to create things, to enjoy things, to have fun, and to do things which are interesting and fun. Therefore Wacom needs a strong idea that will inspire them to innovate further and to push the boundaries and so on.

Ric OK, so what about the public's engagement with the brand, from a public point of view what is the perception?

Keshen Well first of all I see the brand as something that needs to inspire people to change, to do more to innovate. Equally it should encourage and inspire them to do more and to go further. Actually in terms of the current Wacom products at the moment, they do actually push people to go further, and enable people to break through on their everyday tasks and to go a bit further with it. So I think that sense of being able to inspire people, go further and to break through works both internally and externally. I think it's important to see the brand as something which has the same message both inside and outside, pushing people internally to go further, to find new ways to innovate with better products, and inspiring users to do more with it, to have more fun, or to push their work to a higher level.

Ric In the process of unearthing the requirements and hidden knowledge, delving deep into Wacom as an organisation and its various components – what was that journey like for you? You would have been aware of Wacom obviously from a customer point of view, and maybe you had a limited view from within the organisation at the beginning, but then of course the branding process takes you down into the gunnels of an organisation, to come back out with a holistic view. Are there any interesting stories that you'd like to share with us from that journey?

Keshen I think Wacom is truly a global company, in the sense that we'll sit down and decide what Bamboo looks like and what the packaging looks like with all the country representatives present, so everyone brings their own point of view to the table. I witnessed collaboration on a multinational front, which is interesting for me. I think every market has their own taste and issues, and every market presents different views. Our task was to then take on all those views and distil them without compromising. When you listen to a lot of views you can compromise the views and actually come up with something which looks like it didn't go as far as you want it to. Some markets want it blue when another market wants it orange. I think in the end we managed to get a very good working relationship with all the markets together, and I enjoyed that it was a very lively debate and everybody was able to speak their mind – I think that's a good thing.

Ric Is there a bit of a flavour of that also in the concept of the logo?

Keshen No, actually the logo wasn't done in an 'everyone speak their mind thing'. We presented three routes with a lot of options, and then I presented the case for the final design and said why this is different from the other three routes. I think then everybody bought the argument, and I think most importantly they understood the challenge that Wacom faces, and how the world is very different now, and what are the future challenges for Wacom. Because of all that they went for this solution. The argument was clear and simple and it wasn't about saying why wasn't it going to be a butterfly or a frog; we did have a frog at one stage. And so then it becomes clear that this is the right thing. A much more difficult thing was actually deciding on the packaging. Packaging is a very market-focussed exercise – every market has their own requirements but in terms of the branding process, I think that's been quite simple. Deciding on the word Bamboo was much more complex. It was a complex process of deciding whether it is a good name or not. It was a huge debate about whether it is the right name, and different markets thought very differently about it.

Ric Also the challenge of getting a name you could actually use globally without copyright registration issues.

Keshen Yes exactly, what we could register. But you know my inspiration on Bamboo was from the Chinese character Bamboo. The word bamboo is part of the word pen – bamboo is the original pen, because the first pen was a bamboo stick with hairs on it making it a brush. Therefore the word 'pen' is the word 'bamboo' with the word 'hair' on it and that makes the word pen in Chinese characters. So I quite like the fact that it has the origin of pen, although not many people would know that. I just thought it's quite nice to route it like that and just say Bamboo a new kind of ePen if you like. And also it just doesn't sound like you would expect from a new Wacom product, it doesn't sound so technical. I think it's a very good mainstream proposition name.

Ric It's not a Millennium 3000 or something like that. [laughs]

Keshen Exactly. It hasn't got a number behind it, and it just wants to say 'hey this is really simple to use.' Of course there were many other naming options so that took the longest time to decide.

Ric Please tell us a little bit of history about you and your other projects when you were with Wolff Olins?

Keshen I spent 13 years at Wolff Olins as creative director, and then I founded Pajama three years ago. In that time at Wolff Olins I created the brand for Unilever; I created a brand for a country called Liechtenstein.

Ric Wow, you branded a country?

Keshen Yes I branded a country.

Ric Are you an honoured guest if you ever go there?

Keshen Yes, some of the people still remember me. I met the prime minister and yeah it is a very sweet and nice country. And I've also branded a mobile phone operator in Spain and most of South America; Telenor, which is another mobile phone brand in Norway, Sweden, Denmark, Pakistan, Bangladesh, and some eastern European countries, over 13 countries. So those are some of the bigger brands that I have created.

Ric Is your approach similar each time when you engage in the branding process? Do you work with each organisation in different ways?

Keshen Well the process is always through a series of interviews. It's actually through talking to them that you try and get their sense of where the company is going. We find a way to then articulate a vision for them that would be challenging. The idea we create needs to be a challenge, it needs to be something that says 'we are here!' A new idea or vision needs to help take the busi-

ness forward. Once you define that idea, you then think about the values that a company has to have in order to move forward which then forms a 'Creative Brief' that says how we will express that for them. And so in doing that process we make sure whatever we end up with has buy in from the people, and there's an understanding that this represents where the company is going. If you didn't go through that process, it's easy for somebody at the end of the day to say actually it doesn't feel right, because the company has not been through the intellectual argument to say why are we doing this in the first place, and what does it help us to achieve.

So yes it's the engagement with the people in the company that is very important. Sometimes we even talk all throughout the organisation, so that we don't miss any points of view, which may not be from management. What the people think who are actually selling the products or who are making the products as well. So in the case of Unilever we asked the people in the factories who make the products how they thought and feel about the brand.

So a process of engagement is most important. And then I guess listening to everyone, and then playing it back to them, and saying have I encapsulated your ambition, your vision, well enough, and then when you present your creative solution, where is the linkage and how does it marry their vision.

Ric Just going back to the new Wacom mark for a minute how do you see it evolving over time? I want to play with it and animate it in interesting ways. [laughs]

Keshen Yes, you know I think it's interesting to think about what qualities this thing should have. Should it grow up and down? Should it have soft movements? I don't know! [laughs] You know what I'd really like to see is it in different environments. I actually would like to see it in an environment that it feels odd in. Because of the creative field that it sits in mostly, it should sit in any world, and actually have different behavior since it is truly about the five senses. Yes I think it should have the ability to behave very differently in different circumstances. I think it's about also the stretch of what it can do. Actually I think as a toy like thing I see it living in different virtual environments so we would like people to explore it very differently and I think that's part of the adventure of the way we see this thing evolving and so it should have the flexibility to have different characteristics.

Ric Keshen thank you for being part of the Art of Making Marks. It's a great pleasure talking to you.

"OPEN UP. SENSE MORE."

FROM THE EYE OF A PORTRAIT PAINTER / JEREMY SUTTON

JEREMY SUTTON TALKS ABOUT HIS BEGINNINGS AS A TRADITIONAL PAINTER AND TRANSITION TO EMBRACING THE DIGITAL MEDIA

Ric Welcome to the Art of Making Marks. Please introduce yourself, tell us who you are and what do you do?

Jeremy My name is Jeremy Sutton and I'm a professional artist using digital technology as part of my mark making toolbox. My artistic roots are grounded in many years of drawing. Drawing informs all my art, no matter what media I use. My painting process is expressive and improvised. While being in control of my mark making tools, I let go of over-controlling my process, embracing serendipity and flowing with the unfolding paint. When painting a portrait I strive to capture the essence of my subject. In sharing a little insight to my approach to portraiture and the impact of digital technology on my life, I'd like to give you some background to my creative journey.

JEREMY SUTTON

The very first time I painted a portrait on the computer I was just amazed at how intuitive it was and how it flowed just as easily as my traditional media. I expected the technology to get in the way but once I understood the interface it was great... I was using a Wacom pen/tablet with a Macintosh computer and I was just blown away at the ease of flowing with it, just as if I was working with my traditional crayons.

IMAGINATIVE BEGINNINGS

My journey into the world of making marks started over forty years ago when I began drawing wherever I could, covering my bedroom walls as far as I could reach with impromptu frescos of people and assorted animals. Throughout my childhood I loved to draw from my imagination. In 1979, when I was eighteen, while studying Physics at Pembroke College, Oxford University, I started to keep a sketchbook with me at all times, drawing whatever I saw around me, particularly people. I fell in love with sketching from life and for the following twelve years filled up many thousands of sketchbook pages. I started attending life drawing classes at the Ruskin School of Drawing and Fine Art, as well as experimenting with print-making, sculpture and photography.

DR. JEKYLL AND MR. HYDE

After graduating I started a career selling scientific research instruments. While travelling wide and far to places like India, and moving to live in the Netherlands, I kept up my art, leading a 'Dr. Jekyll and Mr. Hyde' existence of scientific salesman by day, and artist by night! I broke through my fear of colour by painting a colossal colourful portrait of Albert Einstein. Up until this time my drawings had all been tonally based, with a limited colour range. I was amazed to observe that the wilder the combinations of colours I used, the more interesting and evocative my portraits became. Oil pastels became my main drawing medium. My first one-man show in the US, in Gordon Biersch Brewery Restaurant in Palo Alto in 1989, was an exhibition of oil pastel portraits on 24" x 30" Arches fine art paper.

THE WONDERFUL NEW WORLD OF DIGITAL PAINTING

My first computer was a PET Commodore in 1978 or so, on which I programmed simple games (using magnetic tape for storage). No art on that machine! Although I had made a crude portrait sketch using a Computer Aided Design program and mouse in the mid '80s, my real introduction to digital painting was in 1991, while drawing a live portrait at a party in Woodside, California, someone came up and said "That's great! You should meet a friend of mine who makes painting software." The rest is history, as they say. Clare Barry of SuperMac sat me down at her Macintosh computer with a Wacom pen/tablet and SuperMac PixelPaint Pro software and I made my first live full colour digital portrait. I was immediately hooked! I knew that this was a medium I had to explore. Within weeks I was painting live digital portraits on the Wacom booth at the SIGGRAPH conference in Las Vegas. I seamlessly adapted to the new digital medium, applying the same approach to portraiture as I had when working with pastels on paper, building up my paintings with quick, loose brush strokes, changing the colour continually and intuitively. Early on I could see some powerful and unique advantages of working with digital media. One of the most dramatic was the ability to record and playback the evolution of my paintings, sharing the process of how they developed, brush stroke by stroke.

AHOY! ALL SPEED AHEAD...

By 1994, a crowded field of competing paint programs had narrowed down to just one stand out: Fractal Design Painter. By this time I had secured my Green Card, painted a live digital portrait of Virgin CEO Richard Branson on the Virgin Atlantic San Francisco Inaugural, and chosen to become a full time artist. I continued to explore the exciting possibilities opened up by digital media, extending traditional techniques such as collage, chin collé and image transfers that I had previously used on paper, to my digital canvas, creating collage portraits such as the one shown here of former San Francisco Mayor Joseph Alioto.

THE SYNERGY OF DIGITAL PHOTOGRAPHY AND PAINTER

In the latter half of the '90s I received an email out of the blue from Jane Conner-ziser asking if she could learn Painter from me. Jane subsequently invited me to teach with her at various Professional Photography schools and share the platform with her at a Professional Photographers of America convention. Consequently I have been actively involved in teaching professional portrait photographers for the last ten years or so, and that, in turn, has led to my own re-introduction into photography, and my use of it as a basis for creating some of my paintings. Photography has been the perfect vehicle for bringing together my passions for dance and art. Through photography I can capture the fleeting moment as two people relate on the dance floor, and then I transform that captured moment into an expressive painting. The example shown here, Moment in Time, is a portrait inspired by two professional Argentine Tango dancers, Christy Coté and Darren Lees. Digital photography and Painter are natural partners in - creativity. The possibilities are limitless. I see Painter as just one step in my creative process—I print onto canvas and then apply acrylic paint and a variety of other non-digital media. I stretch and frame my completed portraits, treating them as one would traditional oil paintings. The end result is artwork that integrates digital and non-digital paint into one unified whole.

Ric How did you come to do Wacom's President and CEO, Masahiko Yamada's portrait?

Jeremy I met Yamada-san in Portland at Wacom's 25th anniversary party with the launch of Wacom's new branding and Bamboo product line. I had the pleasure of talking to him then and was asked if I could come over to Japan and paint his portrait. I landed in Tokyo and went straight to his offices. By that stage it was in the evening and he very kindly cleared some time and we sat down at the Cintiq 21UX in his office. I ended up spending a couple of hours with him and did the digital portrait which was a wonderful experience. We had a lot of fun and he was very animated. At the end of the evening he insisted on giving me a ride back to my hotel, even though it meant going out of his way and delaying his own journey home. I was just so bowled over by his making the effort to accompany me back to my hotel and by his incredibly warm and touching hospitality.

Ric That's fantastic. Mr Yamada seems to me to be a man who is just honestly inspired and interested in creativity.

Jeremy Yes he's certainly full of joy and enthusiasm and on top of all this he gave me a gift before I left the country and got me some special Japanese edible treats and things. You know, he's just like someone who really takes personal attention and appreciation. It takes time and thoughtfulness to do that even though he's an incredibly busy person.

Ric When you were doing his portrait what did you guys talk about, politics, the weather?

Jeremy [laughs] He told me the story of the origins of Wacom which was very interesting and the desire to be able to do Kanji on computer for the newspapers in those days. It all started in Tokyo with a couple of engineers. They were trying to work out a way to do Kanji with their computers and that's where they developed the first technology for the Wacom Tablets. Actually a friend of mine, Sarah Moate is a very respected Zen calligrapher in Tokyo. She was an artist I knew from Oxford when I was there and she actually gave a Zen calligraphy demonstration at my workshop in Oxford last summer. But it was interesting because what she is doing with Zen calligraphy in some sense relates to the origins of what the Wacom pen/tablet was originally created for, which was allowing basically a calligraphic, Japanese calligraphic expression to be done through digital means. I learnt from her the traditional way with ink and a brush and there is a lot of very interesting parallels in the way that I work with the pen/tablet and the way that she works with the Zen Brush! Anyway it was just a really nice experience spending some time with Mr Yamada.

Ric How long did the portrait take?

Jeremy In total it took probably a couple of hours but that is just the actual live sitting part. He sat for me for a couple of hours and then I went back to America with the digital file, printed it out on canvas and then continued work on it with traditional acrylic paints.

Ric Would you call this painting typical of your signature style?

Jeremy In some sense that would be for you to judge rather than for me to say. If you look through my work I'd say yes, and yet it's not that I try to do any style, I just express myself how I feel I can express myself. Sometimes that's very colourfully and sometimes it's not so colourfully. The picture of the tango dancers is a fairly muted colour palette and the portrait of Mr Yamada is fairly colourful.

Ric Is all of this happening on the spot from the point of view of your colour palette? Is it coming from the person's personality or is it more of a visual representation of what you see?

Jeremy It's a culmination of everything. It's definitely happening on the spot as you refer to it. The way that I approach my painting is very spontaneous, intuitive and improvisational. My process is about 'tuning' into my subject and then letting it flow. I'm trying to be as free as I can and let it flow rather than being over-controlled, tight and trying to get everything precise. I actually start off almost abstract and this applies whether I work from a photo reference or from life. I do love drawing from a live subject more than anything else. I have to say, there's no substitute for what happens in a live sitting, drawing from direct observation. The colour choice is very much an intuitive reaction to the person, to how I feel about them, their personality, and their character combined with the ambience and the energy – it's a whole combination of all of the above.

Ric You're like a jazz musician but in a different medium using the Cintiq as your instrument.

Jeremy Exactly! It really is like jamming with the music. The colours come out in a way that has structure, but yet is very free and improvisational. Jazz musicians have structure and they do things which are spontaneous within that structure. My structure as I paint a portrait is that I'm really working with tone and form all the time so my colours reflect that.

I have one thing to say about the portrait painting process and you asked me earlier what did Mr Yamada and I chat about. Actually when I did the portrait, most of the time we were not talking and in fact that's an important aspect of what happens in a live portrait setting. Both myself and the subject enter a zone or a state of being at a level that's not just to do with everyday chit chat. I just ask for people to be relaxed, be themselves, look at me and to ignore everything else. I then enter that zone myself where I'm completely focused on the painting process and completely engaged with them and so there's no need to talk. Most of the painting process was actually conducted in silence.

Ric Obviously you've done this using traditional media for a long time, going into the 'zone' you refer to. Do you find that using digital tools allows the creative flow to occur easier? So you don't have to stop and muck around with different materials or have issues with getting the right colours mixed or whatever. Do you find that using the digital tools allows that zone to be more fluid?

Jeremy That's a very, very good question – Well let me just think how I would answer that – I've drawn all my life and I have really focused on portraiture and drawing for many, many years before I ever touched a computer. I would get into the zone and flow with my pastels and my crayons and my paint in traditional media when I'm drawing a portrait. I have certain colours at my fingertips and I would use one colour and work with that crayon and then change to another, so I would flow with that but there are certain limitations about how

I would work with the materials. Now the very first time I painted a portrait on the computer I was just amazed at how intuitive it was and how it flowed just as easily as my traditional media. I expected the technology to get in the way but once I understood the interface it was great. As I mentioned earlier the first program I used was PixelPaint Pro produced by SuperMac. I was using a Wacom pen/tablet with a Macintosh computer and I was just blown away at the ease of flowing with it just as if I was working with my traditional crayons. Over time Painter has developed and now there's literally hundreds and hundreds of brushes. I have my custom brushes and in an instant switch from 'Jeremy's Mish-Mash Scumble' brush to 'Modern Art in a Can' brush, to the Sergeant Brush, to the Impressionist Brush and in 24 million colours, all in a matter of seconds. There is certainly an incredible speed and versatility to working digitally that surpasses traditional media to a certain extent. There are pros and cons for both. I can work on the computer, do something relatively quickly and efficiently and print out a 40 inch x 60 inch canvas. If I was to paint that same scale of painting with traditional paints, firstly I couldn't have got the same effects, and secondly it would have taken me a lot longer. So there's definitely an advantage in speed. On the other hand there are effects that I get from using traditional paints and materials on the canvas which I can't get on the computer. So as I said pros and cons for both ways and I wouldn't want to be without either.

Ric Do you feel that people don't regard as highly the digital output and the work that's gone into it as much as they would say for a traditional painting or sketch. Is there a perception difference?

Jeremy First of all there's really a couple of questions behind your one question. If I was to just show a finished work of art which was just the computer print as it came off the printer and put it up on the wall it would look like some sort of a flat image on canvas. It would look like a reproduction of something, a print, and so it

"GO FOR IT!

As I create every portrait I challenge myself to take risks and be bold. I encourage you to do the same, to be true to yourself and make marks for yourself. Wishing you joy and strength in your mark making!"

wouldn't communicate – it would look like a reproduction of a painting or a print. It wouldn't necessarily communicate that this is a valuable original work of art. So it's not communicating what I want it to communicate. I think it's only when I work on the digital print with traditional paint that it starts to come to life as an original painting, an original piece of fine art. So I don't put on my wall something that is just a print from a digital printer. I don't engage my audience with something where they're going to look at it and say well that doesn't look like a painting, what is it? I would say the same thing and so I'm not happy with that. In terms of the more general aspect of your question, if people hear that it's involving digital, do they associate that with not so much artistic talent required or skill, time and effort then I think that largely there's still a lot of misunderstanding. People don't understand that working with programs like Painter, you're really painting and I think that there's this misconception that anything that's done with a computer is easy for example that you can edit it. One of the concepts that I teach and I do for myself is that I never undo, so I don't edit. If I'm working with paint I just keep painting and that's one of the things I always encourage my students to do as a painter. If you're designing on the computer then editing is fantastic but if you're a painter and you're engaged in a painting process, then move forward just like you would with traditional media and continue moving forward and then you get a much more interesting landscape on your canvas, much more organic and much richer.

Ric So you're building up the complexity?

Jeremy Exactly and as soon as you undo you take that complexity away. There's just as much commitment for me in painting digitally as there is painting traditionally. I am just as committed to every brush stroke.

Ric Have we already reached the point where it's just as natural to express yourself with a digital mark making tool as it is with a physical mark making tool?

Jeremy Absolutely yes, there's no doubt in my mind about it. I go between those two spheres all the time with every commissioned piece I do and every final piece of artwork I'm producing. 90% are involving digital painting and then traditional painting on the canvas and I'm going between the two all the time. I have more power and freedom with computer paint than with using non-computer paint.

At the end of the day what I really want to produce is a wonderful, beautiful, powerful piece of artwork. It's not something you can just walk past. To do that, no matter how wonderful I feel about the digital painting, I am not satisfied with what prints out on the canvas, it looks flat. It still doesn't have what it takes to be a painting for me. So for me the printing is only half way through the creative journey. I always want to work further onto my prints with traditional paints.

Ric How do you find the difference as a visual artist between using a Wacom Intuos3 versus a Wacom Cintiq?

Jeremy Another very good question. In my studio I use every tablet there is almost. My assistant uses a Bamboo, she loves it and then I've got Intuos3 - 6 x 8, 6 x 11 and I use the 12 x 19 Intuos3 with my 30 inch Apple Cinema display, that's my workhorse. So when I'm sitting down to do a portrait or you know working on a really major large collage that's my favourite place to sit. If I'm working on a photo reference piece and not drawing in a live sitting then I would use the Intuos3 - 12 x 19, you can't beat that, it's comfortable, it's easy – it's really, really good. I like the comfort of having my arm and hand very relaxed on the table while having a good posture for my neck as I look straight ahead at my monitor.

The portability with the the Intuos3 - 6 x 8 is fantastic. When I'm traveling it goes with me everywhere. Having said how much I love using the Intuos3 range of pen/tablets, I also want to share what I love about using the Cintiq range of professional screen tablets. Cintiqs for me have very specific uses and I love using them in certain situations. For instance, I love doing live portraiture with the Cintiq. It's the best. You can see that in the shots of Yamada san featured earlier in this book, how the Cintiq 21UX allowed me to have direct contact with my subject. I'm not putting a screen between me and my subject and the Cintiq sits down low so it's just like a sketch pad. I've fallen in love with the Cintiq 12WX for my travelling, teaching and presentations. Whenever I go around the world and I give a lecture or a talk anywhere I want to have that Cintiq 12WX in front of me which takes me away from the podium. It get's me out from behind the table and puts me right in contact with the audience. I have a little stand for my 12WX and that's all I need. I use those express keys and the touch strips so that I don't need to keep going back and forth to the computer. I love it. There's no substitute for it and for anybody who does teaching or presenting it's a must have.

Ric If you could ask Wacom for a new tool or an innovation in pen/tablets that you've always wanted, what would it be?

Jeremy OK so if you've seen my stage performances then you would understand why I would like a screen of some kind or tablet 4 foot by 6 foot. Something really big that could be used in performance art and that I could do really large hand and body movements with. I know that there's things where you have whiteboards and you write on and it and translates to the computer, I'm aware that there's technology getting towards that but if I could paint digitally with pressure, I would love it as a performer.

Ric OK, a nice big surface to work on but do you want to be able to work with multiple pens at once? Would you like to be able to use your hand to manipulate the image to, say for instance smudge and draw?

Jeremy Oh that would be amazing, the answer is yes, yes, yes – I would love to be able to work with two pens, one in each hand and be able to paint with two different, for instance variants in Painter, at the same time. I would love that of course, that's going to take a bit of work on Corel Painter's side as well as on Wacom's side.

Ric It usually does, but then the combination of hardware and software development together is very powerful.

Jeremy Exactly, so the answer is yes, I would love that. Also if there was a possibility down the road to be able to do finger painting and literally choose variants and then apply them with one's fingers, or even the flat of your hand. Different ways to apply and make marks, which of course gets back to your thesis title for your book. The Art of Marking Marks, I would love more ways to make marks and different types of marks.

Ric Fantastic. Jeremy it's been a pleasure having you on the Art of Making Marks. If there are any last things that you'd like to add please do and thank you again for your interview.

Jeremy I have one historical thing to share with you and your audience before I go. It's really interesting hearing you talk about the whole history of mark making and how you see Wacom fitting into that evolution. A few weeks ago I was teaching a class called the Great Gatsby Impressionist Workshop and giving a little overview of impressionism and the history. What's fascinating and the more I research into it, the more fascinating the parallels are, is that when you look back at what was happening in the 19th Century, there was basically a quiet revolution happening with the art materials available at the artists fingertips. The old oil paints and the method of the old masters based on these oil suspensions were suddenly not available in the 19th Century for the artist. So this old master style of painting was becoming actually more and more difficult to achieve with the physical paints that the colour men of the time were producing. There was such a revolution going on in chemistry through the weaving industry so they were looking at how to expand their range of colours to compete with fabrics from the time. Soon they were producing all these new chemical colours. The colour men were trying to produce paints that could last longer and that could be more transportable and all of this was happening in the early part of the 19th Century. By the time you had the Monets and the Renoirs and the people of the impressionist movement, they had at their fingertips all these paints with brighter colours and a wider range of colours. They were portable, they could pick them out and they didn't need varnishes, unlike oils where some of them never even dried. These paints would dry faster, they were still oil paints, but they dried faster, they didn't need varnishes and so it opened up a whole new set of possibilities which they grabbed and explored and it made me think of moving forward to the 20th Century to acrylic paint which was frowned upon in the 1960s as not being a valid paint medium for creating 'real art'.

Fast forward to the early 90s, late 80s and then suddenly you have this confluence of technology which allows digital painting. Until the early 90s we didn't really have a combination of the computer power with software with the Wacom technology really and you needed all three. Any two of those wouldn't have been good enough to do what a fine artist needs to do in paint. But all three came together and so that launched the whole new medium of paint which I've been enjoying ever since.

So coming back to the relevance to your book and what I do as an artist, is that the medium of digital paint for me is a fantastic medium but it is just another medium and I look at it that way and I use it that way. An artist or anyone who wants to express something will express it with whatever the tool is at their fingertips and whether it's finger paint, digital paint or arranging stones on a beach, they will express themselves in whatever means they have.

I'd just like to thank the whole Wacom team for everything that they've done and contributed to allowing artists like myself to have an incredibly powerful medium to work with, which would not be possible without the Wacom pen/tablet.

→ THE INDUSTRY PIONEERS

▪	John Derry	p.033
▪	Russell Brown	p.049
▪	Douglas Olson	p.056
▪	Bill Buxton	p.058
▪	Duncan Brinsmead	p.063

I ALWAYS FELT LIKE WE WERE TRYING TO BE REPECTFUL TO THE TRADITIONS OF EXPRESSIVE MARK-MAKING TOOLS

SEE EXTRA CONTENT ON www.artofwa.com

INDUSTRY PIONEER:

:JOHN DERRY

// CO-AUTHOR OF
FRACTAL DESIGN/METACREATIONS/COREL PAINTER

Ric Welcome to the Art of Making Marks. John, you were a traditionally trained artist before you started developing and working with digital mark-making tools. Tell us what you saw back then in the early days of working with computers that caught your interest.

John I always felt like we were trying to be respectful to the traditions of expressive mark-making tools, so that they retained all of the same character and richness, but what the computer adds to the mix is that in the digital realm it's a much more malleable medium and by that I mean it encourages experimentation. You can undo your last action and turn on or off a layer. I call these things 'safety nets' and just to know that you have an undo on Painter that goes up to 32 undos back, which means you can do up to 32 strokes. Not that you're going to sit there and count them, but you can do a number of strokes, knowing that you can undo them and in traditional media you can't do that, so you make the stroke you make. Some mediums can be very unforgiving, some other mediums, well, okay, you have a chance to kind of correct it and fix it a little bit, but the traditional mediums are so much more brittle. You do something and to undo it is generally difficult, if not impossible. On the computer, options like undo and layers just make it so easy to go into the situation knowing that you can try things out because you can do it without fear of permanently changing the work and that, to me, is probably the single greatest contribution that digital painting tools has offered. From the walk-on side of that equation, by preserving all of those expressive qualities that we already know through stylus-based instruments, like paint brushes, charcoal and even a pencil, the medium still expresses the same but there's this new extra assisting structure in place that allows you to just try things out and experiment.

I remember when I first started working on the computer after coming out of that traditional world and let's say, for an example, I'd be in some kind of design problem where by there's a decision between a circle or a square. Your intuition and experience says, "I know it's going to be a square." So you go to square. Then the next decision is, okay, red square or blue square and you go, "I think a red square would be right", and you go with it. When I brought that mentality to the computer I remember the realisation of having the opportunity to go red square or blue circle and even though I thought red circle would be right I could try out blue circle, just to see how it works and damned if it wasn't better and all of a sudden, wow, I'm starting to see possibilities I never would have tried out in the past. There it is, that safety net and it's so overwhelming at first, it just really changes your ability to do things when you realise that you can back up and try different ideas and visualisations.

My first real encounter with digital art tools was back at Time Arts when I worked around the guys that were programming Lumena, which is long gone now, but it was also sort of born out of the same kind of thought process. John Dunn, the guy, the artist programmer that originally created it, his whole idea was to create expressive tools for artists and so he was sort of the mastermind of the program. There were several programmers working on it and the interesting thing I discovered at the time and this isn't necessarily across the board, but these programmers kind of hung around in their area. I noticed that they tended to write and work on the code to get a tool working, but as soon as they got it working they would say, "Okay, it's done. I'm onto the next thing", and for me it was like, gosh, the thing I would want to do now is pick up that tool and use it and experience it and figure out what kind of expressive qualities it had. The thing I learnt was that so many programmers, I mean they have engineering minds, what they tend to think about is that the art and craft is in the code itself. It's like architecture. How elegantly can they write this code? How few lines can they use to make a tool do something? How tightly can it be written so that it's fast?

And so their art and craft is kind of - it's like a cathedral. These are the guys that are building the building that is a cathedral, whereas the artists are the people that go into the cathedral and perform music and express their soul and it was just interesting to see that the very people making the tools had a distance from the expressive quality, from the tool itself, but quite interestingly, a lot of people that write code tend to have musical proclivities. Mark Zimmer, for example, Painter's author can write symphonies and software. When you think about it, writing code is very similar to writing music and so there is definitely a crossover there, but a lot of times the crossover stopped there. They weren't interested in using the tool they had created which became my opportunity to work with them, once they had figured it out and said, "Oh, this guy John he is an artist" and I'd say, "Look, I'll try that out. I'm interested to see what it can do" and these guys would come back with, "Oh how does it work John? How does it feel", and so I was able to start feeding back to them what felt good about the tool or how maybe I would want it to be different or better.

This story I've told many times, but is kind of how I got into expressive mark-making software. I had taken a few programming courses, originally thinking I was going to get into the field by learning how to write the tools. I very quickly found out that I'm not a programmer and that I don't have the kind of mentality and mind-set necessary for programming. I'm an artist and that's very different, but it did give me an understanding of how the structure of code works in programming and so the concepts were in place. So I remember one of the early tools that I was exposed to, was when a programmer created what turned out to be an embossing program. It would take an image and make it look like it was in relief or slightly raised. He had it set up so that it had three buttons, being light, medium and strong so that you could get one of three levels of embossing applied to an image. He asked me try it out and then asked, "So John what do you think of it?" Because I knew what was going on under the hood, I was able to say to him, "Well, now, aren't each one of these three buttons attached to what they call variables in programming and so it could be any value?" He said "Oh yeah, exactly", and I said, "Well, here's the thing. As an artist, when you tell me I only have these three choices, I want all the choices in between those three choices, not just those three choices", and that's where I started to kind of push the programmes towards not limiting the choices. I wanted the full spectrum. I want that full range of values available to me, so that I can adjust it to my particular liking. I refer to that as "season to taste." Artists in general all have a different feeling for how much embossing or whatever they want and so this led us to putting more sliders into the interfaces of tools where there was a range of values associated.

Sometimes Painter was actually criticised for this amount of control, because you can open up the brush controls and find dozens and dozens of controls. Every one of those controls gives you a particular control over the way that brush will react, how it's expressing itself or how the hand, through the Wacom pen/tablet, can create an expressive mark and so the downside is, yes, there's lots of controls in there. Of course the upside of it is that you can absolutely, totally control a brush to be expressive in exactly the way you want it to be. I was able to grow up through this sort of software evolution from having very limited choices to being the guy that prodded all the time, saying, "But I want more choices. Can we have more choices?", and that's, I guess, one of the things I have tried to push through all the different engineering teams I have worked with.

I was just on the phone with Mark Zimmer who now works at Apple and I was saying how I'm still making my living with Painter. I never had actually thought of it this way before when he said, "Well, gee, John, if you think about it, basically Painter was custom-programmed for you". When I think about it now I guess that's true. So much of the way Painter works was born out of my requests and so a lot of it, yeah, in a way it was custom programmed for me. Hopefully I represented what many artists would have wanted it to be able to do and so, looking at it now. It just blows me away to see how far people have taken it and without any of our input anymore. People have just picked it up and figured it out.

Ric Well, John, of course, that's why I'm interviewing you for the Art of Making Marks, because in a way it's your fault that we have expressive digital mark-making tools that work in such a wonderful way at all. Tell us a little more about the early days of Painter and where its evolution fitted in with tools like ColorStudio and Photoshop?

John Well, Photoshop timeline-wise, actually I think it came out in 1989 or 1990 and Painter didn't come out until 1991 or 92 and so Photoshop actually was out a little bit ahead of Painter. What was directly competing with Photoshop in that market when it came out was ColorStudio, which was also written by Mark Zimmer and Tom Hedges. Photoshop preceded Painter by a few months and the difference between the two software applications is kind of like the Beta format versus VHS. Beta was actually a better format, but Sony kept it kind of closed while VHS or Phillips, I think it was, had the lesser format quality-wise but it was cheaper and more accessible and so it won out just by being more appealing to the public at large. I think that's a bit similar to what happened between ColorStudio and Photoshop. Letraset being from the world of graphic

arts and prepress, thought of ColorStudio as this very specific tool that would be used in prepress houses and connected to Crossfield scanners and such. So they saw it as a very high-end professional product and so they appropriately priced it as such. I think it was like $3000, so it was priced for a market that wasn't universal, but very specific. So the tools in ColorStudio were great tools, but they were in this high end of the market, whereas the Knoll brothers created Photoshop initially as Thomas Knoll's thesis project, but then shopped it around and it ended up being bought by Adobe as Photoshop. They priced it at I think something like $299 and, even though the tools maybe weren't as precise and as high end as ColorStudio, the price point was the thing that set it apart and just a whole lot of people could get it, whereas ColorStudio was just hobbled by its high price and so the rest is history.

Photoshop took off and ColorStudio just slowly kind of died away, but it was in that same period that one of the tools Mark was working on for ColorStudio was emulating a simple pencil and so, because they were working on ColorStudio, they had a big Crossfield scanner and all this stuff, because Tom was writing drivers for it at the time. Mark scanned some pencil drawings to look at them really closely and try to figure out what do you need to do to emulate a pencil drawing. One of the things he noticed right away was that it's not just the pencil itself, but it's the surface that it's drawing upon and it's the interaction of that lead with an irregular surface that imparts a lot of character into the look of the marks made by the pencil. So that's where he hit upon the whole thing; that he needed to create internal texture that the brushes could be sensitive to and one of the distinguishing characteristics of Painter early on was the fact that it had tools that were sensitive and responded to a virtual texture. Painter came with a whole library of paper textures and by using different textures, even with the same tool, you could make one tool look different based on those textures. It was realised that by the using of pressure sensitive stylus to interact with that virtual surface, the tools responded very much like traditional tools did and the marks made with it were very much the same.

The thing that's probably what I would say a big difference between Photoshop and Painter's internal engines, is that Photoshop was ultimately designed to composite pixels and so, back in the era when there just wasn't enough PC processing power to do nice, smooth airbrush strokes, doing blends and compositing pixels using and doing operations to combine multiple channels or operations of pixels and transparency or different blend modes, whatever, was one way to get around the lack of horsepower. So throughout Photoshop's history I've always thought of it as a compositing engine primarily.

Painter, on the other hand, from day one was created to write pixels to the screen as fast as it could, in an effort to try to overcome the processing limitations and do whatever tricks or cheats you could do to make brush marks seem fast, so that they seemed real time. It wasn't really real time but appeared to be close to real time and so Painter's engine really is kind of a pixel blasting engine that writes pixels to the screen real fast.

So those two different kinds of orientations in the architecture of the products have kind of led them down the paths that they've gone and it certainly wasn't by accident. I mean each product by design was intended to do certain types of computing activities and so Painter just really has excelled at making marks on the screen really fast and then, beyond that, putting in a myriad of different things into that stream from the brush engine, smashing pixels to the screen to do all kinds of interesting expressive sorts of turns and twists to the marks that it makes, whereas Photoshop, if you look at its brush component, it's not bad, but I mean it's only really kind of like Painter version 1 or 2.

I would guess, architecturally, they probably cannot do the same kinds of things that Painter does, with the speed that it does, because architecturally it's so much more built to be a pixel compositing engine and maybe I'm off the mark here, but that's just what I've assessed over the years. It seems like those two orientations give them two very different kinds of things that they each do well, but the good news is, together they're just this amazing broad set of tools, and the fact that Painter can read and write Photoshop format, and you can move the imagery back and forth so easily, is just great.

In the early days I used to hear people complain and say, "If you use this tool or that tool, I wouldn't need to have Photoshop" and I'm sure on the Photoshop side of the tracks they hear the same kind of thing, "If they put this feature in or that, I wouldn't need to have Painter". What's happened in the intervening years is that PC processor speeds are so fast now and machines can easily handle running multiple applications, so that I usually have Photoshop and Painter on at the same time. I no longer have to stop, save the file, quit the application, launch and open it up in the other application. That's all transparent now and so I don't even think of them as separate working environments. It's like your tool box or in your art room you may have Winsor & Newton brushes and you may have Grumbacher brushes and probably two or three brands of paint. I mean you're going to have all these different brands, but in the end they're just tools and you really don't even think of them as specifically as, "Oh this is a Painter tool or this is Photoshop tool." They're just tools and you move to whatever tool does the job best, and so I think the good news is that over the years Painter and Photoshop have become really good, compatible tools and that, to me, there's no competition between them at all. The story that sometimes I hear is, "I wish they would make Painter a plug-in for Photoshop", but for the most part it just seems like they're really nice, compatible tools that occupy and in a few cases overlap, but for the most part they each do what they do best and neither tool tries too strongly to do what the other one does.

Ric Well I guess they are now just part of much bigger production pipelines these days, involving all sorts of applications for editing Vector and Raster files and then there are many more 2D and 3D design and animation tools, music, video, etc. I guess what I'm seeing here though is that the common thread in a lot of cases is the Wacom tablet. John have you noticed that pressure sensitive pen/tablets have become far more relevant with the greatly increased PC processor speeds of today and that it's almost like a renaissance for the pen/tablet? Almost like a forgotten art form lost in time, where once, previous to the PC revolution, multi-million dollar Quantel Paintbox and Kodak Premier systems were the sorts of devices that could actually blast pixels onto the screen quickly enough for real time airbrush retouching and illustration techniques to be developed. On the old PCs we had many work-a-rounds but on all PCs and Laptops today you can paint, draw, and do all of these things with a very high degree of finesse and responsiveness.

Ric With the introduction of innovative new pressure sensitive pen/tablets like the Wacom Cintiq, which allows you to actually work directly on the screen surface instead of getting used to the hand/eye co-ordination required to use conventional pen/tablets, do you think this will help traditional artists start to use digital tools?

John For the traditional artist, yes, but for me the thing that the tablet did originally was that it got my hand out of the way of the image. When you're working with a traditional image, although people have done it for thousands of years without to much difficulty, but the thing that I realised was such a winner for the tablet was that my hand does not get in the way of the drawing. I could totally work without anything occluding any part of the image as I worked and working with the Cintiq, the first thing I notice is that I've got my hand in the way. It really messes me up because I'm so used to not having my hands in the way, so I guess I'm no longer from the traditional school. So for me it seems like it's an impediment to actually have my hand over the image, whereas for the traditional people it's probably empowering or it liberates, being just like working on a canvas or a piece of paper. The fundamental things we have talked about are the safety nets, so I can undo and I can put things on layers and I can move them around and I can experiment so much more than I could. So I guess from that point of view the Cintiq brings it all back together for people in a very natural way to interface with the software.

To me the Wacom tablet is such an essential part of the mix. Kind of like the glue that puts many of these applications in the same playing field. It's interesting meeting people that say, "Well, I use a mouse and that's all I need!" but to me it's their loss because there's so much tactile feedback and control over what you can do with a stylus in your hand, whereas a mouse is not an expressive tool. The tablet is such a standard piece of kit for designers and artists that I very rarely run across someone who actually thinks that a mouse or a trackball is a better interface.

Ric I'm sure many would agree with you, from a very large community of concept artists, designers and visual communicators, who have been using all of these tools with Wacom tablets for a long time and probably find the Cintiq an interesting development but not entirely necessary for them. I noticed with Ron Cobb, who I interview later in this book, says that he just loves the Cintiq 21UX, "I think it's truly a significant advance in the evolution of Wacom tablets", but then later I noticed him working away happily on an illustration using his Intuos3 6x11 and I thought, well, it's going to take a little while for him to adjust after working on a conventional Wacom tablet for so many years.

JOHN DERRY

higher horsepower systems so that we were always on the cutting edge of what kind of processor power was available and then when the software was released the general public, in the most part, had not yet gotten up to that level, but in time they would. So you always had to develop for the future knowing the driving force to be that you're always developing, knowing that more speed, larger memory, cheaper prices, all these things are on the horizon and so you aim towards that.

Ric I remember you once telling me about how at Fractal Design you had a wet lab for working out how to do stuff.

John Oh yeah, the wet lab! Mark and I wanted to continue not just too abstractly figure out things like how paint comes off of a traditional bristle hair brush. So we actually set up a working space separate from the main building where all the engineering went on. I think being physically removed actually was a good thing because it just puts you in a different space. I had been dragging around a lot of art materials with me for years so we got all that stuff together and bought whatever we needed and whenever we wanted to explore a certain medium, like the pastels or charcoals or paint or whatever, we'd play with those tools and work with them, experience them and in some cases I would educate Mark about, "Here's how certain techniques work" or whatever and just through a combination of play and explanation we'd educate ourselves.

I was looking at it expressively, like here's what I want. Here's how this brush does this. I want it to do that. Mark looked at it through kind of this algorithmic way he had of looking at things and he could figure out how he could mimic either the physics or just algorithmically do what this thing is doing, but doing it with pixels on a screen. A major part of Mark's genius was that he could think in that way and he could see the code. So the wet lab just became a great resource for us to interact directly with a wide variety of traditional media and to give Mark the opportunity to view things and analyse them to break it down structurally and see what was going on in terms of writing code to do that same thing.

We'd go to the wet lab and play with things on a Wednesday or a Thursday and then Saturday morning we'd be over at Mark's place taking what we learned from those sessions and applying it. Most times Mark could already see that this tool or this piece of code already kind of does what I want it to do and so he'd start with that. I always describe it as if he'd go in there with a machete and just start hacking code out, cutting, copying, pasting and writing things he wanted to add to it and a large part of my role at that point was when he'd get to say, "Okay John, should this be a radio button or a slider", and I'd always go, "A slider, a slider. Make it a slider" He'd get it running roughly so we could look at it and think then, well, that doesn't quite work. Let's try something different and so, as he was in the writing phase of it he'd bounce ideas off me. By watching on the screen what tools were getting created I could input and say, "Well, can you make it do this or it takes too long for that to happen," or whatever it was and I was able feed back directly to Mark what our intent of the tool should be and then he would write the code. So many tools in Painter are the result of that kind of process. We had to travel a lot, presenting Painter at shows, so when we were on planes, in hotel lounges or waiting for planes, we'd sit and write things in these notebooks and those notebooks became the basis for many tools in Painter. On those Saturdays at Mark's house, we'd start in the morning working on something and it generally seemed to take about 8 to 12 hours. At the end of those 8 to 12 hours we'd either figure out, wow, this is really a cool tool that's going to be valuable or, well, that wasn't a very good idea after all.

I always called Mark the mad scientist. He could write this stuff really fast, but it might be kind of bug prone and it might be slow or whatever. Tom Hedges on the other hand was a Stanford trained engineer and he was able to take Mark's code, and, because they'd worked together for so many years they knew each other's code so well, Tom could take it and just really work at it and craft it to a very tight, elegant piece of code. The combination of the two of them in that way was very dynamic. Mark could very quickly create these maybe sloppy or sort of buggy things, but then Tom could take them and really tighten them up and make them work really well. So the three of us together became like a three-piston engine and certainly as time went on there were more pistons in the engine than just the three of us, but for several versions we were kind of the primary idea factory and forge for Painter to make it walk, talk and spit with nickels.

Ric Now, John could you tell us more about your early training in drawing and art?

John Well, I guess one of the things, and I'm sure you were probably in the same position, going through primary school, I always seemed to be the kid in the class that just gravitated towards being one of the top artists in the class. All throughout my grade school years I remember being asked, "John, will you draw the turkey for Thanksgiving?" Whenever it was that they needed something on a bulletin board or whatever, I tended to be the person that they'd come to. So from a very early age it was always sort of pointed out to me, "Oh you're an artist. You can draw well", and part of it may have come from the fact that my dad was an engineering draftsman, so we always had lots of paper and pencils and stuff around the house and I remember, even as a small child, one of the things that he used to do with me was sit and he'd have me just scribble on a piece of paper and he would then turn it into something, a cartoon character or something. I guess at a very early age it just impressed me about the magic of making marks on a piece of paper and then making them turn into something recognisable. I've always thought that probably had an influence on me at a very early age, plus the fact that there were drawing materials around the house and it was never like, "Don't draw. Don't waste that paper." I mean it was always like, "Go ahead. Draw. Play with it."

So I got encouragement at a very early age and then proceeded through grade school, where I just gravitated towards being one of the top art kids in the class. I was lucky that in my life I never had to go through that experience of, oh god, what do I want to do when I grow up? I always knew it was going to be something to do with art. There was never any doubt about that. So I just kind of proceeded along those lines and eventually found myself going to art school, but the other thing that was probably interesting to me was that I remember I was never interested in duplicating things that I saw and I mean I have great respect for people who will sit and draw and paint from life and create really great pieces from it, but that stuff kind of bored me because I thought well, that stuff already exists. Why should I draw what's already there? I was more interested in making stuff up and ultimately I mean I did go through drawing spaceships and concept kind of things, but I eventually gravitated more towards abstraction, just because I was influenced by the teachers I had. They were from the abstract expressionist era of painting and the thing about that era was that so much expression went into the brush strokes themselves and the marks that they made. I got very interested in just the expression of emotions through mark-making.

The other thing that probably influenced me also was that I always was very interested in the technical side of things. I never actually had a dark room myself, but I was around a lot of dark rooms and the technology of making a photograph into a print was something that really attracted me and then I guess I exercised it when I was in university. I really got interested in print making, lithography and just various forms of how things are printed and got very interested in graphic arts, all of the now, the whole analogue of techniques for creating graphics for print and so that technical side of me was something that I always had and I happened to have graduated from graduate school with a degree in painting in 1981, which is right at the birth, in the first few years, of desktop PCs. I became interested in desktop publishing very early. Some of the earliest applications I can remember even before Apple introduced the Macintosh and programs like MacPaint, very simple - they called them 'paint' applications.

Now we look back at that and I mean you can see where the word "paint" is used to describe that kind of application versus say a drawing application, but I mean they were absolutely crude by today's standards. Some of these early applications I just got fascinated by. That's where I went through this period where I thought, gee, is getting a degree in programming or learning how to program what I need? Back in 1982, 83, 84 there weren't paint applications and there weren't desktop machines that were easily available to just the general public. It was still a few years away. So I originally thought you'd have to get a degree in it. An interesting parallel in the years when I was in high school, I used to work at the engineering and architecture firm where my dad was a draftsman and so I was around engineers and architects every summer. I was very comfortable in an environment where engineering went on and yet I wasn't one of them. I just felt very comfortable working with them and I think that helped me out later when I started to work around teams and groups of programming engineers. In a way it's very similar to how it feels around a typical engineering or architect's office space.

So that helped me out. Instead of thinking "Who are those weirdos in front of the computers down there? I was fascinated by what they were doing. I had a little knowledge about it and so I was able to use that to my advantage to get involved in the tool making process. I did have a little technical knowledge but also had a full background in working with traditional expressive mark-making tools, as well as having my BFA and MFA degrees in painting. So I was a perfect candidate to fit into that mix of people and be a component in a team that had the expertise of how these expressive tools work, and with a little bit of understanding of programming and being able to communicate with the engineers, managed to prod them along. I remember the first brushes on computers. I mean they called it a brush, but all it was a round dot that, if you drew too fast, separated into individual dots because it was actually the illusion of a brush, by drawing and overlapping so close together it looked like you were drawing a continuous stroke. In fact it was a series of independent, individual dabs or circles and so that's why they called it brush, but from my background I kept thinking why would you call this a brush? It doesn't look like a brush at all and so I started to think why can't we get more of the characteristics of a brush? Brushes are made of individual hairs and so it goes.

I was going up through the ladder of processing power, as it became available, using Moore's Law and the whole thing - about every 18 months the processing power doubles. Well, we've been on that curve for 20, 30 years and being part of creating these tools while that same curve was playing out allowed us to keep reaching for the next rung on the ladder. We leveraged that and kept up the excitement to create new tools because the next level in PC horsepower was always right around the corner. So we were constantly developing and saying, "Well, this just basically isn't going to work right now", but in 18 months or so the next turn of the cycle would deliver that extra horsepower or advance in technology.

So sometimes we got criticised for some tools in Painter that would only work on the most high end machines at the time but we had to develop those tools for future machines. We constantly refreshed our in-house systems with those

JOHN DERRY

JOHN NOW TEACHES THE ART OF EXPRESSIVE PHOTOGRAPHIC INTERPRETATION USING COREL PAINTER AND A WACOM INTUOS3 PEN/TABLET.

Ric At what point was the pressure sensitive pen/tablet introduced as an interface tool for Painter? Was a pen/tablet always the preferred interface and then it just kept developing with the evolution of pen/tablets?

John Well, yeah. The first thing I noticed about Lumena when I first saw it in 1984 being demo'd was that it had a tablet attached. It was a Kurta tablet, it didn't have pressure sensitivity and the pen was attached by a tethered cable, so not like a cordless Wacom. The fact that it was a stylus-based instrument, to me, was really smart and that was one of John Dunn's things. He wanted to use a stylus-based instrument and even back when I started working there as early as 1985; GTCO had a pressure sensitive tablet. It was really crude, with this little box that I think the pressure sensitivity circuitry was in and it was really prone to temperature changes. It had a little knob on it and we kind of twiddled with it to get the pressure sensitivity to work. Over time it would drift out and you'd have to play with the knob. It was really crude but you could see in some ways like, wow, pressure is such a major thing. Back in those days there were such limitations on processing power and pen pressure could only address one dimension at a time, whereas now opacity, tip tool width, the blending with other colours, all these things can happen simultaneously, plus you get into tilt and rotation with all of the dimensions that can be pulled now, they can all at once be pulled and all applied in real time.

Back then all you could do was use it to just change the width of a pen. You couldn't do anything else with it and so it was limited, but yet, through either setting the tool up to change width or to change opacity, just seeing those two controlled by pressure was like, wow, that is really important and I think, as a company, Time Arts has probably encountered Wacom in, I guess, 1987/88 and I think, if I understand Wacom's history, that's right around when they'd done very well doing engineering digitisers, but they were exploring and starting to offer pressure sensitive tablets, along with this whole wireless pen capability and that just totally changed the picture, because all of sudden you didn't have that wire attached to the stylus, which always seemed to be too short and it impeded the natural feel of the pen in the hand.

So it had that going for it and the other thing that happened was Time Arts realised that the Macintosh was a platform with a lot of promise and so they ported Lumena over to the Mac and a complete rewrite happened at that point. It was at that time where I remember being in on a meetings and saying, "wouldn't it be so cool if we could have pressure control more than one thing at a time, like if it could change the stroke width and opacity at the same time." The programmers were saying, "Oh yeah, we can do that totally." It was kind of impossible in Lumena because of the way the code had been written, but they could make that possible in Oasis and I remember the first day that they had it running and I started playing. We didn't from day one, design Oasis to emulate traditional natural media tools, but that day when they got pressure and brush width running at the same time was like this revelation "It just feels like, oh my god, look how it's starting to look like pencils and brushes and chalk and stuff." So we immediately capitalised on that and really pushed Oasis much more towards being able to emulate traditional media.

Oasis was probably the first application on a desktop computer to really take full advantage of the Wacom tablet's pressure sensitive pen, and because we'd already had a relationship with Wacom, they were looking for software to show off their tablet and they also, like us, saw that the Macintosh was a creative platform. We very quickly became fast friends marketing-wise and started sharing trade show booths and they gave us tablets to show off our product. They used our product in their demos and stuff. So very early on we had a strong relationship with Wacom and completely independent of that, Mark and Tom were working on Painter. They also had realised that the tablet was a big deal and had got working with Wacom, so by the time I got over to working with Mark and Tom, the three of us had good reputations with the people at Wacom. It was like, wow, these guys really have a lot of ideas about what you can do with pressure and stuff. So we were quite often meeting with Wacom people, they'd come down and meet with us and we'd say, "Can you do this or can you do that?" We started pushing for tilt and bearing and more attributes so I think for quite a long time we worked very closely. I know Tom was always very good at writing drivers. He wrote drivers for devices like Crossfield and Hell scanners so that ColorStudio could directly drive those kinds of devices. He was very comfortable writing drivers for various pieces of hardware and we did a lot of work independent of Wacom for the tablet spooler that's inside Painter that helps it be able to work so quickly when painting directly to the screen. So we had a good working relationship with the engineers at Wacom and we used to communicate quite a bit.

So from early on we had good insights about creating pressure sensitive tools and had many discussions with Wacom about different things, how things could be programmed or how we could utilise the different features. We were involved at a level to help outline how the hardware could be used and different kinds of features we'd like to see in it. So there was a definite synergy there for quite a while between Wacom and us.

Ric John you've been involved from literally the beginning of the digital publishing revolution. You've been very much an instigator and architect in the way in which digital markmaking has evolved. What innovations would you like to see happen in the near future?

John Well, one of the things I like is on the Intuos3 and Cintiq pen/tablets, they have these additional input keys just on each side of the tablet, so that you've got ExpressKeys and you've got the Touch Strips and I haven't seen one in person yet, but doesn't the Bamboo have a little kind of jog wheel kind of thing?

Ric Yes, it's a bit like the iPod's Touch Ring.

John Yeah. So Wacom's developing these associated kinds of tools that start to lead towards thinking more about multi-touch input. I keep thinking that it would be cool if you could have a tool, like a Touch Strip or a Jog Wheel that could be attached to dimensions of colour, so that you could change hue or value or saturation, for example as you're drawing with your drawing hand and your other hand could be used to modulate those kind of attributes. Basically colour control could be adjusted through a second hand input while the other hand was drawing with the stylus. The idea of these additional control surfaces on the tablets is very interesting and then it gets into the whole multi-touch thing, like what's going on with the Apple iPhone and some of the demonstrations you see with multi-touch screens. Maybe there's some kind of multi-touch thing that can happen with products like the Cintiq, being able to take your hand and just touch the screen and by rotating your fingers on the screen, rotate a layer or pinching or expanding your fingers to change the scale of the layer. Then that could be happening with more than one touch on the screen at the same time. That would be cool.

Ric Yes, John that would be cool and I think something not so far fetched as it might seem. So now if Painter is an application developed specifically with the artist in mind then why is it that Photoshop seems to be the application of choice for most motion film concept artists? Later in this book I interview Ron Cobb who in my mind is the father of all film concept art and he uses Photoshop almost exclusively.

John Well, first of all, a lot of that kind of concept art comes out of a need to be able to very quickly depict things and so much concept art, when you look at it up close is amazing how little information is really there, but they're very adept at creating the illusion of a lot of information with really very little information and I think part of that comes out of their heritage. I mean a lot of it was magic markers or designer colours or a very limited tool set because in order to very quickly visualise these things they can't spend the same amount of time as a traditional painter painting them. They've got to be able to knock them out and so they're used to working with a very small toolset and certainly, compared to Painter, Photoshop is a very small set of tools for drawing.

The other thing, I think, is that the people that generally come to that field, they're the talented ones. I mean you've seen these guys. They're incredible with what they're capable of and they're the kind of people I mean you could probably put Vegemite on a paper plate in front of them and they'd come up with something really cool with their finger. I mean these guys are so good. It all comes down to talent and Photoshop is probably already such a big part of their work flow and they're familiar with it and the fact that they're comfortable with a smaller toolset and they don't need all the embellishments that Painter has. They do amazing things with the tools that are in Photoshop. So to me it's

just a testament to their talent. I won't say Photoshop is limited, but compared to Painter's brushes it's somewhat limited, but even with the limitations of Photoshop it doesn't seem to be an impediment for them. So I just think it's largely talent and the fact that they're used to working with probably, in some cases, two or three tools to accomplish what they do and they don't need a broad range. They're not necessarily trying to communicate a personal expression as much as they're executing a vision that they see in their mind's eye and even with a limited set of tools, knowing those tools, they can do it. These guys can take Photoshop and do amazing things with it but, yeah, it would be nice see more people using Painter for that kind of art.

Ric Thank you John. It is my great pleasure to have known you through some of the life and times you have just spoken about. You have always been an inspiration to me and I hope this book will be an inspiration to many more people around the world who express themselves by making marks with digital tools. Those various tools exist today because of you and others like you with vision and the passion to invent new ways for people to be expressive and creative.

JOHN DERRY

JOHN'S RETROSPECTIVE ON TOM HEDGES

DIED NOVEMBER 2007

In fond memory of a pioneer developer who helped make digital painting a reality.

John Tom was diagnosed with lymphoma, a form of cancer about 20 years ago, and at the time the best procedure for it was chemotherapy and radiation therapy. So he had that done and he went into remission for about, I think almost 10 years, and then in 1990 it came back and it was in a lymph node in his shoulder or his neck. So they did more radiation treatment there at the time, but it now appears that that second run of radiation treatment had a damaging effect on him. I mean it killed the cancer, but it caused a weakness in his nerves in his upper body muscles. So over the last few years he's slowly but surely lost feeling in his hands, and I hadn't seen him probably for 2 or 3 years, but in the last couple of years at least he's gotten where I mean he has literally lost the use of his hands and they just kind of hang down.

I just found this out over the weekend. His wife has a store in Los Gatos, which is a nice cosy little community in Silicon Valley and she sold hats, and basically Tom just in order to kind of keep busy worked the cash register and anything electronic, which was difficult without the use of his hands. I saw a picture of him where he actually was using a stick in his mouth to run the cash register and punch individual buttons. When people came in to buy things, he punched it all in and then he'd tell them to 'go ahead and get your change out of the cash register'.

Things were getting worse in the last couple of years and apparently it was actually starting to affect his breathing, because the muscles in your upper body are also the muscles that help you breathe. He died in his sleep last Friday.

And so that was the end. The good news was that he had managed to add 20 years onto his life that he otherwise wouldn't have had.

Ric Which, of course was right through the 'Desktop Revolution' and he was at the centre of it.

John Oh, yes. I met Tom Hedges and Mark Zimmer probably about a year or two before I started working with them directly. I was involved with Oasis, and Oasis, as you know was kind of a precursor to Painter in that it had these natural media tendencies. It was also one of the first applications to introduce the Macintosh community to the Wacom technology. Through mutual industry connections, and the fact that even before they ever showed Painter, ColorStudio, did use the Wacom table and so there were times where Mark and I would be sharing space at a Wacom booth for example at a trade show.

So I mean there was a friendly rivalry, but it wasn't like we wouldn't talk to one another, and occasionally Tom would be around too. So that's where I first got to meet them. Yes, I guess I remember one time in particular, I was coming back from Macworld in New York around 90 or '91 and all three of us happened to be on the same flight going back and, though I didn't sit next to them we did have to wait for an hour or so for the plane. Either they came up to me or I went up to them and we just sat and talked about stuff. So yes, I did know them as friendly rivals for a couple of years prior to starting to work directly with them.

There is an interesting story about Tom I just read on a tribute page that somebody has put up with stories about him and Steve Manousos who was another founder of Fractal Design. Steve at the time prior to getting involved with Fractal had the distinction of having the first on the West Coast of the US, desktop Linotronic print output device at his desktop publishing shop called Aptos Post. Tom was one of the first people to show up for outputs, and he said, 'I have got these files that I want to get them converted into Lino output, can you do that stuff? I will give you some software I am working on and train you on it.' I think it was either ImageStudio or ColorStudio at the time that he was working on. Once Steve saw the software, he said, 'wow, is there any way I could directly drive my Linotronic Image-setter with this?' Tom sat down and in two hours he had a driver working to drive his Linotronic Image-setter directly out of ColorStudio. Not too many people were capable of that back then. It just shows Tom's engineering skill and ability to cut through problems and figure out a solution. It was the same once they started working with Painter; we had a good relationship with Wacom and provided them with a lot of information. Tom was even able to do more from the standpoint of the tablet driver, because they were working on a driver inside a spooler inside Painter, to handle the data from the tablet. I think Dave Fleck at Wacom writes the drivers, I don't know if he still does that?

Ric Oh yes sure, he's still very much involved.

John Yes, they hit it off really well, and for a long time Tom contributed quite a bit to the development of the tablet driver, because he was one of the few people outside of Wacom who had expertise in working out what you do with this data from the tablet? How do you most efficiently take care of it, and do stuff with it? So Tom was very instrumental early on in just providing another point of view and some interesting engineering thinking as to how to most efficiently do driver software for an input device like that. So Tom definitely with his engineering mind touched the early versions of the driver for the Wacom tablet. I remember Dave Fleck coming down to Fractal at times, sitting and having meetings, particularly with Tom just to work through these kinds of ideas of how to do stuff.

Ric I remember in the mid 80s getting a Quantel Graphic Paintbox to 'talk' to a Macintosh computer through ColorStudio's tapewriter driver.

John Oh right, yes of course that was because of Tom. Yes, yes. That's Tom's software.

Ric I was sitting at my computer thinking, 'How can I get files back and forth across these two very different computers?' I actually physically sat the Mac II on top of the Quantel's tape drive device and connected the Scuzzy (SCSI) cables and sure enough, bang it worked! I think I was the first person in Australia to try this out and it ended up being a great cost saving technique to be able to work out my layouts on a Mac and then do the 'expensive work' on the Paintbox after everything was worked out and ready.

John Yes. Tom wrote enabling technology that connected things together that previously hadn't been connected, or had some hand in it. For Tom it was just another interesting engineering challenge. I know later on he certainly did appreciate seeing all the art that was created out of Painter and realising, 'wow this is stuff we did and all these people are using it now', and he liked that. But knowing Tom at the time I don't think that was his key motivation.

He was just interested in the engineering. If it was presented to him like, 'here's something that's just not possible, this can't be done', Tom was kind of like, 'Well I will show you that it can be done.' Techno Tom was from Missouri in the United States, Missouri back when it became the state of Arizona was the 'show me' state. People from Missouri kind of had this 'show me' attitude. Like they wouldn't just automatically believe something somebody told them, it was like 'you have got to show me.' So Tom sort of had that 'show me' attitude.

Ric Wonderful. It must have been great to have somebody around who was able to take, maybe how you were describing, messy code and things that are a little bit out there, and then drive some discipline through the whole thing to end up with something that's very elegant? It seems to me to be a winning combination.

John Well Mark and I were definitely kind of like a Lennon & McCartney I mean Paul McCartney by himself was kind of a little too saccharine at times and John Lennon by himself can be a little bit too bitter, but you put them together and you get this really cool bittersweet unique combination that neither one of them on their own would have done. And Mark and Tom had that as well. They, in some ways were very alike and in other ways they were very different and it was kind of those differences that lead to a richer, more spicier result than you would have got by two people who were basically the same.

Before all this Mark and Tom both worked on software that was used to create the Intel and Motorola chips in the computers that run our software. That's where they kind of had many years of experience working with one another to know how each other wrote code. Tom could take Mark's code and know exactly what Mark was doing. Tom at one point was Mark's boss back in the early days when Mark worked there on a part-time basis.

Ric So a bit of a mentoring thing went on back then?

John Oh yes, but Mark being this overt genius would out intellectualise Tom', and that was a point of friction between those two. They were both very headstrong and they could get into these arguments around the office sometimes in semi-public, where they just shouted, 'This is the way it is, this is how it's got to be done.' And the other one would be like, 'no, you are absolutely wrong', and they would just get into these yelling matches. People outside the bubble would look at them like, 'oh my God is this company going to break up? Those two guys are the founders of the company Fractal and they are fighting as if they are going to start fist-fighting one another.' And the thing was, they just knew each other for so long that they knew that wasn't going to happen, but they also knew you have got to stand your ground for your ideas and so they would get into these sort of knock down arguments. I ultimately had to become their handler in public because sometimes when people started seeing that kind of behaviour, I would have to take people aside and say, 'don't worry, they are like brothers almost, it happens all the time. There's no guns lying around so it will be fine.'

When Tom went through his first round of chemo and radiation therapy, Mark was right there with him the whole time. I mean he sat by Tom's side quite a bit when Tom was really sick. So that was another thing that bonded them together. They went through some really tough times together and when they both made the big bucks after we went public, they bought these really nice houses where there was literally just a big strawberry field between them. Mark had Internet access where he was, but Tom didn't because his place was just enough outside in the country. So Tom being the kind of 'let's make something work that they say can't work', they actually built a Wi-Fi network, like this really high-powered targeted Wi-Fi that they both had these special antennas on Mark's and Tom's houses, so that Mark could transmit the Internet to Tom, so Tom could just hop on to Mark's Internet signal and be able to have Internet access, even though it was like three quarters of a mile away. I think Tom actually just built the antennas. Nowadays you can buy this stuff, but he bought a bunch of parts and stuff and actually made the antennas, transmitter and receiver.

One day, we were sitting around and Tom was looking at something and he just kind of casually said, 'you know I am working on the screen code here and there's a spot in here that it would be literally like nothing to be able to make the screen rotate to any angle. The image is still really in its original orientation, but you could rotate the screen. Is there any reason you would ever want to do that?' Mark and I just looked at each other and said yes, yes, yes. You have got to do that! We have got to have that feature to simulate turning a piece of paper on a desk. So he did that and I always joke and say it was like two lines of codes. I am sure it was more than that, but it was literally like, 'oh let me do that', and then in five minutes he had it working. We were just looking and laughing and 'oh my God look at this, it just rotates like nothing.' No performance hit or anything, amazing!

There's another one where we said to Tom 'we want to do watercolour', and so Tom's responsible for the whole original watercolour layer and making it fuzz out and diffuse, that was all Tom. He was always kind of proud of that whole original technology that we did to emulate watercolour.

Ric Amazing!

John Tom would grab onto something and he would really research it and get right into getting his hands dirty crawling under the engine and working on the code where as Mark and I were more like 'oh, let's put fins on it and paint it with flames on the side, put fuzzy dice hanging from the mirror.' A lot of what we did was about how Painter looked and felt.

Ric Just to change the subject a little as you probably know Microsoft have released Expression Design and I would like to ask you to tell us a little bit about the original Expression from Creature House and Fractal Design.

John Well Alex Hsu was the main guy behind it. He lived in Hong Kong and went to university there where he majored in Computer Graphics. He and a couple of former college mates submitted a SIGGRAPH paper presenting a new style of pressure sensitive vector brush stroke that was the core to Expression. When you submit papers like that which get published, a lot of times your work gets stolen or just adapted so you don't reap the full benefits of it. Even though they had written the paper and other large software companies started adapting the concepts, they still started Creature House and so Alex was aware of Fractal Design and at that point thought, 'these guys would be a perfect company to market our tool in the United States.' We were in the process of evolving our product line with the reintroduction of ColorStudio and ImageStudio (Grey Paint) Painter was doing really well and Sketcher had just been released so Expression was an interesting fit for us.

We really didn't add much to it; we just repackaged it and probably cleaned it up under the hood to be working well on current machines. I think we were probably not selling Poser yet but we had been talking with a Larry Weinberg who wrote Poser because he was looking for a publisher for it. So we were in a mode where we were starting to try to expand our product line. When Alex Hsu was over here in the United States, I think he was probably shopping what was to become Expression around to different companies, but I think he saw in us a really good match. We were creating natural media tools and this vector-based tool would be a great complement to our pixel-based applications.

Ric I gave a shrink-wrapped box of the Creature House/Fractal version of Expression I still had, to Leon Brown, the Expression product manager at Microsoft.

John Oh cool. I don't know when and where and how Microsoft got interested in it, but all of a sudden one day I saw the announcement and it's like 'oh Creature House, all the assets of Expression are being sold by Creature House to Microsoft', and like so many products I thought 'well that's the end of that, we'll never see it again. We will probably watch pieces of its technology turn up in other products but well here it is again.

Ric Yes, in fact they used the Expression brand name to create a whole suite of products and the original Expression product still exists. I am actually thinking we might see some very interesting things come out of this. Quite a lot of ex Adobe and Macromedia guys have joined Microsoft including Douglas Olson the General Manager for Expression. I mentioned to him that I noticed in the first release version of Expression Design, Microsoft had taken out the Raster layer option which turned it back into being just purely a Vector tool. After talking with Douglas, he said that they are doing a whole lot of new things with it and to 'watch this space.'

ONLY FOUR NAMES APPEARED IN THE EARLIEST VERSION OF ADOBE PHOTOSHOP, RUSSEL WAS ONE OF THEM

■ SEE EXTRA CONTENT ON www.artofwa.com

INDUSTRY PIONEER:

:RUSSEL BROWN

// ADOBE SYSTEMS
WORLDWIDE CREATIVE DIRECTOR

Russell Oh I hope you're not going to make me talk about Wacom tablets. I'm not a big pen/tablet user you realise but maybe I'm hoping that….

Ric No, no, no. I want to talk to you about Photoshop.

Russell Okay. Good.

Ric You know a little bit about Photoshop, I gather then Russell?

Russell Yes I know that. I can say that for sure.

Ric Let's start the interview then. So at this point I say welcome, Russell.. Welcome Russell Brown. I'd like to … well I'm welcoming you to the Art of Making Marks and just in opening I'd like you to introduce yourself and tell us a little bit about who you are.

Russell Well. This is Russell Preston Brown from Adobe Systems. I of course have worked for Adobe Systems for twenty-two years. This is a rare thing within Silicone Valley. Most people move from company to company and many people have been to Apple, to Adobe, to Apple, to Adobe and back and forth several times. And myself I've stayed at the same place. That's because, if I were to change jobs I probably wouldn't be hired again. So I have been at Adobe as a graphic designer for the last twenty-two years and have mutated into a Photoshop "guru", (quote unquote), as they tell me, and I travel the world and demonstrate reasons why you need to purchase the latest edition of Photoshop. And so, that's what I do for a living right now - conferences, special events and tutorials on Photoshop. Is that good?

Ric Yes, that's fantastic, Russell. Thank you. Well now I guess I'd like to ask you a little bit about your history. Where you came in with Photoshop, what you knew about Photoshop in those days, its competitors, ColorStudio possibly and just wade in through those early days to now.

Russell The early days! In the beginning of time, there was just Postscript, Fonts and Adobe Illustrator, but I had always wanted to play with images directly, but I never had a program to do that and I believe the technology came along and certain programs started to appear. I believe the first one was Grey Paint (ImageStudio), and then we all saw ColorStudio make its appearance, which it was really quite amazing. I saw an early version of that and of course had played with systems like the Quantel Paintbox. I worked at Atari in the early days and worked on little pixels where you had a paintbrush and the pixels were one centimetre by one centimetre in size. You could paint with big blocks, which was pretty cool. So I had some early exposure to computer painting but nothing quite like the early days when I finally saw John Knoll who came in to Adobe to present and sell to us Photoshop. This was about 1987, if I recall my dates correctly and is the first time I saw Photoshop. Stunned, amazed, I fell to the floor! And then half an hour later when I woke up I realised I had seen the selection tool, the magic wand tool for the very first time and I had seen a soft edge selection which was really quite unique in those times. As I recall the soft edge selection and a mask was new to this level of a program and it was now accessible by the common man, who now could actually combine photos together in a program, an early version of Photoshop, 1987. You didn't have to have, you know, a hundred thousand dollar computer.

Ric Or a million dollar computer for that matter?

Russell Yes, millions of dollars to process images. So a new age had begun. The Macintosh had come of age. Colour was now available and along came Photoshop, and off the world began. And that's when I started to quickly gravitate toward demo-ing Photoshop around the world. I can't recall the first time I came to Australia. Was that the first time we met?

Ric I actually met you in the US, at a MacWorld show in San Francisco and where I first became aware of your work.

Russell You call it work?

Ric [laughs] Well I'm glad you don't. It was an amazing thing, watching you get a room of over a thousand people jumping out of their seats with excitement about combining channels and other Photoshop techniques of the times.

Russell I was just thinking as I'm talking yeah, I'm now conscious of the transcribers that are transcribing this conversation as we speak and I'm now talking to the transcribers! Do they feel strange? Go ahead. I just had to talk to them just for a moment.

Ric I don't know. [laughs]

Russell [laughs] What does a ha, ha, ha turn in to?

Ric Yeah, it will read as ha ha ha.

Russell Okay. Go ahead, I'm sorry.

Ric That's alright Russell. It only cost me an extra few bucks of their time!

Russell That must have been an early MacWorld show then.

Ric US MacWorld shows in those days as you will recall were huge events. I think around about the same time Kai Krause was doing his thing with his Power Tools in the little box and I think at that same show you were presenting Photoshop. Kai's Power Tools was a plug in to make Photoshop do some of the things that you did with lots of techniques, it did it with a press of a button.

Russell Yes. It's hard for me to remember those tools after all these years. I can't remember exactly what they did.

Ric Remember something like a fractal explorer which created beautiful mathematical 'Mandelbrot' images.

Russell Oh, yes. Yes, it's all coming back to me now. Thank you. I can visualise myself running the dials as we speak.

Ric And so we digress.

Russell Ask those questions.

Ric [laughs] Okay, so just going back to those early applications which you mentioned, was Pixel Paint one that you had come in contact with?

Russell I knew of Pixel Paint and I must have played with it at the time. I just don't have a major memory of it. It could be just me having a senior moment, as I say, or my brain is fading but I can remember playing with Grey Paint (ImageStudio) and ColorStudio. Maybe some time with Pixel Paint.

Ric How about Studio8 and Studio24?

Russell Oh my! But by that time I was so involved with Photoshop that I didn't even look up at the others. Doesn't that sound crazy? I just didn't have time to look at the competition because we embodied everything perfectly in Photoshop. [laughs] There was no need to look at any other applications.

Ric Well I just would like to refer back to my previous interview with John Derry to hear your thoughts on this. Not that he's saying anything bad about Photoshop as he's become quite the serious Photoshop user these days. He was saying that in those days his recollection was that Photoshop was built for compositing pixels and when he was with Mark Zimmer working on Painter, they were working on the idea of getting pixels 'blasted' to screen very quickly. Painter does what it does well and Photoshop does what it does well because of their original architectures being quite different. Would that be a fair statement?

Russell All I remember is well yeah, Photoshop, I used for altering images and those that did work with Painter were either starting from scratch and creating the pixels themselves and then I did see some painting on top of images, but you know I think I recall more original drawings and paintings coming out of Painter then I can recall it being used for photo retouching. Is that correct?

Ric Oh yes absolutely. I think really that's the defining difference between the two applications.

Russell The brush behaviors were quite unique to Painter and we couldn't go in that direction, I believe, for copyright reasons. They had a special way in which the brush behaved, and they still do to this day, that made Painter quite unique.

Ric So having said that, Photoshop has some very sophisticated brush dynamic capabilities of its own, and of course has always supported Wacom pressure sensitive pens from day one, I believe. You may be able to qualify that for me?

Russell You could qualify it better than I.

Ric Well now of course when you go into the brush dynamics palette while you have a Wacom tablet plugged in, all of the lovely little attributes become available. Pressure and tilt and rotation, all those and more.

Russell Oh, yeah. It's quite wonderful with pressure sensitivity to take a pattern brush for example and get it to flow with the slightest of pressure, changing the size of the pattern, both opacity and size at the same time is … oh and then, then I just love the possibilities. Me, I love putting makeup on people's faces and especially hair and with some stylised brushes to stroke a brush and the fibres of the hair move in direction of the Wacom stroke. It's really quite amazing to start to build beards and hair and of course being slightly bald myself, putting hair on a subject is quite important to me. Oh my, Oh my!

Ric Is this a new feature you're describing or is this a feature that's been around for a while?

Russell This has been around for a long time, I think, all the way back. There has been capabilities for directional brushes... This goes back to … does that go back to 7 or just to CS?

Ric Oh okay. Now I understand what you mean. Yep, 7.

Russell Oh see, now you understand. The direction of the pattern is aligned with the direction of the stroke of the pen.

Ric Now of course with the Artist Pen feature that could be even more powerful being able to rotate the direction of the stroke with just the angle of your hand.

Russell Oh yeah.

Ric I remember having a conversation with you while cooking Australian prawns (shrimp) on the barbecue.

Russell I thought those were bugs on the barbie?

Ric Balmain bugs? Well, yes those as well!

Russell Yeah, they were some bugs they had the funniest little tails I had never seen before in my life.

Ric Oh, yes okay that would have been some Balmain bugs, [pause] and some prawns too [shrimp]. And so I asked you a question and I still to this day remember you saying "No, we don't think the application Live Picture is going to be an issue for us. We just deal with pixels."

Russell Yes I did say that. I [pause] I felt that - we were dealing with pixels at the time - and I felt that technology was going to get faster. Processing time was going to increase and that Live Picture may have been, you know, it played this role in the beginning of time because there was not the processing strength necessary to process all those pixels so you had to decide, and say let's process this later. And so my comment was that I felt, and I believe it's true, I believe the processing speed has come up significantly since those days and now it is possible to work directly with pixels at a comparable speed. There was some pretty amazing things that Live Picture did, and this is a terrible question, but is Live Picture still around?

Ric Well, it is and it isn't. There are some enthusiast user groups that still use Live Picture. It's not a supported product anymore. I think part of it got bought by Kodak and partly bought by somebody else and gutted for its technology. I have an interview with Dr Philip George in this book who's a senior lecturer at the University of New South Wales - College of Fine Arts, and he's been producing over the past ten years very, very large images still using Live Picture.

Russell Wow.

Ric He's just finished his PhD in something like iconology and images shot from around the world where he's travelled and taken very, very high resolution images. He's composited images as big as seven gigabytes. He said to me Photoshop still can't manipulate the images that he creates so that is why he still uses Live Picture to do it. I thought this could be controversial. Russell what is the biggest file you can manipulate in Photoshop?

Russell I don't have this information. You know, I was never a big user of Live Picture. I never understood how it worked. I knew how the processing was happening, but I'm not a scientist by any way. I think it was described to me once as these little units that it would work. I will throw the question back to you – why is it that their technology didn't catch on? What was about it that people didn't like? I mean with brushes you could lay in a gradient or brush stroke across very large images in real time.

Ric Yes I worked on a poster project for Queensland Tourism whereby I could airbrush a texture in real time on a 256 megabyte file using an old Mac Quadra with only 32 megabytes of RAM. Each of the 10 posters was over three Gigabytes in resource files. Pretty big job for the times.

Russell Why didn't it catch on?

Ric Well I think it's the same reason as why Photoshop killed ColorStudio. ColorStudio was a big, heavy, professionally orientated product with a very large price tag of around $3,000.00 and Photoshop came along and I think it was under $500.00. Everyone could get it and use it and do things with it. Pretty much the same thing happened with Live Picture. It was priced around about $3,000.00, it had a dongle key and it was aimed at the high-end professional. It was a bit different to figure out than Photoshop and although some such as myself used it successfully it didn't grab the mass market. The idea was that Kodak was going to incorporate its unique (Blade Runner like) file format technology into image bank libraries. After talking with some rather large image bank companies I realised that the huge amounts of investments in the TIFF and JPG formats were not going to allow them to start changing anything in a hurry. It was almost like it was just some great technology that came along too late. So at the end of the day, pricing, market positioning and also, you were absolutely right, the hardware just continued to get more powerful. It was always my dream to be able to use my Wacom tablets to paint and draw in real time on the PC/Mac. I did own a Quantel Paintbox for a while but I could see way back then that the desktop PC was ultimately the way to go. Digital real time airbrushing, retouching, deep etching were techniques used on professional high-end systems and then along came Photoshop on the PC. We all trying to get similar results from much cheaper and underpowered equipment and the selection tool, the magic wand and the very powerful capabilities of channel procedures, all paved the way for sophisticated imagery to be created in the new non real time environment of Photoshop. The transform tool is a great example of Photoshop implementing a style of post processing of its own. You've been the master evangelist of these techniques for many, many years and now there is a whole generation of digital artist and designers who know no other way. This is why I meet so many digital media professionals that have always used a mouse. But now finally there is a renaissance going on. The time for using a pen on a tablet, to brush and to paint has well and truly returned. People are discovering for the very first time that these techniques are possible and, what's more, the pen/tablet is actually a better form of mouse. Would you like to comment and give us your perspective on this phenomenon?

Russell You were rambling, you were rambling! So what's the question again and so I get back on track here. I was following you with … so you want to know my perspective on.

Ric Sorry…on what you thought back then about image manipulation in a non-real time application using channels and the ability to make selections and whatever, as opposed to using a Wacom pen/tablet to brush in effects with masking.

Russell Oh okay. I'm an old school and you know I got started before the Wacom pen/tablet came out and so I'm also that … but you know I'm also new school because you know I played around with the Quantel Paintbox and it was totally brush [pause] brush, brush, brush, brush, brush, with a tablet and then along came the mouse so [pause] but I stayed this old school, I'm [pause] [laughs] I'm the stayed guy, I'm the photo retoucher who uses the mouse to this date because I have so much control over it. It's a terrible admission that I don't use a Wacom pen/tablet! But I believe in Wacom pen/tablets, it's the coolest thing and I want a Cintiq!

Ric OK then we must talk!

Russell Yeah, but I got caught up in. [pause] It's a trap! You've seen it trapping users before? We know how to get down the road in our little old Volkswagen and you guys are offering me the latest Masserati but you're driving down the wrong side of the street! [laughs]

Ric [laughs] I think you've definitely understood my question now.

Russell Yeah.

Ric So for me that's why it's like a renaissance.

Russell Oh, if you took away my mouse, I would use a pen but I know how to manipulate the mouse so well and I feel so comfortable and especially in a demo situation. You want to feel as comfortable as possible because there's nothing worse than getting in a demo situation where you get flustered. You've been there before?

Ric Oh yeah.

Russell Everything goes wrong and you get flustered and then the flustered turns in to confusion and then the confusion turns in to a terrible demo. And so the renaissance … the idea that yeah … of course I see more and more people using the tablet but I'm trapped. I'm thinking of Jerry Yulsman who is trapped in the dark room. He makes his prints that look like digital prints but they're all done in the dark room and he uses multiple projectors, multiple negatives to project multiple images on to a single sheet of paper. He composites these images together that look digital and he won't come out of the dark room because he's figured this out how to make his imagery, this really fabulous imagery in a dark room. And so I figured out how to make all this wonderful imagery with a stupid mouse so I'm going to be the new Jerry Yulsman. [laughs] He's still using a mouse, he's the only guy. I remember the only guys using a piece of film to record an image, I mean I think it's the new … there's a good quote for you. I'm the 'new' old guy. [laughs] I'm the guy who's stuck in this mouse world and I should be coming out of it but maybe I won't. I'll be the nostalgic guy that we think of now who still uses film or still goes in to a darkroom. Maybe I'll be looked up to by the young kids with their Wacoms. [laughs] We'll be the next … you know the next thing's going to be the old ones are going to be the ones using the old Wacom and the new Wacom you just move your hands through space and it's a 3D Wacom and you never touch the surface. You just sort of massage the surface of the new Wacom ten years from now. [laughs]

Ric Julieanne Kost who I just interviewed uses a Wacom pen/tablet on stage.

Russell Oh yeah, she's a big time Wacom user.

Ric So I think what we're talking about here is how to narrow that gap, you're in a dilemma in that to take people that are die hard users off the mouse. [laughs]

Russell [laughs] Yes I'm that one.

Ric …and across the line to being comfortable with the pen. I speak to many people who have made that transition in a day, in a week and some may take months because you've got your tablet plugged in but still have your mouse plugged in as well.

Russell But I'm not the artist, more a graphic designer. And if you're a true artist and a painter and you've ever done any watercolour painting or any illustration of sorts, you gravitate more easily to it. I tend to think things more square edged, cut a mask, and the old school … not old school. Just a technique … I think it's a skill that I don't have. I think it's [pause] I think it's certain skills that maybe I don't have that certain artists do have that can handle the Wacom better. You know what I'm saying?

Ric Yeah but I don't agree with you here.

Russell You're saying "well Russ I think anybody can use it." I don't know if I'm as much of an artist as most people.

Ric Wacom has gone through a major mind shift in its whole attitude towards who are or should be pen/tablet users.

Russell Do you think even an accountant should be using the tablet?

IT'S QUITE WONDERFUL WITH PRESSURE SENSITIVITY TO TAKE A PATTERN BRUSH FOR EXAMPLE AND GET IT TO FLOW WITH THE SLIGHTEST OF PRESSURE, CHANGING THE SIZE OF THE PATTERN, BOTH OPACITY AND SIZE AT THE SAME TIME IS … OH AND THEN, THEN I JUST LOVE THE POSSIBILITIES.

Ric It's a business tool. It's a mouse replacement. It's everything that you should be using to interact with your computer in a natural and more expressive way.

Russell Do you never use a mouse?

Ric No, I never use a mouse... well mostly never!

Russell You're a total pen/tablet user?

Ric Yes Russell, I've crossed that line some time ago. But you know, I did for a very long time have a mouse connected at the same time and I would tend to do my email with a mouse. But no, it's a complete interface tool for me now whereby it's more convenient for me in all ways.

Russell And what statistics … do you ever watch the statistics on how many people are using a mouse versus a tablet-based input device? Do these tend to flow up or down? Are they increasing?

Ric Well definitely increasing. I mean, well just look at our worldwide sales figures of so many million per year pen/tablets sold. That's increasing obviously. But then we've also introduced a consumer line called Bamboo.

Russell Yes I've heard about it.

Ric Bamboo is really aimed at everyone from the home enthusiast or even just any personal PC user. Wacom's sites are set on all PC users, especially now that Microsoft's operating system – Vista and soon Windows 7 - is very Tablet PC orientated.

Russell How do you relate to a video person who's clicking forward and reverse or just doing technical editing?

Ric In a lot of cases when working with video applications you're dealing with a lot of screen real estate, so you may have two wide screens joined side by side. You've got timelines, many palettes, and using a pen means that you have the ability to go directly from one point to another point across the screen, rather than to scroll from one side to the other. You've got a much quicker way of navigating large areas of software interfaces and screen real estate.

Russell Okay.

Ric Same thing in the music industry. And later on I have an interesting interview with Craig Calhoun using a Cintiq 12WX with Apple's Audio Logic software.

Russell Not to confuse issues here - I don't know where your conversation with me is going. But wouldn't it be interesting – I'm curious, we've seen a lot of touch screen happening from Apple. I'm wondering what happens if they come out with a machine – you can cut this out of the interview if you'd like – but it's just a curious conversation, if Apple were to come out with some sort of touch screen. I think there are rumors of such animals, a touch screen PC where you would do everything right on the screen. Menus would pop up, keyboards would pop up and I'm assuming you'd have some sort of way of drawing with your finger or whatever. I want to say just have you guys thought about these sorts of things?

Ric Absolutely. RRFC™ touch technology!

Russell Oh okay. That was just a side note. I was just curious. I was just sitting here playing with this new iPod touch … I can only sense the next thing from Apple is to push that technology even further to the bigger screens. Start small, get bigger and bigger.

Ric Yeah and you know interestingly at the moment the Mac OS is actually trailing a little bit with the pen/tablet user scenario and Microsoft have actually pushed ahead here. Demos of surface technologies being used in Medicine and Entertainment are available on the web. I think Wacom will just make sure that it's well positioned in all camps to deliver commercially viable, well evolved advanced human interface solution.

Russell Sorry to push the interview back on you. [laughs]

Ric That's alright.

Russell Okay. You can switch it back on me again. Put me on the spot again. Have I said anything logical yet?

Ric Well then Mr Worldwide Creative Director of Adobe we've gone from where everything's been to where everything's going. Can we get any little sneak hints about Adobe's visions for the future?

Russell Well, you can see that … for Photoshop? You can see our vision and our goal is just to expand Photoshop to get more areas, more users through other recent changes to Photoshop in CS3 extended, which is really extending itself out to other professions like doctors with DICOM files. 3D artists who have been painting on their 3D objects in Photoshop and then posting them back to their 3D applications to put the maps on to their objects. Adobe is moving in that direction. Working on your 3D images directly for film, video, artists. And then with motion graphics now brought in to Photoshop we're looking at the motion area and with video as well, we're just seeing this explosion, this YouTube explosion is making everybody into a video artist, and they now have a forum to go show everybody what they've just done and creativity gone wacko. So that is certainly a hint of the future of Photoshop. Looking to new avenues and new places to take it. And my goal is to promote that so that it's all a seamless connection. I think video tools should all work in harmony with each other, like you know bringing Photoshop files into Illustrator and InDesign I hope to see that same thing happen with video files.

Ric With the introduction of things like Smart Objects in Photoshop I have found that my work flow has actually started to centre around Photoshop far more than to be jumping from Illustrator to Photoshop then to In Design as a work flow in print. To the point where … and one of my colleagues was challenging me on this, that I shouldn't be using Photoshop as my layout design tool. But now with Smart Objects and the ability to embed all my logos and postscript elements, I'm really literally using InDesign just to roll the combined file out to a PDF.

Russell I'm curious – here's another question for you. When you place a logo as an Illustrator file in to Photoshop as a Smart Object, then you place that whole composite in to InDesign and create an Acrobat file and it was really complicated. Sounds intriguing and I'm interested. I haven't done that yet. Is the logo still size independent?

Ric Yes, absolutely.

Russell Embedded?

Ric Of course.

Russell Oh wow. That's amazing!

Ric I didn't think it was my discovery, I thought you'd [laugh] you had actually engineered this. It was a revelation for me because it just means that I only need to work in one program. I don't need to keep going back and forth across three. I've found the design process is far too cumbersome that way.

Russell I was just thinking I hadn't tried it before. You know I haven't done any Prepress in the longest time. Either sorting pictures, working on video – I totally forgot about prepress. I just haven't done it in the longest time but I was thinking, you know, if you did embed all of that and get a PDF and then you send the PDF off to be printed, I was thinking it might have rasterised everything but maybe since it's embedded I … how is that magic happening? [laughs]

Ric Well that's what I thought all the magic of Smart Objects was about, that it was retaining the vector information right through the process. I'll believe that until someone proves me wrong.

Russell It is. And so … and in fact my next few demos I'm going to be focusing on printing from Photoshop and if you place an Illustrator file into Photoshop and it's colour managed, what buttons do you push to make sure that the colours appear the same all the way through the whole process all the way to Acrobat. I just watch my wife sometime as an independent graphic designer struggle a bit when she has to deliver something as a PDF, answering all the right questions that the PDF has been processed, and then they show export it as version eight, for example, but her clients only have version four. Do you ever run in to that problem?

Ric Oh yeah. Absolutely.

Russell Yeah. Do you sometimes lower it to the lowest common denominator and export things in Acrobat 4 format [pause] you know, come on you guys. Upgrade already!

Ric [laughs] Well yeah, I guess mainly I'm sending stuff to publishers who are reasonably up to date, so I haven't really had to worry too much about backward compatibility but I can imagine how that would happen. I also find that writing out a PDF from InDesign as opposed to Illustrator does a better job and I don't understand quite why.

Russell I wonder..

Ric And I was thinking now if Photoshop can embed EPS files with Smart Objects then why not write to Acrobat from Photoshop?

Russell Mmhm. I don't know the technology I never heard myself. Okay, I spun you off and tried to interview you. In a closing statement, do I make my closing statement … you ask me for a closing statement.

Ric Well I'd like to actually take you through this narrowing area of transition between the mouse and the pen/tablet and I'm just wondering if there's any chance of seeing Russell Brown on tour in the world with a pen in his hand?

Russell Oh, definitely. Maybe I'm just looking for the right pen/tablet. Maybe I'm looking for the Cintiq which really lets me get in contact with the screen. I've seen early versions but you say the technology has changed.

Ric Yes you need to have a look at the Cintiq 12WX I think you'll like it.

Russell The Cintiq Twelve? Twelve inch? What is it?

Ric A Twelve inch screen. It looks like … physically it looks like our Intuos3 6x11 tablet, so it's got all of the Express Keys and Touch Strips and all those great features, but instead of just having the tablet surface, it's a screen surface. …and it's light, it's thin, and has a nice long cord, so it's very cool.

Russell And do you look at the screen or do you look at the tablet?

Ric You can do both. It has a nice little button which allows you to flick between your monitor, your big monitor and you can be using it just as a normal tablet then, or you click the button again and bring the cursor back to the screen on the tablet so you can be working directly on the screen of the tablet.

Russell Wow. This is new technology.

Ric Fairly new.

Russell Yeah, would you ever see me [pause] yeah, I just have to … I just have to do it. I know that my next event - if you want a closing statement - my next event here in the US is my Adam conference coming up in April of next year and one of the areas that we're going to go in to is painting. Giving a painted look to classic movie posters. My theme is classic movie monsters; Dracula, Frankenstein, werewolf, mummy and we'll be taking images and making these posters and I wanted to do this painted look and so I was investigating the possibility of everybody in the room having some way of painting and this new Cintiq sounds like just the ticket to bring this to a room of graphic designers who want to paint over an existing photograph.

Ric Fantastic let's do it. Well again thank you Russell Brown for participating in the Art of Making Marks. It's an honour and a privilege to have you with us.

MORE INDUSTRY PIONEERS

SEE EXTRA CONTENT ON www.artofwa.com

:DOUGLAS OLSON
// GENERAL MANAGER / MICROSOFT

Ric Welcome Douglas to Wacom's the Art of Making Marks. Please tell us a little of your previous life at Adobe Systems before joining Microsoft.

Doug Well I'll tell you about my time there and just so you know was involved in the first support of Wacom technology at Adobe, primarily the pressure sensitive tablets. Those things happened in my teams. I ran the Illustrator team and the Photoshop team's starting in 1992, eventually incorporating Wacom support into numerous products including ImageReady through 1998. So those were my times and most of the beginnings of those products. I'll say, there were really serious sales ramps happened during that time. So that was me. Now of course the funky thing here is I'm a Microsoft guy now and still in love with all the other products.

Ric I am really interested to find out from you about what is going on in Microsoft with Tablet PC technology, Multi-touch and Surface technology. Things like that are really quite exciting. I think Wacom probably plays a good partner role there for the future so if there's anything in that area that you'd like to comment on from your inside knowledge and experience that would be great.

Doug Yes those are two good points. Those teams are connected to some degree, in the group that I'm working with and the Surface product line for a couple of reasons. One, our product Blend, which I don't know if you know much about but you can compare it to any of a number of interactive authoring environments. It happens to compare closest to the Flash authoring tool. I think it's now called Flash Professional. Surface actually uses WPF, it's basically our client technology, for doing rich user interfaces. And Expression Blend uses this, or should I say creates many of the applications that are being put onto Surface. So Surface is inherent WPF driven device. WPF used to be code named 'Avalon' and you may or may not have ever heard of that before…

Ric Yes, I have.

Doug Good. So basically you have a general idea of what I'm talking about, which is good. So yes that's somewhat interesting. The other thing that's interesting is that both the Surface group and my group in general, the Expression studio team are working with some top designers in creating basically new innovative user experiences that haven't been seen before. Both teams are working hard along with a guy name Bill Buxton; you may or may not have heard of that guy. He's really the father of multi-touch surface technology. He's been at Xerox PARC, he's spent a bunch of time at Alias Wavefront, he just wrote a book called 'Sketching User Experiences' that published under Morgan Kaufmann publishers, and it's subtitled 'Getting the Design Right and the Right Design'. He's an amazing guy, he's been around forever! He happens to work today as a personal researcher at Microsoft but he's a Canadian and he's on the faculty of a bunch of different universities and things. He's been working with us as well with the Surface team incorporating some of his ideas as well as just a champion of great design. I'm pretty new to Microsoft, having come from the world of… I was on the founding team of Authorware, one of the two companies that merged together to become Macromedia. I've been doing this stuff for a long, long time, way back when in 1982.

Ric Authorware was a product I used so many years ago. My background is in digital media production and design from the early, early days of interactive media just to let you know.

Doug Yeah, exactly from the early days. So I was one of the primary contributors to that product and also to the merger.

Ric It was a great product used a lot for educational CD authoring.

Doug Yes well actually and more so than education, the corporate training plays. I have mixed feelings about that though being a major contributor to the product it definitely taught me some lessons about how important it is for the run-time to perform well. It helped me learn quite a bit about the true nature of user experience, meaning no matter how good you make it for the users of your product, it's actually the end user that really counts. The things that you create from the authoring tool have to perform or it doesn't matter how nice you've made it for the users of your product. It's taught me a lot about why things like Flash are just intrinsically better even if it's somewhat harder to get your arms around.

Ric Well now you've painted a little bit of a picture about yourself I'm actually intrigued now to find somebody like you working at Microsoft. Were you there during the Macromedia the Adobe merger?

Doug I actually left Adobe in late December 1998 to run a new start up which a year later was acquired by Macromedia again. I was on the other side of Adobe in Macromedia and I stayed at Macromedia until, again, just before the merger with Adobe so it's a crazy world.

Ric I would have a lot more questions for you if I had had a glimpse on the inside of Microsoft to see what you guys are up to so I'll keep this interview fairly focused around our tablets. Of course this is still user experience but more from a hardware device point of view.

Doug Oh I totally understand believe me. Not being an artist per say, although I care a lot about aesthetics, obviously my interest in user experiences is a testimony to that but I'm not an artist myself. I have a couple of Wacom devices actually that I use from time to time however it's not my primary input surface. But you know, I care about these things and I care about it for a lot of reasons. One reason of course is that ultimately our users care about those things. And the reason that Leon can't say a whole heck of a lot about the future of design is the same reason that I can't say a whole heck of a lot. Let me take a quick step back.

You might wonder why I'm here at Microsoft. I'm here at Microsoft because I believe two things. I think that for much of Microsoft's history they've kind of grow up from the inside to do just about anything in this world and yet here they were thinking about how do they break into the market for creative professionals. Microsoft didn't have a great name in products for creative professionals and I was actually impressed by their interest and conviction that they needed to have leadership that really understood this market space if they were to be successful in creating a whole suite of design focused products. So I was brought in from the outside, not quite two years ago, to basically build the Expression Studio team and now it is almost completely staffed with former Adobe, Macromedia, Softimage and Pinnacle folks. So we have very deep domain knowledge now.

Of course the other reason I'm at Microsoft is that in as much as I loved my time at Adobe I hate to see just Adobe to be the 'only game in town.' There's only one company in my mind that has a chance at competing with Adobe. Not in wiping them out in the classic Microsoft style of stomping which just shouldn't happen. Frankly competition in this space is important and right now with Adobe being the only player in the space in kind of sustained engineering mode, no longer even pushing the products from an engineering an innovation stand point. I'm actually very intrigued about the future of a product that would incorporate, and I don't want to say too much here, but just to say we are working hard working on a new graphics product, and I'll just leave it at that for now. We believe it's going to be quite innovative and new for this space. It will of course incorporate fundamentally the whole Wacom API for both pressure sensitive pen and inking, so it's a super important thing.

Ric So that's a 'watch this space' and hopefully a reality by the time of this book's publication.

Doug Most definitely 'watch this space'. And for a lot of reasons. I don't want to say too much about it because obviously it's all about how we're going to innovate in this space and really have a product that is fully competitive with Photoshop and Illustrator.

Ric Are you aware that Wacom has been developing multi-touch and point devices for some time now?

Doug Oh yeah, smart stuff!

Ric So where I see, obviously any traction in this area for innovation is going to be through strong partnerships with innovative developers. It's all very well to have these capabilities but unless they actually do something meaningful for the user, it's really not much point at all.

Doug I would very much enjoy being the Expression team touch point for Wacom and I would also encourage you to connect with my good friend Bill Buxton.

Ric Yes I hope to do my PhD in 'Expressive Human Interaction technology' with Wacom and Bill certainly sounds like someone I should get to know. Thanks Doug your interview has been most enlightening and we will be very interested to see what comes next in the Expression Product Suite.

MORE INDUSTRY PIONEERS

SEE EXTRA CONTENT ON www.artofwa.com

:BILL BUXTON

// PRINCIPAL RESEARCHER /
MICROSOFT / 1997-2005
// CHIEF SCIENTIST / ALIAS
WAVEFRONT / 2005-PRESENT

Ric Welcome Bill and thanks for joining us in the Art of Making Marks. As Chief Scientist at Alias in the early days you did some very innovative work involving Wacom pen/tablets. Please tell us about your work from then until now as the Principal Researcher for Microsoft and how your work has evolved.

Bill Very few people have ever taken much advantage of the stuff that was in the UD series of Wacom pen/tablets in terms of their capability to sense multiple devices on the tablet surface at a time. We started doing that very, very early in terms of being able to support two handed inputs. One thing that we did was build perhaps the first digital airbrush worthy of the name. Up to that time, there was a huge gap between how a real airbrush behaved, and what their digital counterparts actually did. For example, there was little resemblance between the skills required to use one versus the other. You almost never see anybody using a real airbrush without holding a frisket in the non dominant hand in order to dodge and mask the principle image. The visual language of an airbrush is a soft feathered edge on one side and a very hard edge on the other and that only can be achieved using a frisket or stencil in combination with the airbrush. There are some programs that give you very awkward ways to position the frisket using your mouse or stylus, which does double duty as the airbrush. But we actually let you do the thing you couldn't do with any other digital technique and that was to hold the frisket in your non dominant hand and hold the airbrush in your dominant hand and work in a very natural way. That was only possible using the UD series of Wacom tablets and there are other things too that we started to do where you could hold rulers or other constraints in one hand and your primary tool in the other. For instance if you were doing a pivot point and rotating something in 2D or 3D you could push down with your left hand holding one device, say a puck in your left hand, thereby specifying the pivot or anchor point, and then use your dominant hand holding the stylus to control the degree of rotation.

We started to develop these tools from about 1989/90 to really take advantage of Wacom's dual sensor technology, though mostly experimental systems, we actually did support some of this stuff in a product called Studio Paint when I was at Alias. There's a video of that stuff on my web page. (www.billbuxton.com) The problem with these sorts of things was that, if you think about it, the mouse took about thirty years from invention to the point that is caught on and became ubiquitous. So, some of the ideas that we were doing back from 1989/90 are only just now becoming mainstream, using other techniques like multi-touch on devices like the Apple iPhone. Scaling things with a two-point gesture, such as we see today with "pinching", or rotating by grabbing something with two fingers or two hands, are things that we were doing with Wacom pen/tablets way back then. These techniques became well known through publications and demonstrations by us and others. Wacom had a huge impact in terms of enabling much of this work.

So back in 1994 when I first joined Alias, one of the first places I visited was Wacom headquarters in Japan. There I met one of the co-founders, the person who did the original hardware whose name is, Murakami-san. He didn't speak English and I don't speak Japanese. He didn't really know who I was and I'd never met him before. It started off as a typical Japanese business meeting, fairly formal with the guests on the one side, and hosts on the other side of the table. But very quickly he started to get excited. I showed them a couple of things that I'd been doing. Then the meeting just broke into chaos. Now this just doesn't happen and all of the other people sort of looked like this never happens, you just don't do this in typical Japanese business meetings. But here we were. Murakami-san expressed to the interpreter something like, 'I've been looking all my life to find someone like you! I've been having all these dreams of hardware and what the hardware can do but I've never found anybody who understood the idea from the software.' I was saying to him back through the interpreter, 'I've had all these ideas about how software could work but I've never found anybody who made the hardware.' The meeting broke up completely at that point. He then just grabbed me and took me up into the lab behind the doors where visitors normally wouldn't be permitted to show me some stuff that they were working on. This included things that have still never been released, including things like an industrial designers full set of digital markers, where he'd have a handful of styluses each one marked with a different colour - just like markers in a traditional marker set. So, there was no menu. You just grabbed the marker you wanted and started using it. He also had an eraser that really was, built from an actual eraser, that you just used on the tablet to erase your digital work. It was a remarkable concept at the time. There was just this wonderful degree of inventiveness at Wacom that has never been commercialised and he was exploiting the ability of the technology to do more things that exploited the subtle properties of the hardware. The key was the ability to sense what specific physical tool, or device was on the tablet surface. Basically you do that by changing the frequency in the coil. In those days, in the UD series, you changed the actual induction coil in the sensor so that different objects all had different resonance frequencies. Murakami-san was pushing those types of systems to do very interesting things. He pulled out another system that he allowed me to try and videotape so I actually still have a videotape of this paint program and I have an article on my web page if you want to read about all this stuff. Let me tell you about it.

Under Recent Work and Activities there's a paper called Surface and Tangible Computing, (www.billbuxton.com/#recent) in preparing that paper I had the videotape which I'm happy to make available so you can take a look at it. I've also still got the paper written up, in Japanese about this system and it was one of the first examples of what has now become called Tangible or Graspable computing, a new emerging area that this is one of the two first instances of. It was a paint program with no graphical menu. Instead there were these little tangible objects or what today are calling physical icons or 'phicons.' One was a little filing cabinet, one was an ink pot, one was a stylus and one was an eraser. When you wanted to paint you painted with the stylus. When you wanted to pick a new colour you put the paint pot on the tablet and you pushed down on the lid and your paint palette came up. You then moved the paint pot to select the colour you wanted. You then picked up your brush and started painting with the new colour. When you wanted to erase you just used the physical eraser, which could be sensed because of the particular coil embedded in it. If you wanted to file something or retrieve something from the file system you put the little filing cabinet on the screen tablet and you'd push the drawers which were spring loaded. In essence, the whole menu, all the menus were held in your hands not on the screen. Yet, they were physical icons that represented the function, the same way that icons do on the screen. That project was extremely influential and it helped lead to a whole stream of research with a student I had at the time named George Fitzmaurice. We'd been working on graspable computing. He saw the Wacom work and some other work from Denmark which was unrelated to this in which I'd been involved. His PhD thesis is still a classic in this area. Then the work was taken on by Hiroshi Ishii, who was a visiting researcher in my lab at The University of Toronto at the time and took the concept to the media lab and really put it on the map. So the work out of Wacom had a huge impact both in technology and the underlying concepts that are still shaping new ways of thinking about human interaction with computers.

Ric Fantastic.

Bill The other thing that may be of interest is the work of Duncan Brimsmead at Alias. Duncan was an absolute creative genius. He developed a technique to allow you to paint with these natural elements instead of just a colour. You could paint with a 3D texture and 3D elements and so on and so forth. It was just mind boggling. It's still is mind boggling but there were a whole lot of other things that went on there in terms of developing techniques surrounding the pen/tablet. You'll find a paper called T3 which really pushed what you could do with two hands, a puck and a stylus. The culmination of the commercial side of this work was perhaps the first application for the Tablet PC that was designed from the ground up to be pen based and take full advantage of Wacom technology. This project that I led was done in five months, starting with no team, no concept, yet still shipping in 2002. It was called Alias Sketchbook, now it's called Autodesk Sketchbook Pro.

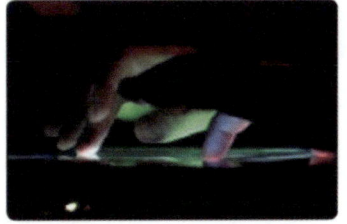 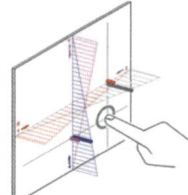

Ric Yes I love using that tool, it is very elegant.

Bill I was the lead on that project which came out of my research team at Alias. Gordon Kurtenbach was my PhD student and he was my first hire when I became head of research at Alias. He became head of my research team and took on the role of lead engineer on Sketchbook. His Thesis on making menus was called T3 http://www.dgp.toronto.edu/~gordo/papers/thesis.pdf and George Fitzmaurice's PhD thesis on grasping www.dgp.toronto.edu/~gf/videos/GraspableUI.mpeg is full of stuff around innovation with Wacom technology. Marking Menus and the Hotbox, which kind of defined the interaction language of Maya, grew out of their work, Radio Menus and Hot Box has driven the Alias stuff and were all developed for the Wacom tablet. Scott Rawlings and his group at Wacom as well as the folks in Japan were very, very helpful so there's really a lot of history there and the reason why we were able to put Sketchbook together so quickly. It is still one of the most highly rated programs in terms of useability and user satisfaction. Also the reason why it had no bugs was because we were building on stuff that we already knew how to do as we'd spent years figuring out some of the basic stuff behind it. It's a great example of how research can inform product development really effectively.

In doing Sketchbook, I wanted to prove to my colleagues and the executives at Alias that there was a different methodology to use when developing products where you actually employ a proper design process, a process that an industrial designer would recognize, for example. I talk about that in my book Sketching User Experiences. Sketchbook was the first product I took from beginning to end following that process and also it's one of the only products that ever came out of Alias that was designed from ground up and shipped on schedule and on budget. We'd gone through a period of several years developing products that didn't ship on time or failed or were withdrawn or were highly compromised and so the thing about Sketchbook was that it was the first product that from beginning to end followed that methodology where you really did the design up front and the business planning up front and how you're going to build it up front and then you go ahead and build it.

Ric So you were innovating in both Process and Product design methodology?

Bill That's right and the fact that we had no team and we didn't know what we were going to build on July 1st and yet the product shipped on November 7th which is the day the Tablet PC was to be launched. We had no Tablet PC's in house until very close to October and we had no deal with Microsoft until probably around September. That we still made the press date for October 1st is a testament to that methodology and the team.

Ric Brilliant.

Bill That's not a well known story but we would never have been able to do that had we not been doing our development on Wacom tablets. We knew that the drivers worked and everything worked and we would never have been able to do it had we not had known a lot about the user experience or really understood the technology. When we saw this opportunity it was just like 'man we've done our homework' and it really was a team effort. There were about eight full time equivalent staff or less and, as I said, it was actually five months from the beginning day to end shipping day. It was a great experience.

Ric Sketchbook continues to evolve, have you had much to do with version 2?

Bill No, in fact I think that what it has evolved towards is more of a paint program which was never the intent and I think that's unfortunate. I would have liked to have seen it go a different direction but I'm not going to try and second guess the business reasons for that. It's not for me to say what's right or wrong. I would have liked to keep it as simple as possible so that you have as much user flow as possible. There are a few ideas in there that were pretty powerful, there was a zoom/pan tool that was never developed to reach its full potential and it started to go more and more like other paint programs rather than being very distinct. My view about that class of product is that you make a number of things very light weight and easy to use and then you design with clean interfaces so that the way you get real fluidity and personalisation is by the combination of the components that you use as opposed to building more and more features into a single application. That's just a philosophy of design and I'm not saying that everybody should follow it. It's really just my personal view. I would say that for the most part Autodesk have retained the heart of Sketchbook and they've kept it up to date and they've kept the quality there so who's to complain.

Everywhere I go I see people using Sketchbook which reflects my view of the importance of sketching and how I'd seen it in the context of industrial design. Digital technology has enabled us to do all kinds of wonderful things but actually this has hurt the design process because of the lack of sketching. Designing on computers has tended towards people doing less and less sketching. The question was, so how could we make it so that they did more and more? Make it a better experience than paper by having simple layers and being able to try a couple of different things without risking your entire sketch. So I'm really quite happy with it.

Ric How do you find using it with the Cintiq 21UX?

Bill Yes, the Cintiq has many positive things especially as they get larger and I think there's nothing I can say that I don't like about it for what one does with it. If you put a really powerful computer behind it it's like a Tablet PC on steroids! The challenge with the Cintiq is that until it gets larger even than it is right now it's difficult to do two handed stuff on it. Like everything it works for something and is bad for something else and in no way am I saying that the Cintiq is a bad product. Just sometimes a pen/tablet is better, and on the other hand sometimes a screen/ tablet is better.

Working directly on the screen is really good and Wacom have done a very good job on the Cintiq in terms of the texture of the glass and minimising the problems of parallax. What you can't do is work two handed with the stylus and puck and even if you could your hands are now obscuring your work whereas on a tablet the coordination actually to work indirectly is extremely quick to learn and then your hands never cover your work and therefore you can have different tools on your tablet without obscuring it. So there's pros and cons to both and I think that it's like no one really use the same kind of pen or the same kind of car and just because I don't drive the same car as you doesn't mean yours isn't a great car, you just have different purposes. Maybe you live in the country and you need a four wheel drive and I live in the city so I drive a Smart car for example. Not that I own a smart car but just that I'm trying to make a point.

That's the whole idea of a product line and I think for other people just having a tiny little Bamboo brush is fine and they don't need anything more. I believe that what is going to happen is that pen based stuff is going to move increasingly out of just the graphic arts field. For example I own almost every eBook Reader there is. I have a Sony Reader and I have a thing called iRex which has the Wacom technology in it and I have the Amazon Kindle but I can tell you that for my day to day work the only one I use is the iRex, which is the least well

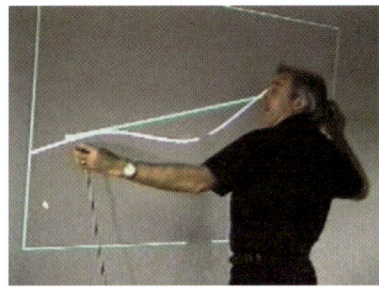

known of all. I had one of the first ones to ship and it's the most expensive and probably the one that's going to fail in the market but it's the only one I'll use. My life involves a lot of reading and commenting on documents and so without the ability to annotate with a pen it's just not an acceptable experience. Reading for me cannot be disassociated from the activity of marking up and annotating. On the Kindle I can do text notes like you can in Adobe Acrobat but I want to do graphics, circles, draw arrows and that sort of stuff and I want to be able to do it out on the dock in the summer in the sun which I can't do on my Tablet PC. I carry the iRex with me everywhere. I also think on mobile phones touch technology is a great thing, I know as much about touch as I do about pen based input so this isn't one against the other, they're just different, and for me this touch versus stylus phone debate that's going on right now is totally bogus. It implies that it has to be just one or the other when in fact of it just depends on what you're doing as to which type you should use. It's absurd to have something that's a palm sized application device with a screen that I can't use as a virtual post-it-note type of device. So again if you come back to the stylus and I can only write down on a post-it-note instead of being able to just sketch or scribble on the screen, it's just as absurd. If I only have touch on my phone I can't take notes, I can't write, I can't do quick drawings and save the file and send it on, and so forth. My fingers are just too damn fat to do anything but finger paint which is the work of a child, not of a professional.

Ric So of course you must be very well aware of Wacom's developments in RRFC™ touch technology, what's your opinion of this in combination with our EMR® pen input technology?

Bill My first surface was a three foot diagonal display that I built back in around 1992 which had a high resolution digitising stylus, it wasn't a Wacom because Wacom didn't make this type of product but I used a transparent overlay system from a company called Scriptel and so the left hand had gesture recognition and you held the pen in the other hand so you're talking about something I've been doing for about fifteen years. Being able to use a stylus in one's dominant hand and touch with the other just makes sense. Bring it on!

Ric What I meant though is the actual technology we are bringing to market now.

Bill There is a number of people playing in that space right now. It's already shipping on Dell. I haven't actually used the Wacom. I don't know whether you've got the palm rejection right or what kind of gestures, what kind of touch. So while I haven't used the Wacom technology yet, I'm interested in it. Somebody's going to do it right and here's the thing about Wacom. Wacom's been an outstanding hardware vendor but Wacom has been at best a mediocre software company, that's for your drivers and other things. You've either farmed that out or not controlled it, and the support from the software side has not been good and it never has been. The challenge is, as we move into touch coupled with pen this is absolutely not a hardware only problem. You can put the best touch surface and combine it with the best stylus technology and you still have an unusable system unless you've got the software layer right. Wacom has never taken ownership of that and that is the challenge. I'll be very curious to see how that goes. I track these technologies still very carefully and I'd love to get a sample of the units and actually try one out and see for myself.

Having said what I just said my area is in the software side of things which sits between the hardware and the devices and the user as well as the applications and Scott will tell you that I've been a total pain in the arse repeatedly in terms of asking for things and him having to say no or maybe, or helping me. He's been really good. He's a very good friend and has always been open to me trying to push the company and help them gain the insights that will make them get the products right. It's what I've always done and what I will continue to do because I just want to have the right technologies available from the vendors which our software runs on. It's as true now with Microsoft, as it was when I was with Alias.

The thing with Scott that I really respect is that he would never go and do something that might be cool and innovative if it might compromise the quality of the product or brand. I think that's absolutely the right decision. I think the real trick right now in terms of this particular space is that it's really competitive. There's a lot of threat in some ways to Wacom's position if the touch stuff takes off and holds back the stylus, even if in many cases it shouldn't. A lot of times the market looks like a bunch of lemmings. The iPhone has had a really large impact on what people think they need or what they think the future is. While I think the iPhone is a wonderful piece of design, I also think it has some gaping flaws. The note taking and sketching difficulties and the lack of a stylus are not the least of them.

Ric It amazes me of Apple's lack of attention to pen input in this whole area. It constantly frustrates me and my colleagues when presenting pen technologies for medicine let's say and somebody says well you know I don't want to use Vista, I'll be using the Mac OS and so I have to say 'Well I'm sorry but the pen experience is very different'.

Bill [Laughs] The thing is you should be able to be more blunt. Apple does no research, they have no research. They don't push that. Every once and awhile they'll acquire something. They acquired a company they called Fingerworks and if you read the PhD thesis of the technical guy from Fingerworks they acquired, it's all about the work we did in Toronto. Steve has been very adamant about their iPhone and that it is not going to have a stylus, he's made statements like 'if God wanted us to use a stylus he would have given us skinny drawing fingers.' Fine, he's been very successful with it. I respect what they've done and I really enjoy a competitive marketplace. By making such a strong statement in such a strong product you define the space and the value of looking at input. So I would say that my ability to get other approaches to input implemented was actually easier because of Apple and so they helped me as much as themselves.

Ric Are you able to talk a little bit around the Microsoft's Surface Technologies and your work in that space?

Bill I think the best I could say is that surface technologies are going to develop pretty quickly - faster than anybody predicts. I think they're going to become more cost effective, faster than anybody thinks for a number of reasons but not the least of which is what's going on with some of the technologies which I've been happy to put on record in a key note talk I gave at the International Solid-States Circuits Conference in March 2008. I discuss this in the Tangible and Surface Computing paper that I mentioned earlier. These include new thin technologies that incorporate multi-touch right into the display itself. It's not a deeply technical paper because the audience didn't know much about applications. It's just trying to talk about some interaction concepts where I think things are going in pure science and how we're going to get back to the computers and how this might help shape how you approach design of inner line circuitry. I think that the whole aspect of tangible computing, such as Wacom helped initiate, is also going to be a big factor. What becomes especially cool is when our gadgets, such as our MP3 players, digital cameras, and mobile phones, can also be tangible objects that we can use in interacting with Surface. www.billbuxton.com/#recent

Ric I saw a very good video presentation from Microsoft addressing health and medical markets which took a number of user scenarios and outlined the opportunities for Microsoft's Surface technology in that space.

Bill I know the video you speak about and yes we do a lot of those types of envisioning videos to try and frame ideas because it's not about any single product, it's about the larger ecosystem. The value of those types of videos is to show the devices in a larger context and the relationships to the other technologies that would be part of the ecosystem. Even when working on an individual product you're always keeping in mind the larger ecosystem, the value system and the conceptual framework in which it's going to exist. Those types of videos are futuristic but it's actually trying to say okay so if we've got ubiquitous computing and we have these things we carry around with us and we have these venture networks and everything is embedded in the environment, what are they really and how do they work together? What does it really look like? And I'd say that Medicine is one of the areas that is of very high interest to the company, It's a priority.

Ric Our CEO Yamada san has a similar vision as to the partnerships and how our role as an interface solutions organisation in those ecosystems you suggest may manifest further down the track and he has set the organisation on a path to work in harmony with these sorts of visions of the future.

Bill What I see in the hardware vendors and so on is the biggest threat to Wacom, though I've never heard anybody express any disappointment with the quality of the Wacom technologies. If they are trying to find alternatives it's largely just simply due to the pricing. It's a financial thing about trying to cut down on the cost of goods compared to touch and other technologies. I think in many cases the movement to other input technologies whether it be stylus or touch based is behind that a significant consideration of cost reduction and then using the current visibility of touch as the external reason and just not speaking about the other cost part. For Wacom to be a player the bets are off and if someone else can come up with a great stylus technology that's cheaper I would say there is significant vulnerability.

Ric Well with the technology patents being twenty-five years down the track and other various players coming into our space this may be an issue but of course with Wacom's position of market dominance and the Bamboo brand positioning hopefully will at least segment that competition a little for us and there is new technology innovation going on...

Bill My sense is that Wacom is adapting and it's always just a tough thing. I think rather than seeing that as a negative comment it's just being honest and by the way, you could say that this is always true with companies that have a major market position and the challenge is how to stay in front of things. In fact these types of changes in the market sectors are in fact challenging for all companies. But for the good companies like Wacom, ones that are well managed, they are actually very healthy challenges in the sense that it accelerates the ones that survive towards openness and to investment in innovation and it forces out complacency. Wacom has always been trying to push so I've never seen them as a follower or as a complacent company. What I'm really trying to say is that I'm not telling Wacom anything they don't know from their own marketing analysis and trends analysis. What I am saying is that knowing the company what you do next is based on what you've done in the past and so I'm really excited to see it.

Ric Thank you Bill for sharing your very valuable insights with us today on Art of Making Marks.

MORE INDUSTRY PIONEERS

SEE EXTRA CONTENT ON www.artofwa.com

:DUNCAN BRINSMEAD

// PRINCIPAL SCIENTIST / AUTODESK
// PRIMARY DEVELOPER OF MAYA PAINT EFFECTS, MAYA HAIR AND MAYA TOON, ALSO MAYA FLUIDS AND NCLOTH.

Ric Welcome to the Art of Making Marks. Just to open the interview could you please introduce yourself and tell us a little bit about who you are and what you do?

Duncan I'm Duncan Brinsmead and I am the principal scientist at Autodesk. I am the primary developer of Maya Paint Effects, Maya Hair and Maya Toon. I worked a lot on Maya Fluids and nCloth more recently.

Ric So you're the mad scientist that has made it all happen for Maya.

Duncan Yeah, I get called that.

Ric Fantastic. So how long have you worked with Wacom's pressure sensitive technology in developing these tools?

Duncan Gosh, It would have been a long time ago when I first encountered Wacom pen/tablets. The first time I really started using them in any real capacity was when I worked on Maya Paint Effects. We had pressure support with that and created all kinds of ways you can map the pressure channel to the brush. The size of the brush, say for instance the size of a tree, a plant that's generated as you're stroking or it could be like the number of leaves on the tree or the number of branches so you're actually controlling 3D shape aspects by how hard you press. So if you want a really big tree in the forest you just press hard and scribble. If you want little bushes and shrubs you just press more lightly and put your shrubs around the trees. So all the brushes in Maya have those attributes included when you select from the presets. Although to be honest I think most people aren't aware of that because they probably just use the mouse but really the mouse is like pressing full pressure on the brush. That's like the upper limit and you don't normally want it at full pressure because they work much better when using pen pressure sensitivity.

Ric So you can have a lot of control over the brush.

Duncan Yes.

Ric Does that include using tilt information from the pen?

Duncan We were talking about that but never did include tilt. It could have been quite useful for Paint Effects because of just the range of 3D controls you could have used with it.

Ric Any thoughts of still implementing that one day?

Duncan We might, yeah. It could be useful. To be honest I haven't done a lot with pressure sensitive stuff on the pen/tablet since the Paint Effects work. I've gone on to do other things.

Ric I'll have to send you lots of emails from our customers and get it put back on the radar!

Duncan We had a person who knew a lot about your technology.

Ric I'd be very happy to come in to your office and make sure you're all set up! Have you seen rotation working with our Art Pen?

Duncan Like twirling it? That could be useful. I never thought of using that motion, so it captures that?

Ric Yes it does, it's basically two sensors in the tip of the pen so that it's capturing the swivel motion. Both Adobe Photoshop and Corel Painter have brushes that can give the user a more natural fluid motion when using the pen. ZBrush or in your case Mudbox would be interesting 3D tools for using this feature.

Duncan Well, that would be nice. Something like that I would find a lot that can be done with the pen. For example it would be nice to have a two-handed input where you've got a pen in your right hand, if you're right handed, and then you're just using touch on the left hand so that you can grab things and manipulate them, move them around and then hit them and do even more precise things. Sort of like a hammer/nail scenario.

Ric We are now incorporating that kind of technology though still in the labs at present it will be coming in future products.

Duncan Oh really! Multi-touch would be great because I think there is many interesting uses for that.

Ric So if you could ask Wacom to create for you a special feature or some crazy new innovative product what might that be?

Duncan Well what I'd like to have is some sort of a surround screen that's not touch sensitive but just for most of the upright viewing area. You generally don't want to lift up your hand to the screen and touch it. What's the point? But then combining it with a desktop surface that is a multi-touch screen device which you can use physical devices on to interact with more precision. Also perhaps you'd be able to use just your fingers on the surface as well so that your keyboard could then be just a little Plexiglas thing you have as a multi-touch display. It would function like a regular keyboard but the display could shine through the Plexiglas and put whatever you wanted in the keys for your keyboard. You could actually use the display to be your keys but at the same time have the physical keyboard so you get tactile feedback where you're touching.

Ric Right, so it's all sort of integrated as one constant surface with different areas that physical surface devices could sit over and interact to create more tactile interaction.

Duncan Yeah, one surface that's your display with sensitivity, but then you have various devices you can bring in, stick on it for different types of interaction.

Ric Maybe using something like Microsoft's surface technology where there's a relationship between the objects that you put down on the surface and it automatically works out what it is and how it should relate to the other objects sitting on the surface.

Duncan Yeah. Actually you do want some sense of touch so maybe even a surface that's not a keyboard but it's a surface where you've got an image on it but you also have some relief to it and various hot spots you can touch and the software's designed to know where those hot spots are. You'd have a physical touch sense when you touch it. In general you have to look at where you're touching or see the interaction points but it would be nice to be able to work blind and just go by touch a lot of the time. The keyboard is great for that reason and many people rely on the little dots to centre the keyboard and know where their fingers are positioned. Having something like that and can sit on a tablet might be kind of nice.

Ric So in summary you would like tactile feedback on a multi-touch screen device with rap-around heads up screen display?

OK so now I'll just get that off to our engineers at Wacom! Thank you, Duncan for participating in the Art of Making Marks.

CREATIVE INNOVATORS

- Ron Cobb: Film Designer — p.067
- Nick Pill [RSP Pictures]: Film Designer — p.073
- Marco Nero: Film designer — p.077
- Jake Hempson: Character Animator Modeller — p.081
- Steve Stamatiadis [Krome Studios]: Games Developer — p.084
- Ken Lambert [Ink Project]: Broadcast Branding — p.087
- Gerry Haggerty: 2D/3D artist — p.089
- Allan MacDonald: Automotive Designer — p.091
- Tin&Ed: Graphic design Duo — p.095
- Julieanne Kost: Adobe Senior Photoshop Evangelist — p.098
- Dr. Phillip George: Digital Media / University of New South Wales — p.103
- Richard Luxton: Fashion Photo retoucher — p.108
- Ted Blore: Paintbox / Photoshop Artist — p.111
- Bryn Farrelly: Digital Compositor and Editor — p.117
- Craig Calhoun: Audio Engineer / composer — p.120
- Steve Rosewell [Studio Kite]: 3D props and sets — p.125
- Julian Tylney Taylor: VFX / Technical Designer — p.130
- Nigel Allen: Cinema 4D evangelist — p.133
- Matt Taylor: Sixty40 Animation — p.135
- Cindy Bower: Traditional cell animator — p.138

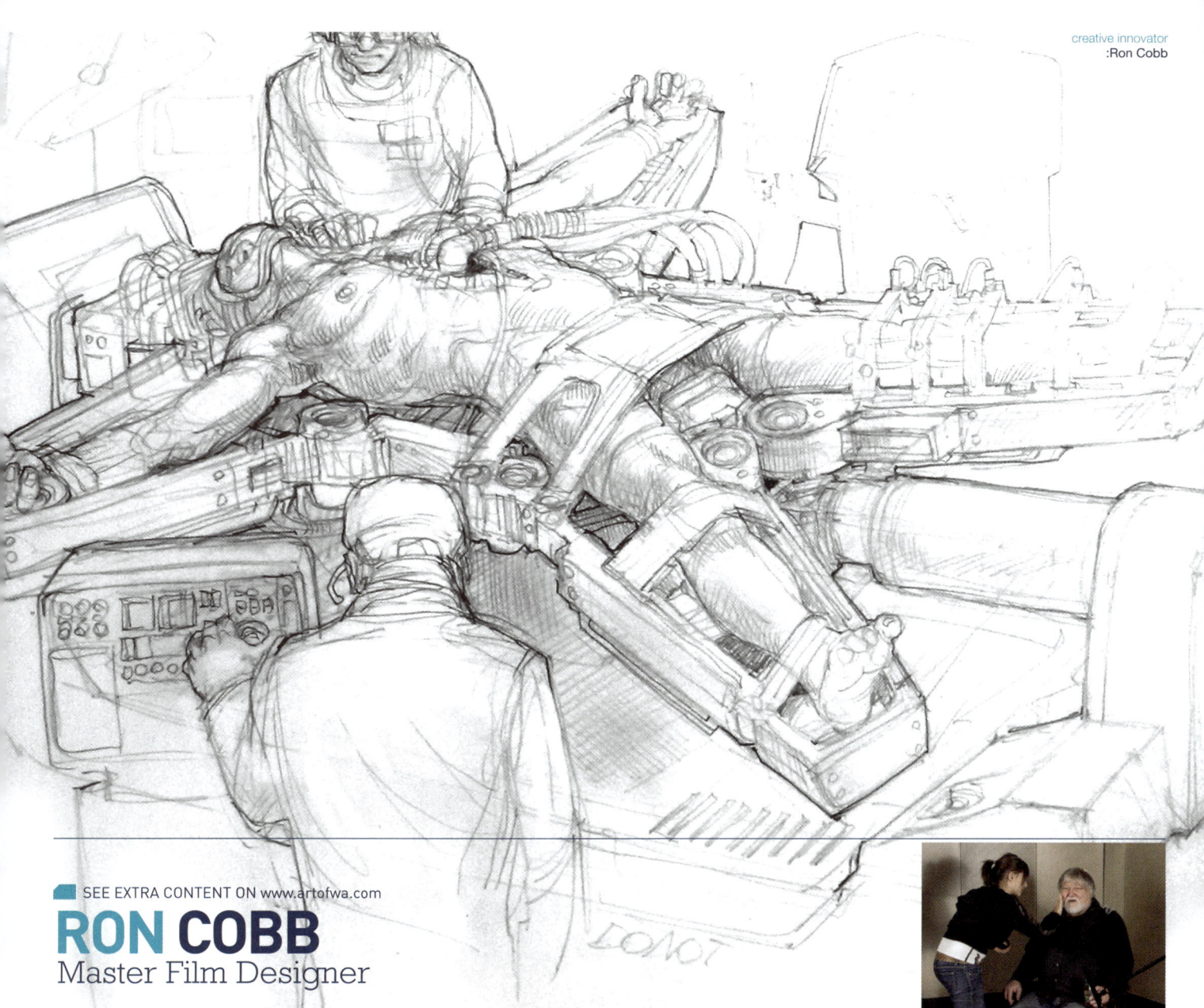

RON COBB
Master Film Designer

SEE EXTRA CONTENT ON www.artofwa.com

Ric Welcome Ron to the Art of Making Marks. Please tell us who you are and what do you do?

Ron [laughs] Well I'm still trying to figuring that out. I've been told all my life, I'm an artist, an inattentive student, a frustrated writer, a nerd, even, a know-it-all. Truthfully I was never very good at anything except drawing. So I found myself posing as an artist for most of my life. This ongoing ambivalence about my ability results directly from having to grow up limited to a methodical, certainly slower, process of learning. As a result I have always been aware, of how very much I do not know. At some point in my middle-class upbringing I became a political cartoonist for a sixties style underground newspaper in Los Angeles. That's when I discovered I liked thinking about human behavior and commenting on the motivations of my fellow humans, famous, infamous and insignificant. I would then illustrate the result in pen and ink after learning the technique, on the job. I think the key to my central method in pursuing the arts has always been an emphasis on content, far more than subjective self-expression. That's why I always refer to what I do as illustration. I like to illustrate my ideas, designs and enthusiasms. My earliest and strongest enthusiasm was a deep obsession with the sciences. So to this day, both art and science motivate me with no clear boundary between. Even my political cartoons were drawn from my best understanding of cultural and physical anthropology, brain science and, most pointedly, endless speculation about Darwinian adaptation. I kept up, as best I could, with whatever research or informed speculation that was ongoing at the time. For the cartoons this opened a door of commentary and insight into who we are and why we act as we do, far more fruitful than a hundred years of socio-political debate. I also used sci-fi-like images of the future, post-nuclear war, automation, etc. to comment on technology and the social challenge it always brings. I avoided drawing endless caricatures of politicians because scape goating individuals seemed too predictable and far too easy to dismiss. Most of the time I preferred to depict the plight of the common man caught up in our history of cleverness, belief, creativity and folly.

Another major passion of mine is film. I had always been thrilled by motion pictures. When opportunities to be involved in filmmaking begin to appear I couldn't believe my luck. Could I possibly write, direct or invent my own films? As it turned out, over the next two decades, I contributed a great deal of design, a bit of writing and some directing to a stream of major and minor features. With film, the blend of art and science was unavoidable and my obsession became how to infuse believability into even my most fantastic designs. By now I'm an advocate of secular rationalism and a sceptic of all unwarranted belief and revealed certitudes. Of course, right in the middle of my film work drops the digital revolution. Suddenly the tools for altering, enhancing, creating and perfecting images began to radically alter all the arts and, to my way of thinking, elevated the motion picture to near miraculous power. Also the use of these new tools became increasingly accessible. So I guess I'm a commentator and an image-maker.

creative innovator
:Ron Cobb

Ric Fantastic Ron! How long have you been using pen/tablets in your production process?

Ron Well I can't say I remember. It was during the time they were being developed. I tried quite a few because I liked the enhanced control.

Ric Well, like you said, it doesn't matter, any pen/tablet I guess. We don't specifically have to be talking Wacom here.

Ron Wacom was the real discovery, when it emerged, because prior to that pen/tablets were too slow, though anything has got to be better than drawing with a pack of cigarettes.

Ric Do you mean drawing with a mouse?

Ron With a mouse yes. [laughs] That was rather strange.

Ric I've heard of drawing with a brick...

Ron Pack of cigarettes. Why'd I say that? I've never smoked.

Ric That's good.

Ron I've always appreciated the way a new tool closes a larger circle by connecting a human more effectively to another tool. This was when I could spread the word and sell a lot of pen/tablets, a lot of Wacom's, by saying to my artist friends "look you're right back to hand-eye coordination, though you can draw with a stylist that can be a brush, a pencil, an eraser or an airbrush using paint that dries instantly on a surface that never wears out. And now with Photoshop's layers, you should have no fear of it." Digital art should be seen as just another medium. If anything the Wacom helped me solidify my view that Photoshop and high-resolution image making was the real purpose of Photoshop, not collages derived from altered photography. I never used Photoshop that way. To me it was the ultimate blank slate. I could sit anywhere with my Wacom and a white screen and start sketching, scribbling, erasing and shuffling layers until I had a finished image. Yet, I don't see it as a huge departure from the traditional way in which artists work. Now that I've got my Wacom with Photoshop looking over my shoulder, I can easily derive an image the way I used to, but with so many additional advantages.

Ric Now with layers, yes!

Ron Yes with layers, so it's been hugely satisfying over the years, and Wacom was a major part of it.

Ric Well I remember seeing the early work that you did for PixelPaint. Were you using a pen/tablet when you were doing those paintings?

Ron [laughs] I think I was actually doing them with a mouse.

Art of Making Marks

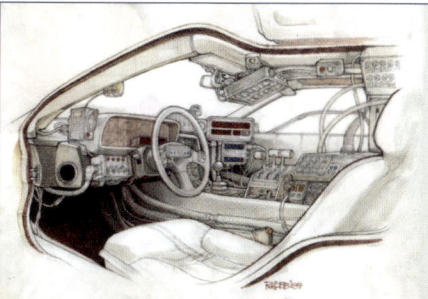
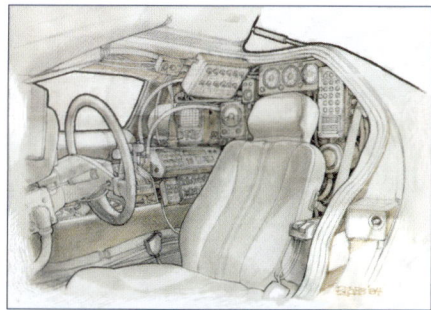

Ric With a mouse? Wow, because that was real frontier stuff.

Ron Yes, I did some of the very earliest photo-real, computer images with PixelPaint. As I said before, I tend to see myself as more of an illustrator, illustrating imaginary places or distant landscapes wherein the subject matter is the created element. This was very powerfully derived from my childhood discovery of the astronomical paintings of Chesley Bonestell. His name may not mean a lot to many people, but when I was very small, the discovery of Chesley Bonestell and his work set a fire in my brain that has never faded. The beautiful photo-real oil paintings he created in the 1930's and 40's were utterly unsurpassed in showing us what we might see if we were standing on the surface of the moon appreciating the landscape, rather than looking up at the moon as a sunlit sphere in the earth's evening sky. His work was so evocative and convincing I think that's the point I was branded by my lifelong commitment, that art must always be in service to discovery and one's best grasp of reality. Bonestell went on to show us our future on many worlds and events that we could never see or photograph. I did some of my later cartoons on the computer as well by graduating to digital pen and ink. [laughs] You know, on the Mac.

Ric And that would have been early Photoshop days?

Ron Yes, early Photoshop. I found I could do cartoons with the same spontaneity, complete with thick and thin lines of digital ink by using a Wacom pen.

Ric What tablet are you using now?

Ron [laughs] Well I'm trying out Wacom's Cintiq with the image on the tablet's screen which is, for me a Godsend in terms of needing to physically turn the drawing as I work on it. That was one of the things I couldn't do before Cintiq. Now, the image is right where I can hold it in my lap like a drawing tablet, as it runs with all the advantages of Photoshop, but turn it when I need to and hold it while drawing horizontal strokes toward me as opposed to away from me. You see, we all have different motor skills.

Ric And so is the jury still out do you think, as to whether this is going to be your preferred method in the future or will you still use the more traditional Wacom pen/tablet?

Ron No, I see no reason, I mean Cintiq is a genuine addition to image technology, though I don't always have to use the addition. I don't have to put it on my lap, I can still use it as a desk top tablet but the convenience of drawing right on the image is very, very – how would I say – satisfying.

Ric Fantastic.

Ron Very comfortable. Comfort's important! [laughs] You don't want to be frustrated.

Ric Tell us more about your work.

Ron After phasing out my cartooning in the early seventies I starting working in film by contributing some designs to Dan O'Bannon and John Carpenter's student film, Dark Star and later (also because of O'Bannon) I helped out on the original Star Wars. Then I acquired a permanent reputation in the film industry when Dan O'Bannon and Ron Shusett wrote Alien and asked me to help them sell the script by adding some illustrations. As a result I ended up going to London to work on the 20th Century Fox version of Alien as an illustrator/concept artist. Ridley Scott was the director. Later Jim Cameron got in touch with me about inserting designs into the second Alien feature, Alien's. Then John Milius capped it all by hiring me as Production Designer of Conan the Barbarian and a short time later I did The Last Starfighter with the same credit. At this point I was well into evangelizing the emerging use of computers for the generation and modification of imagery. Remember, when I started working in the film industry in 1974 there was no such technology even remotely available, though, I was aware of its development in computer science labs and industry. I tried to convince the producer's of Alien that we should try to use some early wire frame images for the Nostromo's control screens, but there was no one in the UK that could do it. CGI still had a long way to go, at this time, and I had a lot of convincing to do before I could get my hands on it. This was also true, I might say, with

creative innovator
:Ron Cobb

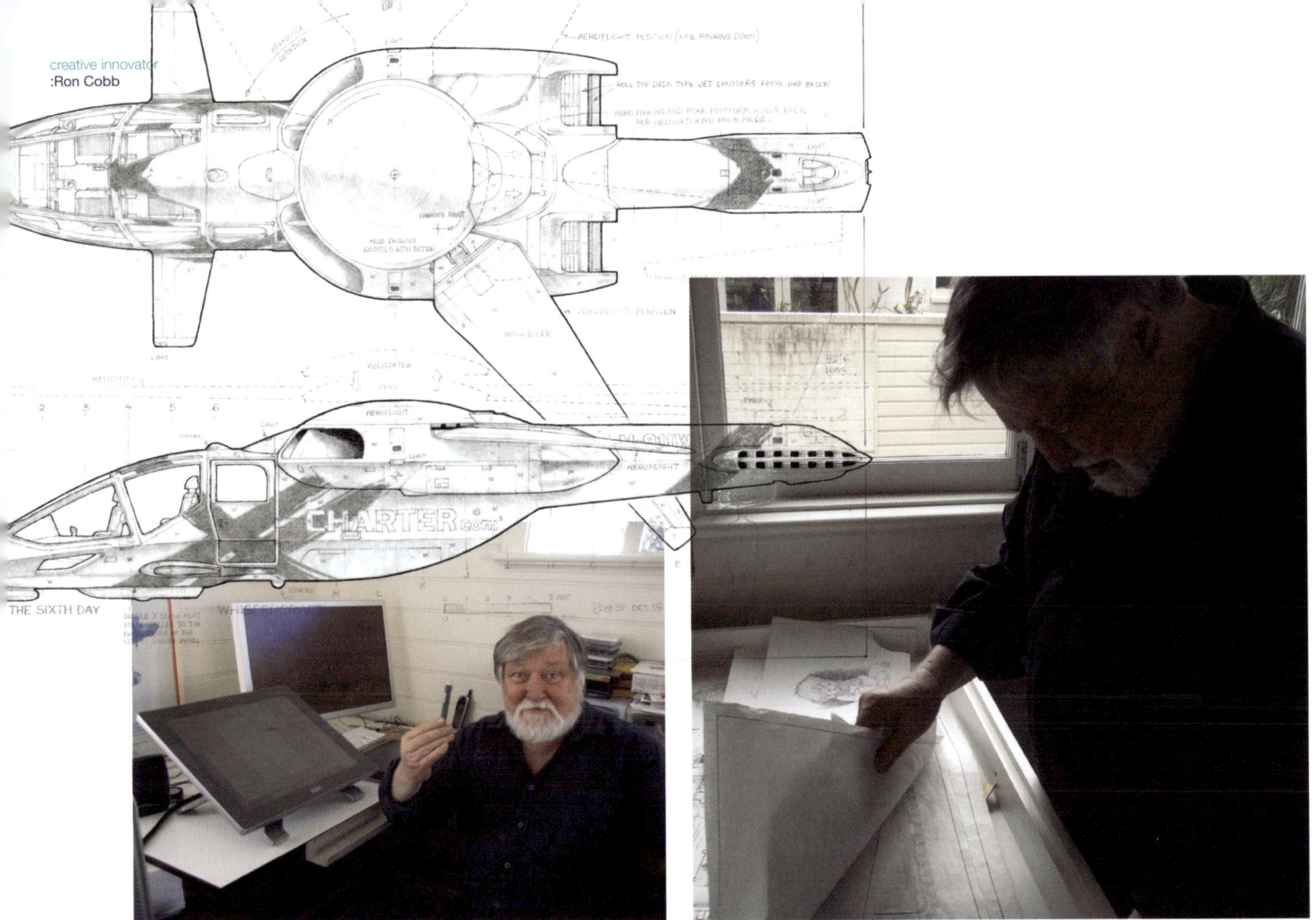

my late, very good friend, Douglas Adams, because Douglas dearly loved to poke fun at our human entanglement with machine intelligence. When I met him to work on an earlier US television version of Hitchhiker's Guide to the galaxy, one which never happened, he felt computers and digital watches were something to laugh at and, considering the way he wrote about it, I had to agree. [laughs] But I went on to counter this by saying, "There's something very appealing and desirable about what computers might become some day and you might want to reserve judgment for just a short while" and he pretty much did.

Ric Well, he turned around didn't he?

Ron He admitted that I turned him around, he became the biggest Mac-nut that ever existed as we all know now.

Ric I wonder if any of that related back to his deep thought in Hitchhikers' [laughs]

Ron Oh yes, well it was all, you know, there was no reason for him to ever stop satirising all that but he fell in love with the whole, I mean his whole life was just dominated. He became an Apple master of course.

Ric Which of course you are too.

Ron Well I was trying to be, I never quite made it even with Douglas backing me. They cancelled the program before I…

Ric I think we'll have to reinstate that… You're definitely a Wacom master.

Ron Okay, very good. But what happened was Apple sent Douglas all over the world to represent Macintosh because he did it with such charm and humour he helped Apple prevail through some very bad times. I'll never forget going up to, his house one day in Santa Barbara, a few years after being declared an Apple master, and being shown a spare bedroom, which was stacked to the ceiling with obsolete Macs, monitors and modems. [laughs]

Ric Like a museum?

Ron This was true for his house in London as well. He had every iteration of every model of Macintosh that ever was. [laughs] Six times over.

Ric Well I'm sure you're probably a bit like that as well.

Ron Well I have been, I've gone, yeah I've had, it's a little fireplug. I did my first drawing on the little Mac Plus (fireplugs), again with a mouse and I found it irritating. Irritating, I really wanted more resolution.

Ric You persevered.

Ron I persevered. Stuck with it, you know.

Ric Well Ron you have been an inspiration to just so many up and coming artists in so many fields…myself included in that.

Ron Well I'm glad to hear that.

Ric What innovations in your work are due to the use of technology?

Ron The techniques have always merged painlessly into whatever I was trying to do. However even to this day, I do analogue. I sketch and I draw and I even paint occasionally, so there's always been this mix. The digital control of imagery has been a real godsend for me. It sped up my productivity and clarified my creative process. But as far as milestone breakthroughs in innovation, I can't recall, any that stand out, except possibly, winning a few prizes or being able to do something I never thought possible like automating perspective by using 3D modelling.

Efficiently eliminating all the repetition and drudgery between someone who wishes to create an image and the resulting image. There have always been traditional artists who maintain the virtues of having to wait for paint to dry then knowing how to layer a medium, glaze and varnish in just the right order so the whole image doesn't explode off the canvas, you know. I still know artists who won't use a computer and pen/tablet because they miss the feel of the canvas.

Ric Oh, yes the smell of wet paint!

Ron I know, [laughs] I can walk away from my large flat screen anytime I want and paint and draw on my easel …as I inhale the smell of the linseed oil. But it works the other way as well. I like the feel of the little Teflon point skittering across the

Art of Making Marks

creative innovator
:Ron Cobb

"..It's like the completion of a great circle wherein image making and manipulation is once again as natural as scratching on the wall of a cave"

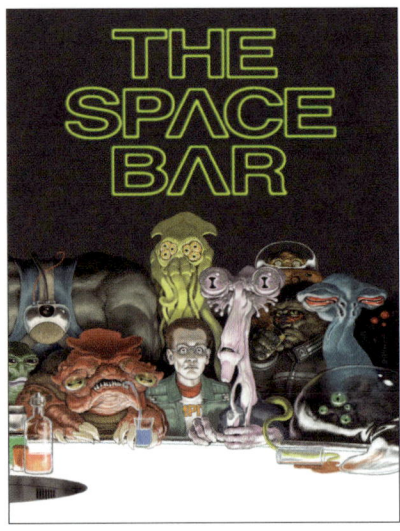

surface of the tablet; I love the colour and the glow of the phosphors in a dark room, the soft whirr of the drive, and on and on. You could wax just as poetically about all that as well. So to me, what's very real about digital image making in that a lot of things that I would consider elements that impede my desire to get to an image are being systematically eliminated. The fact that I would have to redraw something entirely just to move it an inch to the left in an analogue composition is very discouraging. To shift a layer in a Photoshop composition two inches to the right is a breathtaking form of empowerment for me. So improvements in this technology on any level at any time will only offer me expanded the tablet, well speed and response and detail and all of the capabilities that it commands in Photoshop or similar programs are just indescribably desirable to me. I mean, they just help me in every way.

Ric If you could ask for any new features or future innovation with Wacom pen/tablets what would that be?

Ron Not a great deal. I'm very content with a lot of what now exists. I look forward to the Cintiq 21UX being a little lighter and a little brighter, I do have a very bright studio here. Other than that I can't say. If anything, surprise me. I'm waiting to see what you guys might come up with next.

Ric Well a lot of people have said they'd love to be able to touch with their finger and point with a pen at the same time. Your finger being able to move an object and then paint on the surface, scroll the page with a multi-touch capability. Is that of any interest to you do you think?

Ron Possibly it would be something I would never use, like fake brush strokes. I've always developed my own techniques with the pen/tablet and Photoshop wherein I can get a paint effect that I prefer by using the tools as they are. So in some respects I'm kind of conservative in the way I use them. Something like that doesn't sound like I'd find it particularly interesting except maybe I would. I might discover that it's useful.

Ric Maybe if there was good software/hardware collaboration that went on there?

Ron Possibly, because I'm always concerned … I like pixel precision; I like things to stay where they are. I like the fact that I can … I often move things by counting pixels to get very precise proportions or to follow a lot of perspective lines on a layer, and some of it is making things work that weren't meant to work that way but they work well for me. But aside from just ever-increasing responsiveness, resolution and brightness, I'm very content.

Ric I'm interested to know what your thoughts are about pen/tablets in education, you know for children to draw and write with. Wacom's brand directive for the future is the message that everyone should be using a pen/tablet instead of a mouse to be more expressive. I see kids picking up our pen/tablets and drawing and just having fun quickly and easily. Do you see that being an important part of a child's development?

Ron Yes, I see it as an important part of human comprehension because it's putting hand-eye coordination and the precision grip back into play. Again it's like the completion of a great circle wherein image making and manipulation is once again as natural as scratching on the wall of a cave, but now this tactile manipulation is a two way street that will first deliver the astounding enhancements of digital image mastery and ultimately invite the child to flow into motion, sound and the modelling of three dimensional space. Obviously having to draw with a mouse was not as easy as scratching on a cave. So great improvements had to be made just to consolidate the promises of this new technology and connect it to the primal interface of the human mind. So what we can offer our children now is the ultimate blank slate that is deeply complementary and responsive to their writing and thinking skills while keeping pace with their expanding mode of perception. So with these elements all in a row I would think it would be a very powerful tool for education.

Ric That's fantastic. Well thank you Ron. Thank you so much for being involved in the Art of Making Marks, we're honoured and privileged to have your thoughts.

Ron Well, very good.

Creative Innovator: Nick Pill

SEE EXTRA CONTENT ON www.artofwa.com

NICK PILL RISING SUN PICTURES
Film Designer

Ric So Nick if you could just introduce yourself …

Nick Well my name's Nick Pill, I'm the Visual Effects Art Director at Rising Sun Pictures. I've been here a good two to three years now and my purpose here is to give an overall visual guide and direction to film projects we're working on.

Ric So how long have you actually been using Wacom pen/tablets in your daily work?

Nick It first started I think on Happy Feet, is where it became the most important while I was doing environment design. So that was a year's worth of that. It was probably about three years ago now when I first started on the Wacom as full time equipment. Previously before that I had a Wacom for just private use at home which I used on Photoshop for doing simple illustrations, a lot of comic book work in my own time. So I think in total I probably started using the Wacom about seven years ago.

Ric So your background is as an illustrator?

Nick Yeah originally it was graphic design that I got into and then I moved into working at Disney doing layouts and backgrounds. That was all very traditional using pencil and paper, graphite paper. But in my spare time I was always interested in doing things more digitally and a lot more finished. That was something that was never around when I was younger, going through college, so it was nice to finally come across a means of drawing digitally as opposed to drawing on paper. So I have been working on a Wacom for seven years roughly I guess and these days mainly the Intuos3 pen/tablet.

Ric And it's great to see you sitting in front of this beautiful Cintiq 21UX interactive pen display.

Nick I'm becoming very fond of this Cintiq.

Ric So now if you can tell me just a little bit more about your work.

Nick Well my job here predominately is concept art and the purpose is to read screen plays for upcoming feature films, selecting things with more of a visual effects spin on them that Rising Sun Pictures is more likely to pick up. I concentrate on conceptualising the environments, characters, mood or atmosphere and then create digital paintings for sending off as part of the bid package, as well as cost structure from the producer's side of things, just too kind of sweeten the deal and then make things look beautiful.

Ric So what areas do you feel Wacom tablets have given you an advantage or allowed you to do something that you just couldn't do otherwise?

Nick I think Wacom tablets with their pressure sensitive pen support through any sort of digital medium, whether it be using Adobe Photoshop or Adobe Illustra-

Art of Making Marks

creative innovator
:Nick Pill

tor, It enables me that confidence of actually being able to explore a lot more. I can be fast, fluent and it's easier to understand and get right down and get working because speed is of the essence generally. I mean time is expensive. There's a lot of things that you can try that you normally wouldn't do if you were using traditional mediums and you can re-grade colours, you can paint straight over with another colour and grade that in and change the complete atmosphere of what you have just done.

Ric At the whim of any Director?

Nick Exactly and then there's a lot more iterations and people can comment on those much faster so it's about turn around time basically. It's a lot quicker than using any traditional pencils or pens.

Ric So if Wacom could give you some new innovations in the tablet, what might that be? If you could have anything that you wanted, or is there something that you don't have right now that you would like?

Nick Yeah, I think Wacom tablets and the pens seem to be fairly responsive. They've come along way since Intuos2. I've got an Intuos2 at home for my private use which I use occasionally and I find those just aren't quite as sensitive when you're doing art and illustrative work and so I borrow the Intuos3 from work for use at home.

Ric So there was a good reason to upgrade then.

Nick That's right, oh yeah, a very good reason to upgrade. I haven't specifically found anything that I feel at this stage is lacking. It's one of those things where the technology of it doesn't get in the way of what you're doing artistically and I think if it's operating at that level then it's working fine for my purposes. Once I start finding it complicated and I'm getting lost amongst it then I think there would need to be changes, but at this stage no problem.

Ric Things like the ExpressKeys and Touch Strips you're not finding useful by the sounds of it, you prefer to use the keyboard short cuts?

Nick Yeah I still use the keyboard rather than ExpressKeys. But I think that's just from my own laziness. I think what I need to do is probably start using the ExpressKeys and setting them up for particular needs that I have. It would probably help my posture a bit more and whatever instead of leaning across.

Ric But I noticed when you started working with the Cintiq that you liked putting it at a portrait angle. So of course then you'd probably like to have the software reorientate itself for portrait.

Nick Yeah something like that would be pretty cool.

Ric Possibly an innovation for the future.

Nick Yeah, I think the automatic orientation would be a pretty handy thing. Especially if you're twisting and rotating the screen quite fast while you're working. Because once you actually get in the zone it's kind of cool to almost twist yourself. But if you could twist the canvas it would

creative innovator
:Nick Pill

"I concentrate on conceptualising the environments, characters, mood or atmosphere and then create digital paintings for sending off as part of the bid package"

be excellent. That to me would be pretty cool.

Ric We might have to talk to the Adobe Photoshop development team about adding that feature. So what do you think about the various accessory pens for Intous3 and Cintiqs?

Nick I've had a look at them, the Airbrush and the Art Pen as well and it's almost like you can get that response anyway from the standard stylus pen.

Ric The pen that comes standard is very good.

Nick I think as well people just get used to it… which is a great thing because mostly when you make an outlay like that for a Cintiq you don't want to be making anymore outlays in a hurry.

Ric Whereas if you were typically an airbrush artist and you're crossing over from traditional to digital tools, then that's probably where that airbrush pen comes in handy. You get a similar flow control.

Nick Yeah and it feels a bit like an airbrush tool to hold. It's like digital cameras still making that clicking noise but they don't really need to anymore so it links you with the feel of the original tool.

Ric Yes, very true. Well now thanks so much Nick for giving us your time and to see your beautiful work that's displayed in this book and good luck with your next feature film.

Nick Thank you.

creative innovator
:Marco Nero

● SEE EXTRA CONTENT ON www.artofwa.com

MARCO NERO
Film Designer

Ric How long have you been using Wacom pen/tablets?

Marco For the last 6 years I've used Wacom tablets for all my work. Prior to this, I was executing all my work (including Mattes) with a mouse which drew the odd gasp from fellow staff from time to time. I had heard that the tablets were good for photographic retouching and eventually requested one for my work computer.

Ric What type of pen/tablets do you use now?

Marco I have two Intuos3 Wacom tablets of my own and two older models which I have recently passed on to friends to try. One Intuos3 is for my laptop and the other is currently used on my desktop computer. I'm eying off recently released Wacom models already and like the new additional features concerning ratio-to-screen on the newer 'widescreen' Wacom tablets. But the rugged nature of the tablets make it unlikely that the owner needs to upgrade regularly and I have never heard of a tablet failing.

Ric Tell us about your work?

Marco As a Film Designer, my job covers Conceptual Design, Retouching, Matte Paintings and Texture Maps for 3D Models. Projects for Film & Television that I've produced work for which required an interface such as the Wacom tablet include Happy Feet, Farscape, 28 Weeks Later, House Of Flying Daggers, Stealth, 300, Revenge Of The Sith and dozens of book covers, magazines and television commercials raging from Optus, Smirnoff, Nintendo, Visa and Holden to the exotic Chanel No. 5 commercial with Nicole Kidman. I also enjoy traditional illustration and photography, both of which I can enhance greatly with further digital manipulation when required. Retouching pictures for a catalogue or a portrait is many times faster and more efficient with a tablet than any other means for me. I can't bear to think about going back to the days without one actually.

Ric What innovations in your work are due to the use of Wacom pen/tablets?

Marco There's a lot of subtle effects and specific techniques which can only be achieved efficiently and professionally with a pressure sensitive tablet and pen. The Wacom tablets have been a steep learning curve for me after trying one out in a store some years ago. The work I do ranges from Digital Matte painting to Photographic work on a professional level and almost every project benefits from the freehand potential of this particular type of interface. It's easier to use when applying gradient tones to scanned illustrations than a computer mouse or track pad can and the increase in speed is one of the reasons I'll actually pack a tablet in my backpack when working in the field to enhance a commercial photograph etc prior to burning a disc straight from the laptop. I can recall sitting next to an annoyed rattle snake in the Badlands of Alberta

Canada whilst digging for dinosaurs and photographing the fossils around me. I needed to quickly edit the images and transmit them to a publisher the moment I returned to the hotel. The Wacom tablet I'd bought with me allowed me to conserve battery power on my laptop whilst splicing and compositing several dozen images together to form panoramas and to remove unwanted elements. I made it back to my car just a few minutes before a twister slammed into the ground where I'd been working and made the deadline without a hitch due to the speedier work flow that simply couldn't be achieved with any alternative such as a mouse or track pad. I won't go anywhere without at least one of my Wacom tablets these days if I can help it.

Ric What applications do you use in your work flow and what functionality is driven by using a pen/tablet.

Marco Primarily I use Adobe Photoshop, Painter and occasionally Adobe Illustrator. Photoshop is one of the most versatile programs afoot and I must confess that I avoided computers altogether for some time until recent years. Now I have to kick myself just to pull out the brushes and inks. One of the biggest advantages for me with the Wacom tablets has been the ability to produce work which looks to have been airbrushed or even applied with oils. I usually switch between Painter and Illustrator and more than once I've been asked by major studio producers how I achieved a particular effect because the work looked to be hand painted. I recently coated the inside of my home with blue paint from an airbrushed acrylic painting on art board. Even the cat took on a decidedly blue tint on his otherwise pristine, white fur and we were sponging residue from surfaces and fixtures for nearly 6 months afterwards. With the Wacom tablets, I can execute the same degree of quality in illustrations without the need to rinse brushes and cleanup afterwards. In fact, I even ended up retouching the painted and scanned image using the Wacom tablet to allow for more details and gradients in the painting after I scanned it into the computer. I find that applications such as Painter are perfectly matched with the Wacom tablets since the recording of individual brush strokes can be applied more concisely with the digital stylus-pen. I just can't do this with a mouse. I've been able to paint book covers for Penguin Books using the tablets, giving the resulting images a more organic and hand rendered feel. Working with multiple layers in Photoshop is a breeze with the tablets and I love the side buttons on the tablets these days... especially the sliders which make zooming and pressure settings even more versatile. Occasionally you only have a few minutes to produce an image during production and the Wacom tablets allow me to move very quickly to build up layers of colour and highlights to produce a final image. The 'chunkier' style that I'll sometimes switch to for such work hints at being far more detailed than it actually is. And I think that when you break art down to its simplest form, a sign of the skill of the artist is often found in very minimalistic approaches. Capturing as much information with the least possible number brush strokes is an interesting exercise to me. I also just love the freedom to manually manipulate the pixels by painting an image freehand. But it's not always about applying colour. Sometimes the best application of subtle contrast and highlights for an image is achieved with my Wacom tablet. I think the orientation and ergonomics of the pen & tablet lends itself better to the hand for freehand work than any other method.

Ric Conclusion - If you could ask for any new features or future innovation with Wacom pen/tablets what would that be?

Marco Perhaps I'm just content with the tablets as they are but I find them to be a natural extension of the hand and thought process. If you make a few bad strokes with a digital pen and tablet, you can erase them and start over... ink and paint are unlikely to yield with as much ease. I wouldn't mind seeing self-illuminated LCDs fitted inside some of the side buttons to identify recorded functions or even allocate their strength assignment. The recent sliders are already great for tracking in and out of an image and even altering brush sizes etc... I'd be interested in seeing a colour sensitive pressure-based track pad which would show what preferences have been selected by the user so that an adjustment could be made at a glance. In this respect, whilst the pen itself is already pressure sensitive, perhaps some of the controls for paint 'injection' or eraser 'sensitivity' could be applied visibly via optical fibre to the tablet buttons rather than require a manual selection via the software application. Modern iPods and some Computer Screens today use an advanced form of touch control which may also find their way into peripheral devices and this may make future drawing tablets more versatile than they already are. But simplicity is obviously paramount and I can't ask for much more than the current range of tablets today.

SEE EXTRA CONTENT ON www.artofwa.com
JAKE HEMPSON
Character Animator Modeller

Ric Welcome to the Art of Making Marks. Just in opening the interview could you please introduce yourself and tell us a little about who you are and what you do?

Jake My name's Jake Hempson. I am a character animator/modeller and I've been working in games for the last eleven years. I started working in games as a concept artist back in 1996 at a company, in Oxford, England called Rebellion Developments and we were working on the Alien Versus Predator game for, at that stage the Playstation one. But gradually I moved on to just doing PC games and pretty much since then I've been working at different games companies in the UK for about seven years. I moved to Australia in 2003 and I've been working at Krome Studios for the last three and a half years. I'm now a lecturer at Qantm in Brisbane and I'm primarily focused on teaching just animation and modelling concepts. I've been using a Wacom tablet since about 1997 when I was working on a project and had some RSI issues with my hand so I started using a Wacom. I've been using Wacom tablets for 3D modelling and for animating so I don't actually use a mouse, I've always used a Wacom tool.

Ric Really it was purely a mouse replacement issue at the beginning and so how did that then transfer to your workflow?

Jake Well from 2D background work, transferred into concept work so I'm using it for 2D concepting and also within 3D when I'm using more refined modelling applications like Softimage. Softimage is a XYZ translation with different mouse buttons which was a bit strange using the pen, but more recently now with Mudbox and ZBrush which is an extension of 2D concepting but it's like 3D concepting which I'm using more and more. Obviously that's where I initially want to see how Wacom integrates with the 3D aspects of the tools in terms of using it for the conceptualisation.

Ric So what type of Wacom tablet are you using now?

Jake I'm using an Intuos2. Yeah, Intuos2 with the two side scrolly things and the little button shortcuts. That's pretty much what I've been working with since the whole Intuos/professional range happened. I do have a couple of Graphire tablets which is like my walk around tablet when teaching. I've got that at my desk so if I want to do some quick stuff, whip up something and then obviously the school has Intuos2's I believe.

creative innovator
:Jake Hempson

Ric So could you tell us a little more about your workflow and describe more about your actual work.

Jake With game development generally the character design concept work is 2D. Then we block out a character in 3D using 3D Studio Max or Maya. Just in my case, I work in Maya now. Once you've blocked out the character, then it's pretty much using standard processes which is throughout games development now. So you take the blocked out character which is effectively your low res character model and add some extra rows of geometry to help support the subdivision modelling when you take in to ZBrush or Mudbox. From that we basically export into OBJ file and import it into our 3D package. In my case I work with Mudbox primarily then rework it. I physically sculpt in Mudbox using the pen pressure sensitivity of the Wacom pen/tablet which is a big feature in that application. So you can actually, by pushing down harder you can actually manipulate the geometry and sculpt it. In a 3D sense it feels like clay because you are actually applying pressure to carve into areas, cut into areas and sculpt it.

Pretty much once that process is finished, as a games developer you'll then re-export it and either generate normal maps or ambient exclusion maps and bake that down into the low res model which would have well placed UV's and be unwrapped, and then those will be used as shaders for the final game engine. That's the very simplest way I can describe the process. Some people might work from a high res model for the user concept and that would get signed off. You'd then make the low-res model to match the contours, and that does happen. Sometimes I'll model a character in ZBrush or Mudbox and I'll rework the hands to become bigger and more expressive. When I take that back into Maya I would perhaps rework the low-res geometry to fit the silhouette and closely approximate the hands to what the high res model was. So I make changes back and forth, and again 'bake' my texture maps, my normal maps, my colour maps, all that sort of stuff.

Ric Obviously Wacom tablets are used extensively in films and game production/development but do you see opportunities for Tablets as an actual interface for game functionality? Like how the Nintendo DS is developing with pen interaction.

Jake I suppose you're also looking at the Nintendo Wii model of gameplay.

Ric Yes there are many new styles of human interface systems for games starting to happen also the very popular Guitar Hero on Xbox 360 is very interesting.

Jake Yes this is happening. I know a couple of games where you actually make a mouse movement in a certain shape that you draw and that would represent a particular spell casting technique. I can't remember the game off the top of my head but the game designers are talking about the fact that you draw a square shape that would represent you and then call up a set of commands. It was for the style of role playing games that are happening these days.

Ric Yes I have seen a prototype called Crayon Physics that's also very interesting. You draw a square and then it takes on the physical properties of a 2D square. Things like putting pressure sensitivity recognition into Adobe's Flash Player would open opportunities to develop all kinds of browser based games or new kinds of interaction with websites for annotation and navigation.

Jake I think it's probably a deeper discussion Wacom should be having with game designers/developers in general. I even tried to play Quake once with a Wacom tablet and that was interesting. [laughs]

Art of Making Marks

creative innovator
:Jake Hempson

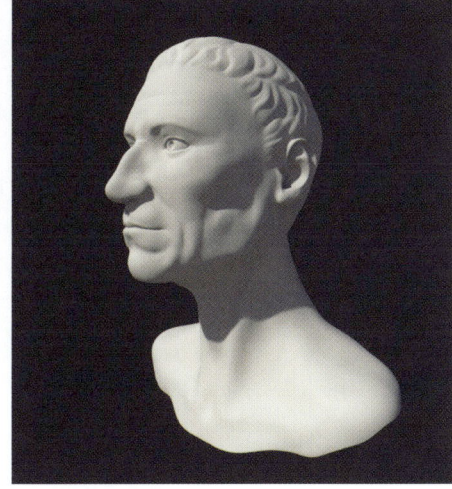

Ric My son finds the Cintiq very, very good for sniper shooting in Counter Strike. [laughs] What new product or innovation would you like from Wacom in the future?

Jake I guess something moving into haptic mechanisms although I don't really want an armature attached to my pen. I'd like to have different overlays for a range of tactile surfaces. I'd also like to see tighter integration between the hardware and the software applications like ZBrush and Mudbox. Like maybe a button switch on my actual stylus to say 'okay I'm switching from this mode to this mode like changing tools from a brush to knife but using the same stylus'. So that's probably a thing you could think about I'd use the same stylus but have different modes I can allocate to it. There's a hook tool in Zbrush which would be wonderful to be able do that with.

Ric The notion of utilising the rotation sensor of the Wacom Art Marker in ZBrush would be amazing but after some discussion with a developer it sounds like a lot of work to implement that kind of feature. We need more people like you asking ZBrush for this feature.

Jake Wacom should also talk to the Mudbox developers at Autodesk. They would probably be receptive to that kind of idea. The whole concept of being able to have a sphere and slightly tilting the brush to select an area behind the 3D same to pull the geometry out a bit would be great. So I can see that with your different type of stylus pens there could be some great tools developed for 3D.

Ric Thanks you so much Jake for sharing with us your interesting world of character designing for games on Art of Making Marks.

"I physically sculpt in Mudbox using the pen pressure sensitivity of the Wacom pen/tablet which is a big feature in that application. So you can actually, by pushing down harder you can actually manipulate the geometry and sculpt it."

creative innovator
:Steve Stamatiadis

Greater Frill
With Chainsword

SEE EXTRA CONTENT ON www.artofwa.com
STEVE STAMATIADIS
Krome Studios/Games Developer

Ric Welcome Steve to the Art of Making Marks. Just to open the interview could you introduce yourself and tell me a little bit about who you are and what you do?

Steve I'm Steve Stamatiadis, I'm the Creative Director at Krome Studios. My job involves pushing projects along from the creative point of view, making sure they're fun and look good and I also work on a day to day basis making games. The last one I did was Star Wars. I do a bit of art direction, game direction and game design, characters and all that sort of stuff. I do a bit of everything.

Ric Great. So how long have you been using tablets in your work and for fun?

Steve Well the first time was for work and that was I think 1994. It was a large A4 size one at the time which was the big beefy one but not the biggest, it was pre Intuos I think, the UD series of Wacom tablets and I've been using them ever since then. I've gone from different sizes, a little 4x5, then I was running the 6x8, previously I had a 6x11 and then the large Cintiq 21UX. The large display tablet which is one of the best things ever.

Ric Fantastic. At this point in time, is it your primary pen/tablet or secondary?

Steve I have the one tablet and I work with two displays but the big Cintiq is pretty much the primary pen/tablet for everything. It's my favorite by a long shot. I don't think I could go back to anything smaller.

Ric Do you see the Cintiq giving you an advantage or creating a more innovative way for you to approach your working process and creativity?

Steve I think what happens with the Cintiq, well just with pen/tablets in general is it gives you the whole thing of Undo, it lets you experiment more. But I'm finding with the Cintiq I'm actually drawing differently because of its size. I'm actually using my arm the way I'm supposed to be drawing. I know when I used to draw, I used to do very small sketches, working small with little wrist movements and now it's sort of elbow movements with a proper drawing style. It's intriguing because I never used to draw that way but it's the way you should really open up your arms to do actual big sweeping movements. So it's changed the look of my artwork a little bit - in a good way.

Ric A bit like getting the butcher's paper out and being able to do sweeping movements.

Steve It's exactly like that. Before it was more of an angular style and you do a lot more work to try and get the lines right but with the Cintiq 21UX you do the mark and if

creative innovator
:Steve Stamatiadis

creative innovator
:Steve Stamatiadis

and the way they work together is very intuitive. I think Photoshop has become very much like that, the way it's set up. So you can set your brushes up a certain way and it's got a good workflow now with the layers and stuff.

Ric Do you combine Illustrator in that process? Are you using Vector tools or are you just doing everything within Photoshop?

Steve I pretty much do everything within Photoshop. Photoshop's become even my pencilling tool where originally I'd pencil stuff on paper and scan it and then maybe ink in Photoshop or colour it in Photoshop. Now with the Cintiq it's gone from doing my layouts in Photoshop on the Cintiq, then I'll pencil it properly on the Cintiq. It's just like the whole process has just gone from paper to digital in the space of about less than a year, which is pretty amazing. It was just so easy to do. I don't need paper anymore because I can do it on this amazing thing. Yeah so working in Photoshop just makes it really easy to do that stuff.

Ric So that process could work into the workflow of your entire operation, everyone being digital and slotting in on that pipeline at some point depending on what they do?

Steve Yeah… because we're not tied to paper and if we need to make changes or move things around the guys are in the habit of working with layers so that we can have a nice quick interaction on the artwork. Sometimes we need to change things quite radically for publishes if we're getting approval. When we were doing concept art for Star Wars we'd go through maybe 8 to 10 versions or something and then they would go off and we'd have to get some feedback from Lucas Films of how they wanted stuff to fit in with the 'universe'. Sometimes it was only a couple of changes and we had the ability to do that digitally, because the guys at Lucas Films would be painting digitally as well.

Ric Cool. I guess one of my favorite questions to ask is about the future. If you had a crystal ball or wanted something from Wacom that solved some problems for you, what might that future innovation be?

Steve You know how Sony's got that paper display that looks like paper? Once we get that, where pen/tablets can feel like you're drawing on a pad of paper and still undo, I think that would be the most awesome thing. But that's requiring displays and stuff down the track to get much better. That kind of digital paper look and feel would be nice.

The new surface on the Cintiq is great, it feels more like paper when you use the optional grey nib in the pen. It feels like you're actually working on a piece of paper. If the screen had the brightness of paper as well that would be really great.

Ric Okay I'll get straight onto that one for you and let you know when it's ready!

Steve Digital paper would be a really big one I think. That way you wouldn't feel like you're drawing on a screen it would feel like you're just drawing on an A3 sketch pad, with texture.

Ric Would you like the Cintiq to be larger or a different screen format?

Steve Oh definitely a wide screen, 23 inch wide screen display I think would be great. And the technology that the new Cintiq 12UX has where it's really thin. We need more buttons on the side as well.

Ric How about with touch capabilities too… programmable touch surfaces or something?

Steve The ExpressKeys were a great addition to the system but even more of them would be good and programmable ones would be really cool with visual displays so you know what they are. That sort of stuff would be great.

Ric Has the ExpressKeys been significant for your productivity?

Steve Well I'm using that really thin Microsoft keyboard at the moment which compliments the tablet really well. Photoshop only uses pretty much just the one side of the keyboard; even a keyboard on the tablet would be kind of cool come to think of it.

Ric There is so much more you could do when you bring touch into play with the pen/tablet it's open to just program and arrange what you want. Visually you could put a keyboard right there on the screen.

Steve Or actually turn the whole tablet into a computer.

Ric Well of course we've got Tablet PCs for that, our technology is in most Tablet PCs already but it is a question that's asked a lot 'Are we going to produce one ourselves?' I think the answer at the moment is 'we're just concentrating on the interface technologies and let other people who build computers utilise that technology in different ways'.

Steve I think it's good to work with your strengths. It hasn't hurt Wacom so far.

Ric So thanks Steve that's fantastic. Good luck with everything and great work.

the mark doesn't come out quite right you might rotate the Cintiq and then undo and try a couple more times. Before I'd be doing a dozen more goes on a normal tablet, just trying to do it lots and lots of times, trying to get it right. With a normal tablet you're trying to do that hand eye coordination thing, matching it up with the screen. But being able to see it actually there where your hand has been, it's just a whole different feel. I love it.

Ric Fantastic. So Steve tell us more about your work?

Steve Most of my stuff is more comic book cartoon based which I enjoy most. I do some painted work as well but I really do like playing with the line width for comic style artwork, where the outlining is really the integral part of the image. So a lot of what I do is character design but costume design is a better word for it really.

Ric So you're designing the look and feel of the characters.

Steve It's like trying to bring the actual character or personality to life by what they're wearing clothing-wise. Because a lot of what you see in the game is visual short hand – hey this is a character and they might be wearing these types of clothes and you can tell immediately that this is what they're doing on a day to day basis. Then you add the personality to the clothes as well. So that's why I call it costume design as well as character design because really it's both elements that have to go together.

Ric What applications do you use mainly in your workflow?

Steve I'm pretty much just using Photoshop CS3 at the moment, extended version actually, because it gives me everything I need. Like it's a workhorse set of programmes, ones that aren't trying to be too pretty. When I got into the industry I was using Deluxe Paint on the Omega, which is one of the best paint packages ever because it was like 'hit these functions' and 'these functions work with other functions'

086 Art of Making Marks

SEE EXTRA CONTENT ON www.artofwa.com

KEN LAMBERT INK PROJECT
Broadcast Branding Design

Ric Welcome Ken to the Art of Making Marks. Please introduce yourself and tell us a little bit about what you do.

Ken My name is Ken Lambert. I'm the Creative Director and co-founder of Ink Project, and we're essentially a brand communication company specialising in the fields of print and broadcast design which also involves us in strategic thinking, creative development and also production. From there that can go anywhere from Animation to Live Action to Cross Media. There are no boundaries so it's completely open.

Ric So the technology can take you in many directions?

Ken I don't really rely on technology that much. It's a relevance play so we always want to be about ideas. That's the forefront of where we are, and we're about servicing those needs for clients and ourselves. So where I think Wacom is interesting is that I have been using the tablet for about 15 years, and I've come to a point where I'm actually totally reliant on it. When we hire new people and they come here I actually encourage them to go through that process. It's about two or three weeks where it's awkward, it's uncomfortable, but I actually feel that as we're working with the Wacom tablets it's actually more akin to drawing, it's more akin to a creative process, so I think the mouse is actually redundant, and for me, I can't actually use a mouse. So that's really important, and that comes down to even laying down technical things like topographic roles and that sort of thing. So in terms of that I think the Wacom tablet is incredibly important, however I don't actually encourage my guys to design on the computers. We design on paper and again it's more akin to the creative process, and so the natural step from that is pen to tablet. I've always thought areas that I'd really like Wacom to improve on would be to have more mouse functions in terms of the scrolling ability. To actually have a scrolling function on the pen, I think that would be cool. The thing with the pen is that it's actually quite good and that in terms of software I think that Wacom can go a little bit further with screen capture and recording mouse and pen strokes, that sort of thing, giving us data that we can actually use like scripts that can be used within programmes like After Effects, and other applications. I think things like that would be really useful and also for Wacom to step into the media side, actually start giving us tools that connects it all better.

> "I don't actually encourage my guys to design on the computers. We design on paper and again it's more akin to the creative process, and so the natural step from that is pen to tablet."

Ric Of course we're very reliant on other developers and most of our development is around just making sure that the drivers all talk to everything properly.

Ken Yeah. Look, I love the product, I think it's fantastic and I'm really encouraging us all to use it.

Ric What type of tablets do you use in your studio? I notice a lot of designers here using Intuos3. Is there any particular size that's preferred?

Ken We used to use really big tablets, because we were using Flame, Flint and all that sort of thing, but it's not very portable, and I think the A4 size works for me and it seems to work for everybody else. We've actually got rid of all of our large tablets because they take up too much room, and they are a little bit large in terms of the art becomes bigger and that sort of thing. The A4 seems to be adequate size. Any smaller seems to be too small for us, but A4 seems to be adequate, because again it equates to your wrist movement and that sort of thing.

Ric So tell us a little more about the work you produce?

Ken One of the main things that we do is branding, like for example we've just branded a well known advertising agency in Sydney, and that all goes throughout Australia. More so we're known for branding television stations, so things like TVNZ, SBS, we work in the United States with companies like the Sci-Fi Channel, AETN and Showtime. It's mostly to do with channel branding and all the auxiliary things that go with that.

Ric Fantastic. So we've touched on it earlier, what future innovations, would you like to see come from Wacom.

Ken I like the touch screen thing. Only the thing I feel is we're so used to that it's almost like third party now, and we concentrate so much on the cursor that when we go over it, I still think there's a gap between what you can do with technology and what you can do by hand, and so I guess that's what you guys are trying to do to make that gap smaller and smaller. I look forward to those sorts of innovations, but I don't have any big dreams for anything. To me it would be great to eventually have no tablets and no strings, and you're basically in this particular virtual world where you're grabbing things off shelves and manipulating them and placing them, and so actually physically involved so you're up from your seat and you're actually pushing things around in a dimensional space.

Ric So something like using VR or a holographic heads up display?

Ken Yes, I think that would be cool. I've seen some innovations from Sony where they've done things like, they would have a brain storm where they actually write a piece of text and it comes out in script, and then they're able to actually take that piece of type - being projected using lasers - they can take that piece of type and put it on the wall. But I think that you've got to be really careful about gimmicks. The industry moves so slowly that I think it's much like the iPod. If you can find that one thing that everybody wants, and right now it's, for me the thing would be the ease of use. You know what would be great? Do you guys have a portable Bluetooth version of the Wacom?

Ric Yes but only in our consumer range not in the Intuos range.

Ken OK well that's enough for me.

Ric Thank you so much for participating in the Art of Making Marks and good luck with all your future projects.

Ken Thank you.

SEE EXTRA CONTENT ON www.artofwa.com

GERRY HAGGERTY
2D/3D Graphic Artist

Ric Welcome Gerry to the Art of Making Marks and so just to kick things off I'd like you to introduce yourself and tell us a little about what you do.

Gerry Well my name is Gerry Haggerty, I've been working with Computer Graphics since 1987, which is the year that I met the man who gave me my first Wacom pen/tablet. That man happens to be you Ric Holland! When did we get that first Wacom tablet Ric? I think it was about 1988 or 1989 was it?

Ric You are probably right there Gerry although you may not remember but I had a few other brands of pen/tablets previous. The first was actually a Summagraphics tablet around 1985-86 which I used with Cricket Draw then I bought a Kurta tablet to use on my very first Mac II with I think Studio 8 and later PixelPaint. I then moved on to the Mac IIfx and bought my first Wacom pen/tablet, the SD-420. I had used one on a Quantel system and wanted to try and get the same experience on my desktop system. Unfortunately the computers were still very slow but we got by.

Gerry They did look good with our computers back then I must admit, but they work a lot better now. [laughs]

Ric Just for our readers benefit, Gerry and I worked together for many years as colleagues at my various design studios through those early digital pioneering days of uncertainty. There was hardly anyone else doing the level of digital work that we were achieving and there were never any guarantees that anything was going to actually work.

Ric So, Gerry through those pioneering days I often would say to myself when things weren't always going right, 'What are we doing all this for anyway?'

Gerry Well, apart from the obvious, which is keeping the wolf from the door I think it was just that we were always up for the challenge.

Ric [laughs] I think pens and pencils were actually a lot cheaper.

Gerry Yeah but we got dirty!

Ric Yep, Gumbo rubber adhesive then came wax machines and spray adhesive, anyway our readers don't want to know about all of that ancient technology. So how long do you think you've been using a pen/table, you do maths?

Gerry Oh, that must be about 16 - 17 years, something like that. I use it for everything basically now, apart from Illustrator.

creative innovator
:Gerry Haggerty

Ric You still don't use it for Adobe Illustrator?

Gerry No, I can't stand it for Illustrator, because I get clicks when I don't want them, so I just flip over to the mouse when I'm using Illustrator. But for every other piece of software that I use the Wacom is definitely the way to go, especially with just getting around the desktop, never mind painting, etc.

Ric I'd agree with you except for one point in Illustrator and I guess leading into Flash, pressure sensitivity in things like vector brush strokes are cool. So Gerry tell us about some of the work that you are doing these days. Apart form all the 2D Photoshop imaging and After Effects compositing you've done for years and years the architectural work you've been doing sounds very interesting.

Gerry Yes, the work I've been doing for Pro Pacific Architects is visualising a property that they were developing in the headland at Cairns in Queensland Australia. I get the architectural model files from ArchiCAD and I've got a very accurate terrain mesh as well, but I had to populate it with thousands of trees and bushes and make it look photo realistic. In Autodesk's 3D Studio Max I used this little program called Forest, with the Wacom tablet I can interactively use the pressure sensitivity of the pen/tablet to paint on the trees, which was great, it saved me a lot of hard work, trying to make all these thousands of trees. I ended up painting 270,000 gum trees onto the terrain model. With pressure sensitivity the more you paint the denser the bush line becomes and it was just beautiful. It was almost like playing god!

Ric So Gerry, tell us a little bit more about the way you use pen/tablets in your work flow.

Gerry The pen/tablet is the most useful tool for all the software I use, because going from 2D in print, into all the different types of media we use now, to be an effective designer/media artist these days you've got to know how to do vector, so that means Adobe Illustrator and able to use Photoshop and then bring it all into Adobe After Effects or Apple's Shake. Then of course there's 3D programs as well as pixel compositing programs. In all of that I use the Wacom tablet quite extensively for everything from dragging assets into compositions and imparting special effects and particle effects, modelling with meshes, pushing and pulling, so that you are sculpting in 3D with your Wacom tablet. Adding hair and other particle objects to 3D objects, etc, etc, as well as all the image retouching that I do on a daily basis. When you work in 3D and composite in 2D you have to be able to use Photoshop. It's just the tool of choice for image manipulation.

Ric How do you use the Wacom tablet with 3D Studio Max?

Gerry I have been using the hair plug in with the Wacom pen/tablet. It's just beautiful, you can paint hair on people and then comb the hair and style it interactively. When you're using the tablet you can save a lot of time. You don't have to go clicking back and forth with your mouse to increase the amount of hair coverage, etc. As well as painting on trees and flowers onto landscapes and manipulating the landscapes in real time, which is a great thing. It saves you having to go back into Photoshop and create new displacement maps and bump maps and all that.

Ric Fantastic, so what would you like for the future, what innovations or what things have you wished for that Wacom could provide to you as far as a better human interface?

Gerry My wish list for Wacom would be for a very cheap Cintiq that I could afford.

Ric Well how about half the price of the Cintiq 21UX?

Gerry Well now we're talking! Has that come out has it?

Ric Yes

Gerry Oh brilliant. Is it wireless as well?

Ric [laughs] No it does have a cable, but it's got a neat cable system, which is two and a half metres and all of the bits go into a need little breakout box, so you've got this nice thin screen/tablet, with a little fold out stand at the back so you can tilt it up, you can have it on your lap.

Gerry That just sounds wonderful.

Ric It's a beautiful little screen, nice resolution and you can also run it with multiple monitors and and your cursor can move back and forth between screens using the extra button on the ExpressKeys .

Gerry It exists now?

Ric It exists now, so your future dream is here already.

Gerry [laughs] I feel as though I've found a new religion. Let there be Wacom!

Ric It's great fun to talk with you as always Gerry, thank you so much for participating in the Art of Making Marks.

Gerry I'm very honoured Ric.

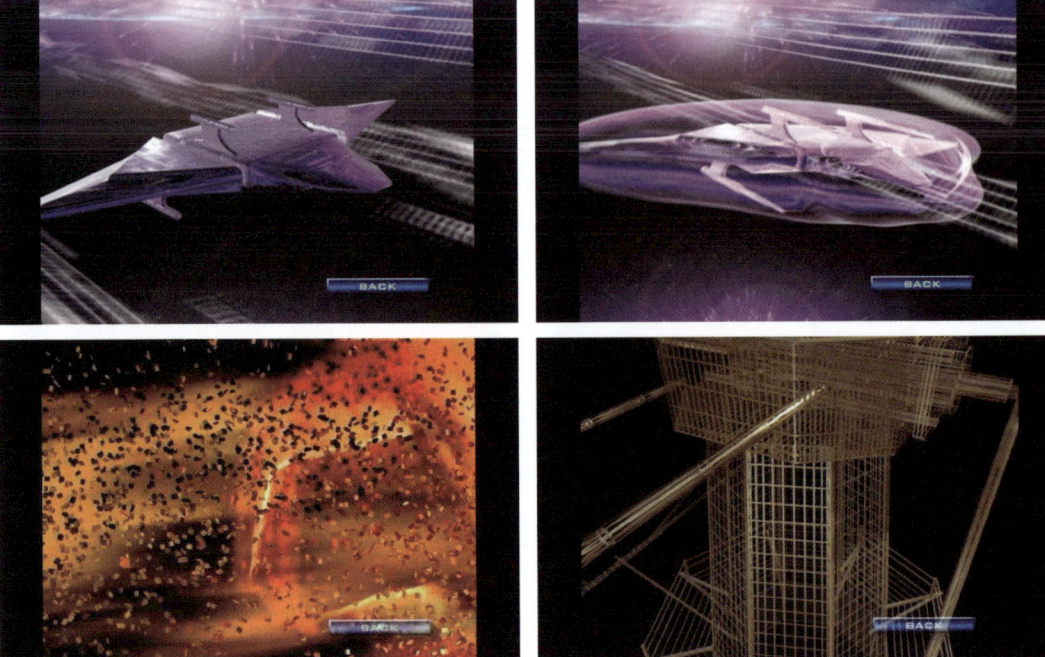

Art of Making Marks

ALLAN MacDONALD
Automotive Designer / Scania Trucks, Stockholm

SEE EXTRA CONTENT ON www.artofwa.com

Ric Welcome to the Art of Making Marks Allan. You are a designer at Scania of great big trucks. Please tell us how you got into the field of Automotive Design, specialising in truck design?

Allan My dad drives trucks, so I've always been around trucks and of course all boys are attracted to cars and stuff, so I was always interested but it hadn't actually occurred to me that somebody could actually design cars. I don't remember exactly why or when, but sometime near the end of school it just popped into my head for some reason that somebody actually must design cars. I don't really know why, but from then though it was just to try and find a route to be able to do that. So I started looking at the different universities and found out about the course at Coventry University in England, which has a course specifically for people who want to be car designers. The more I looked into it I realised it was actually a reasonably famous course with very good links to the industry. A lot of the people who are designing the cars we drive today have been there. So I actually decided, okay, that's what I want to do, and spent some time putting my portfolio together and applied to Coventry. Actually I was so sure that I wanted to be a car designer it was the only course I applied for. I think some people apply to different schools and hope to get in one or the other, a back up plan, but this was all I wanted to do so I went for it and got in. I studied there for four years and it was good fun. I also did a placement, six months work experience at Volkswagen in Germany in Wolfsburg which was a lot of fun. They were a very good studio and I learnt an awful lot. Not to take anything away from my time at Coventry, but when you're actually in an environment with some really good designers and some really professional people it's amazing.

Ric It's the beginning of a life time of learning really isn't it?

Allan Yes that's right, and I had a fantastic time there, just to see how it all happens was a dream you know…I am in a car design studio! So that was fantastic, and then after that I graduated and started working at quite a large consultancy in England called Design Research. I was there for a year and then spent another year at Rover Cars which was a lot of fun. It was quite interesting actually to contrast those two companies because at the consultancy it's a lot of different projects, you have a lot of things coming in and obviously you have to know the business as well, but when you switch to a car company you tend to see things through to fruition a lot more, taking projects the whole way through. I'd always planned that I wanted to design trucks though, so I wrote off to Volvo Trucks and after a couple of interviews they said yes. I was there for five years and did a lot of enjoyable work there. I would say that in my five years there that's where I learnt the most. I was there for a long time and I saw a lot of different projects through. Then about a year ago now I just decided it was time for maybe a little bit of a change, try something new, so a year ago I moved to Scania Trucks in Stockholm. And that's where I am now.

Ric Do you have to take on a new philosophy in design or do you bring your own philosophy and concepts with you?

Allan That's an interesting question. I think a bit of both, but of course as a designer you have a little bit of your own style, especially in the way you draw. I think it's inevitable that something of your style will come out, but of course it's very important to spend some time to find out the values and the look and feel of the company you work for…what they stand for. Your designing a product for them, it's not for you. Does that make sense?

Ric Yes absolutely.

Allan And of course since my Dad's a truck driver I've been around trucks a long time and I understand them very well. They're in my blood.

Ric That smell of diesel?

Allan Exactly and I feel that I intuitively understand the differences between the brands just given that I've been aware of them for such a long time.

Ric You've spent a lot of time building up your drawing skills, at what point did you adopt digital tools as part of your drawing process?

Allan My first job actually, so that's an easy question to answer. At Coventry, I don't know the reason why, but we didn't have those tools available so it never really happened. I'd never even actually used the internet which seems really bizarre when you look back on it now.

Ric In a lot of ways it's good to keep everything fairly focused and pure at the training stages. I trained completely traditionally, but then again there weren't any digital tools in those days.

Allan I wouldn't say there was a reason for it, I don't know if it was a budgetary thing or something, but I just never came across them. I don't even remember it crossing my mind that you could really draw digitally. Having said that when I think back to my first job I don't remember it feeling strange working digitally with Photoshop and such things. Are you familiar with Alias?

Ric Absolutely, Alias Studio Tools?

Allan Exactly so they had the tools. It was my first introduction to using a Wacom pen/tablet with Photoshop, and using Alias, all of those things. It wasn't so fun at the time but I do remember one of the ways I learnt Photoshop. Every time there was a presentation they would scan in all these different drawings and sketches and have me using the lasso tool to cut out these sketches and put them onto a presentation board. I guess you're pretty familiar with Photoshop too and remember the first time

you used the lasso tool. It can get a bit complicated, it's a weird tool the first time you use it.

Ric Well with a mouse it's pretty cumbersome.

Allan Exactly, but I got into working with it, and just slowly picking up all these skills. The first time you really get into digital rendering is a revelation. I'm sure you're aware of that too. You suddenly find you can try so many different things. For myself I thought the most exciting thing was the development in my drawing skills. You can learn how to draw better and much faster because you can try so many different things, things you might be scared to do on paper. You've got to get it right on paper, you make a mistake and you've got to throw it away but Control Z is a fantastic feature.

Ric Of course layers was a god send when that occurred.

Allan Exactly, you can try different lighting situations with what you've drawn, try out different headlamps. It's really so versatile.

Ric How long have you been using a Wacom pen/tablet?

Allan About eight years and actually on Cintiqs for around five years.

Ric So you've gone through the evolution of Wacom pen/tablets?

Allan Yes the first one I had was I the big beige one, I don't know which model that was.

Ric Do you notice much change in sensitivity and control with features like tilt?

Allan To be honest no and when you mention the tilt that's one part of the function I've never used. I have some colleagues who use Painter of course.

Ric Yes, you get tilt functionality in Painter that's correct.

Allan To be honest I don't think they even use the tilt functionality. It's a little bit of a better program for drawing, sketching fast movements for example. The maths behind it is a little bit better than Photoshop for doing this type of work. Photoshop doesn't seem to support the tilt, so I've never used it, and the pressure thing… I'll be honest I don't notice the difference. At least it's nothing I've ever thought about.

Ric And so, you're working on a Cintiq 21UX these days?

Allan Yes. I think I've tried them all. I had the Cintiq 18SX, the first one that came out with the big frame and then so on and so forth.

Ric And have you had a chance to play with the Cintiq 12WX?

Allan To be fair everybody here has a Cintiq 21UX, so of course coming down to the little 12" one felt a little bit like a backward step. One of the nice things I found about it though, and you might find this a little bit funny, was that it is fantastic for surfing the internet. It was so light and small you could just sit it in your lap. I was discussing with one of my colleagues what he would look for with regards to improvements to the Cintiq 21UX and of course it's the size and bulk of it we would like to reduce. I guess you're all aware of that. I don't really know anybody who's ever really lifted it off the stand to actually sit it on their lap and sketch. The one time I've done it is when you have some engineers coming for a meeting and you just want to show off…you do it then.

Ric I've heard of people mounting them on mechanical arms so as to have a little more ergonomics that way.

Allan I'm kind of used to it now, and I actually don't think about it now, but at first I remember wondering where to put the keyboard and I had ideas to mount it above the Cintiq amongst other things. Now I don't even think about it, it's not a problem.

Ric Tell us a little bit more about your work?

Allan I enjoy my work. Basically I get paid to draw things, which is fantastic.

Ric Is your work all in 2D or 3D as well? You mentioned Alias Studio Tools so are you actually involved in taking your visualisations through the 3D modelling process?

Allan I use Alias, now called Autodesk Studio Tools, so yes, and of course I'm designing 3D objects so I have to understand what I'm drawing. Whether I give it to an Autodesk modeller, a CAD modeller or a clay modeller, I have to at least understand what my drawings mean in 3D. So yes, you're correct; I work in 3D as well with the first rough model usually being built by me.

Ric And so what other application do you use?

Allan I build in Alias/Autodesk so yes I make a rough model. My job though isn't to be an Alias/Autodesk modeller but it's an advantage to be able to use it and thrash out some shapes.

Ric What about applications like Autodesk's Mudbox and Pixologic's ZBrush, are they tools that are starting to be used in car/truck design?

Allan I've never even heard of those.

Ric ZBrush has been used a lot in the film industry for sculpting and facial detail. It crosses the digital bridge between 2D and 3D.

Allan It's interesting you mention film production because I think one difference certainly in automotive design and

perhaps as well in product design is the importance of surface quality. In film it's purely sculpture, but in automotive design you have to think about highlights, lead in, curvature and such things. I'm assuming there's different kind of maths involved. I know for example when working with 3D Studio Max or Maya there's a different way to model. Autodesk Studio Tools is much more precise in what it does for surfaces.

Ric Of course Alias Studio Tools was built from the ground up for an industrial designer although it's interesting because Autodesk has bought Mudbox from its previous owner and they've been doing a lot of work with it and I would imagine to bring into their suite of products as part of the workflow so you may find it popping up at some point as something useful.

Allan It's an interesting thing you say because bringing different ways to sculpt and model can always bring different qualities to the process. That is always going to be interesting and exciting.

Ric There's some interesting stuff on YouTube showing this type of product being used with multi-touch and a more human and tactile interaction to the software. Maybe it's too early to ask you what you think about this but it's certainly a developing field that I'm very interested in.
www.youtube.com/watch?v=wh1Qy6OvI1A

Allan I always find the thought fascinating that you could be looking at the model on the screen and actually just push your hand against the surface and have it move to your touch. It could be really interesting but probably is one of those things you don't really know how it would feel.

Ric How do you sketch down your thoughts?

Allan I use Photoshop for 2D work. Other people may just draw on paper, some use Painter and other tools like SketchBook Pro. In the beginning of a project working in 2D is the fastest way to get as many ideas, thoughts and suggestions as possible down in order to have something visible to discuss. Generally when a project starts that's what we do, we sketch a lot of things and get them up on the wall. The design chief can then come in and say they like the direction or that we should maybe try this sketch with some of the details from another, and so we start a discussion. Of course more sketches follow and at a certain point it slowly starts to progress into 3D. Usually it begins with some CAD, either by the designer or a CAD modeller putting something together. Sketching is continuous through the whole process, but now you also have a 3D model to discuss as well. In most cases in the automotive industry at some point clay models are also developed, and you begin to work on that as well. Even sketch on it. It's interesting because I noted down that one of the nice things about being digital is that you can take pictures of the clay, bring it back to the computer and sketch direct on the photos. It's easier this way to explain to your modeller what you're aiming at, which would be not so easy to do on non digital photos.

Ric Is the design process constantly evolving?

Allan For me personally I don't see a great deal of change. Of course the digital thing has become stronger and stronger, computers get faster and faster and the CAD programs get more powerful. 3D rendering tools have become much stronger because of this, for instance Autodesk Showcase, the new tool from Autodesk for rendering 3D models to a photo realistic finish. You can spin the model around in real time and see the car from different angles. Those kinds of things are progressing very fast now since rendering CAD eight years ago was something that took a lot of time. Setting up the render and getting all the lights in the right place, doing test renders and making adjustments could take many hours, if not days to get a really nice render. Now it's something we can do

creative innovator
:Allan MacDonald

virtually in real time. HDRI technology allows us to build a photo realistic environment around the model which fulfils all the lighting as well as the reflection needs. It's a much faster part of the process. Generally though it's still a 2D process we begin with, before progressing to 3D and then eventually ending up as a product. I guess it's fair to say we still rely on the real aspect. We still want to see some kind of physical model, because as good as these programs get it's absolutely no substitute for seeing the thing in front of you with your own eyes. Being able to walk around it and touch it is very important.

Ric Are these full scale?

Allan We do both. We do smaller scale versions at the start.

Ric That must be pretty impressive seeing a full size clay truck?

Allan They weigh a lot I can say that. The process usually starts in some kind of a scale model though, maybe a quarter scale, since you can move the clay around faster, allowing more design time. I remember when the digital thing really started to take off and you'd hear a lot of talk about not needing clay anymore. I think you will always need something physical in front of you at some point in the process. Having said that, the digital process makes the clay modelling stage faster and more efficient since you can try things out in the computer first. You can experiment before having to move clay around. We can also use rapid prototyping machines to build quick models, we can print small items in 3D to hold look at and discuss.

Ric Is there anything that you would like Wacom to develop in the future.

Allan Wacom Cintiqs or any of the Wacom tablets for that matter are still a two dimensional interface. I was thinking more along the lines of bring it into a three dimensional interface with up, down, left, right and near to far if you see what I mean?

Ric A spatial interface?

Allan Yes exactly. Though you will need the right kind of feel if you're trying to push a surface. It might feel so unnatural that it doesn't work … but if it does work then it would be fantastic.

Ric It would need some sort of field that creates friction.

Allan Yes that would be great, when you close your eyes it would feel like you were really manipulating the surface with your hands. I think that would be awesome.

Ric The movie Iron Man presents some nice concepts for the industrial designer or engineer. 3D prototyping is done using holographic projections, moving things across screens just by pointing a pen. Minority Report presents the glove concept and throwing images around the screens. There's some interesting stuff there and certainly some innovation is going on in this field of interface technology. I think it's really got to do a lot with good collaboration between software and hardware technologies also the end users themselves bringing the right questions to be answered.

Allan Well if we look back to my Cintiq 21UX it is not very mobile and when I'm working with all these different people, including CAD modellers, clay modeller's engineers and so on there are a lot of meetings. It would be fantastic to have a drawing tool which could come with me. Where I could sit in these meetings and sketch out ideas directly.

Ric So portability but on the scale of the Cintiq 21UX?

Allan Yes. We tried the Cintiq 12WX but personally I just felt a little bit cramped on that size screen.

Ric The thing I feel the Cintiq 12WX really has in its favour is this ability to move from one screen to the other with a new button that's included on the top of the express keys.

Allan Aha, I didn't try that.

Ric That really opens up a few things because then you can think of it as an Intuos3 6x11 pen/tablet which also can function as a small and light Cintiq.

Allan Exactly, opens up a new way to work.

Ric It's really a hybrid between Cintiq and Intuos. That's basically where I saw the greatest advantage with that particular product and the fact that you can sit back with it to do a bit of sketching and so it doesn't replace the Cintiq 21UX. Allan thank you for being on the Art of Making Marks.

Allan My pleasure.

"For a long time whilst studying in high school my intention was to become a graphic designer. For many reasons however this prospect did not excite me, but at the time I could not see any other options. I was doodling a car one day when the idea came to me that somebody must do this for a living."

creative innovator
:Tin&Ed

SEE EXTRA CONTENT ON www.artofwa.com

TIN&ED
Graphic Design Studio

Ric Welcome to the Art of Making Marks. Thank you for this interview. Can you just introduce yourselves and tell us a little about what you do?

Tin Well I'm Tin, and he's Ed, and together we're Tin&Ed.

Ric Fantastic.

Tin We do graphic design and moving a little bit towards doing full motion.

Ed It's hard when you say graphic design, I suppose we're not sort of traditional like that, we're always up for a challenge of something that we haven't done before and, like on the weekend we were painting trees for a video clip and we seem to get involved in anything and everything.

Ric So from the technology side of your studio, how long have you been using Wacom tablets in your workflow?

Ed Well, actually not long enough. We only got them at the start of the year, well Tin got one at the start of the year, it's just something that we've been meaning to do and didn't realise what a difference it would make.

Tin It made such a…

Ed ….difference!

Tin We do a lot of illustrations and that sort of involves drawing and scanning in and cleaning up and all that sort of stuff. All of a sudden we were just drawing straight into the computer. You have almost the same, well pretty much the same control as working on paper.

Ed More control over the way that it works with different variations. You're not so restricted.

Tin So we haven't actually been using the Wacoms for that long but it's totally changed the way that we work which has been fantastic.

Ric So, I noticed you're using a combination of Intuos3 and Graphire4 pen/tablets on various computers.

Tin We just got the one that was quite easily available in a Mac store, but then when we decided to get our second one we looked into it and did some research to find out what would be best for us and bought the better one. Tin uses it for absolutely everything. I don't really use my mouse anymore. [laughs]

Art of Making Marks 095

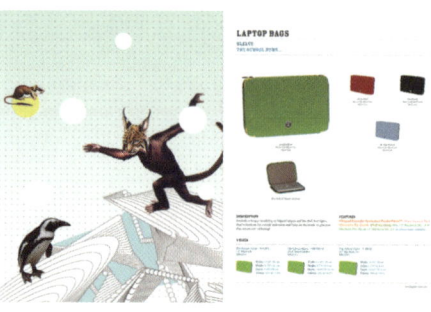

"We do a lot of illustrations and that sort of involves drawing and scanning in and cleaning up and all that sort of stuff and all of a sudden we were just drawing straight in to the computer. You have almost the same, well pretty much the same control as working on paper."

Ric So it's become a mouse replacement?

Tin Yeah, it's a mouse replacement, but in terms of our work we use a lot of Photoshop for illustrations and also Illustrator for illustrations as well. Illustrator has probably been a very surprising in terms of more control.

Tin The fact that you can actually get different line weights in Illustrator surprised us, and now since we're moving real big into animation using Flash we can use this same feature.

Ed I don't necessarily like the tools as much in Flash, After Effects has been really good. We're only just starting to get in to Adobe After Effects though.

Tin Everything that's drawing related is done with the Wacom, the other thing that we use it for is visualisation, it's really good just to be able to sketch and brainstorm ideas.

Tin We don't' really use our scanner as much anymore, which is good. [laughs] Because we would sit there for a week just scanning and cleaning things up and now it's just straight in.

Tin It's changed the way we draw as well, we just draw bits in different places and move it around here and there. The undo thing is amazing; you can't draw with a pencil and go oops, that's a mistake. Undo!

Ric If you could ask Wacom for some cool new innovation what would it be?

Tin That's a hard one. I wish they had more tools. I know there's the airbrush and art pen but some different pens and brushes that feel more like traditional charcoals, markers, and different size brushes.

Ed Also a future thing could be like a sort of touch sensitive thing, so that you can start designing a bit more with your hands. Obviously you still want to use the pen as well.

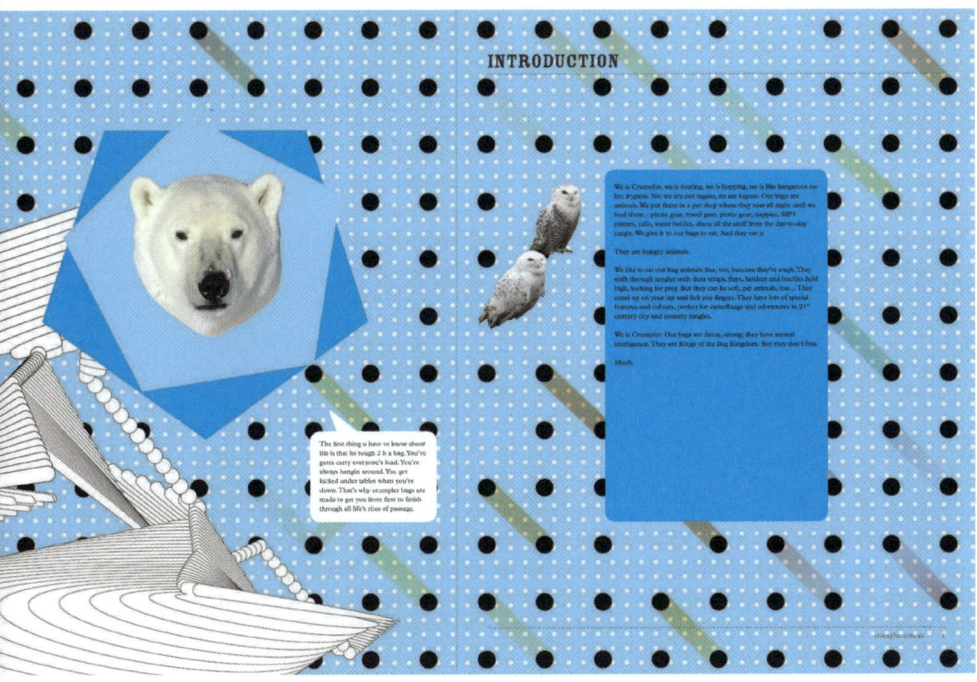

INTRODUCTION

We is Crumpler, we is roaring, we is hopping, we is like kangaroos on hot poppers. No, we are not lagans, we are lagans. Our bags are animals. We put them in a pet shop where they roar all night until we feed them – picnic gear, travel gear, plenty gear, nappies, MP3 players, cells, water bottles, discs, all the stuff from the day-to-day jungle. We give it to our bags to eat. And they eat it.

They are hungry animals.

We like to set our bag animals free, too, because they're tough. They stalk through jungles with their straps, flaps, holders and buckles held high, looking for prey. But they can be soft, pat animals, too... They crawl up on your lap and lick you finger. They have lots of special features and colours, perfect for camouflage and adventures in 21st century city and country jungles.

We is Crumpler. Our bags are fierce, strong; they have animal intelligence. They are Kings of the Bag Kingdom. But they don't bite.

Much.

The first thing u have to know about life is that its tough 2 b a bag. You're gotta carry everyone's load. You're always hangin around. You get kicked under tables when you're down. That's why xtrampler bags are made to get you more feet to finish through all life's rites of passage.

Tin   Yeah and smudge it with your hands! Or put on a special glove and it's like wet and dry paint and then smudge it.

Ric   Wacom gloves! Excellent. Well thanks guys for this interview and I'm sure all the readers are just fascinated with your work and how you do it. Is there anything else that you want to share with us before we go?

Tin   Creativity, it's cool.

Ed   You should all do it.

Ric   What are your plans for the future?

Tin   We just finished art directing a video clip, like a music clip, so we sort of want to do a bit more motion stuff and work a lot more with Adobe After Effects and that sort of thing.

Ed   Go to the US. Well, it's a world trip but mostly just to go to New York and show of our stuff and, I don't know, having fun and all that.

Ric   The world's your oyster! Thanks guys.

Tin   Yeah thanks. [laughs]

SSENGER BAGS
ARNEY RUSTLE BLANKET...

FEATURES

JULIEANNE KOST
Adobe Senior Photoshop Evangelist

Ric Okay, so just to kick things off Julieanne, could you introduce yourself and tell us a little about what you do.

Julieanne Sure, my name's Julieanne Kost and I have been working with Adobe since 1992. I went to work with them because I couldn't afford the software at the time and knew that I wanted to be a photographer. I actually got a degree in psychology and biomechanics of movement and my parents weren't fond of sponsoring the arts at the time, which I totally understand now.

Ric So they wanted you to get a real job.

Julieanne Totally yes, and I now understand what they were saying. My mum was a silk screener and did elaborate artwork that she sold for barely enough to cover her costs so my father I'm sure looked at that and said "no, let's not go the art school route". But I went back and got a degree in photography, afterwards.

Ric Psychology then photography!

Julieanne The degree in psychology was very helpful when I went to work with Adobe in tech support and a little awareness always helps. So I've always wanted to make images and that's why I have my day job.

Ric Did you know that psychologists and sociologists make good graphic designers?

Julieanne No.

Ric They can reverse engineer a piece of visual communication you know by working out what people are responding or reacting well to first, and then go and design something appropriate.

Julieanne It makes sense.

Ric David Carson a well known designer from New York once told me that he trained first as a sociologist and then later became a designer and this he believes is one of the secrets to his success. Hope I haven't given away too much there David.

Julieanne Oh yeah. I know who he is. I love his work. He probably will forget more about type than i will ever learn!

Ric What do you do currently?

Julieanne I actually travel around the US and around the world and teach people, try and educate them on Photoshop and its features and hopefully get the technical part across so that they can focus much more on the creative part.

Ric So at what point while using Photoshop did you start using Wacom tablets?

Julieanne It was actually kind of late in the game. Probably like eight years ago I started using a tablet. I think the reason is I bought the really big one, but it took up to much space on my desktop, I went and got the smaller one (Intuos3 4x5) which also took me a little while to get used to, bit of a slow learner, I guess. It probably took me a week to get really comfortable with it. Maybe it was more like two weeks because I kept going

creative innovator
:Julieanne Kost

back to the mouse, because it was something that I knew and then one day it just kind of clicked. You know, you just … it's like, you can't really teach anyone how to use it. I mean you pick it up and it seems intuitive but it doesn't because I was using the mouse for so long.

Ric 'Mousing over' is the key; after I show somebody how to 'mouse over' which is to actually float the pen point over the tablet, people start to get it. First time tablet users often don't realise you can do that.

Julieanne Another interesting thing is that you can do that also to make sure that you get a brush stroke right. It's like you mouse over without doing anything to practise first and then you can go back and lay down the stroke. It's beautiful, yeah, it's great.

Ric What Wacom tablets do you use now?

Julieanne I use the Intuos3 4x5 in my demonstrations because it travels better and I have the Intuos3 6x8 in my office at Adobe plus I have a Cintiq 21UX at home. So I think that the thing that's interesting to me is that coming from the darkroom I knew how to dodge and burn, and then you really have to relearn that when you start working with a mouse and it was like I finally got comfortable with that, just because I learned to adapt to the mouse. So as soon as I got a Wacom tablet it was quite a lot easier than using the mouse itself. It wasn't so much as me being a slow learner but again it was just me adapting to another technology and, you know, that was eight years ago and obviously I've never gone back to the mouse for any of my creative work.

Ric Talking with Russell Brown over many years and as my career has spanned using systems like Quantel Paint Box, Lumina and other painting systems like that, I originally learnt to paint and retouch digitally in real time. Then PixelPaint, ColorStudio and Photoshop came along on the Mac/PC, trying to do the same things without enough processing power, so that nothing worked in real time. I found Russell's presentations always fascinating because he showed his techniques for creating selections and blends to create similar results but just not in real time. Channel operations, Airbrush blends, all done through a selection process, editing channels, and whatever rather than to just paint the thing in. I feel that the last 10 years have been like a renaissance of sorts for digital photo retouching and illustration. Finally being able to digitally paint and draw on a PC in real time is very empowering, would you agree?

Julieanne Yes it is incredibly empowering. I will say that the biggest benefit for me is the control, because I mean I can manipulate images in a way that I could never have done in the tractional wet darkroom. Some people can but I don't have the patience, and the same with retouching. I've seen people do it traditionally but I would not have the patience to do that.

Ric When you say traditionally do you mean using acid washes in the dark room?

Julieanne Yes absolutely and cutting friskets and then using the dyes. Yeah, no way. I would not have the patience for that.

Ric In my interview with Richard Luxton a professional photo retoucher from the original discipline, who's now probably one of the most experienced in the country for digital fashion photographic retouching, he says he went

"I love the fact that i can take pictures from different points in time and assemble them and make something that does not exist... It's somewhere between that decisive moment where you're capturing what's happening......"

directly from the dyes and masking to a Kodak Premier system, which used a Wacom tablet. And so he's been using that from the very beginning, and then from there to a Mac based Photoshop scenario to the point now where it's just how he does everything. And he says it's just that he can't understand how anyone ever, at any point, used a mouse for this kind of work. I'm often talking to people in conferences and trade exhibitions and someone will come up to me and say 'Tablets Oh yeah, but I can do all this photo retouching stuff with a mouse", I just say "Well, that's great and I'm pleased for you but maybe really you're holding yourself back. If you can do all that with a mouse, well it'll be amazing to see what you can do with a pen!"

Art of Making Marks

creative innovator
:Julieanne Kost

Julieanne It's also their speed. It's so much faster with the pen on a tablet. All you have to do is look at someone's history palette in Photoshop while they work. When they are working with a mouse you can watch each stroke whereas watching them with a pen, it's just a blur and it's done. If I'm doing hair or if I'm doing skin or retouching or anything, you can't do it with one stroke. You have to do it with a lot of small strokes or it'll look like you painted one stroke and it doesn't look like an eyelash, or you remove something and it looks like you did it with one stroke. You really need to get in there and dodge and burn. I know with my illustrations I could never get the masks just right without using a tablet.

Ric You have two very interesting sides to your career, one side being the on-stage Photoshop master and the other side being Julieanne the published artist. Tell us about Julieanne the artist?

Julieanne Julieanne the artist is not very in balance [laughs] because Julieanne the evangelist seems to take all of her time.

Ric You have to sneak that art in there when you can.

Julieanne I try, I do.

Ric I noticed that it comes out in your presentation.

Julieanne I don't nearly spend enough time making illustrations. It's because I do them for myself, and I really enjoy that and I want to do them and you know, an illustration can take me three to six months. I mean, people always ask "well how long did it take you to make that" because I'll use a lot of the illustrations to then demonstrate features and I tell them "thirty-eight years it took me to make that", because it's like that. They are the sum of everything that's come before and I like that. I love the fact that I can take pictures from different points in time and assemble them and make something that does not exist. It's not just a place that doesn't exist but it's a feeling that doesn't exist and it's a point in time that doesn't exist, so it's somewhere between that decisive moment where you're capturing what's happening, and then cinematography where you're telling a story over time. I've got snippets of time and place, but in a still image. And I like that. I like that a lot.

Ric It's like you're conjuring your own reality.

Julieanne Yeah, oh yeah it's not a reality that's out there at all, and that's where the psychology comes in too, because every time I finish a piece I can look at it and go "oh, I remember when I did/saw/felt that. I know what that's about."

Ric You're using a tablet as a mouse replacement, to your dodging and burning, to illustrate, so tell us a little bit about your workflow using a tablet? Is there a workflow?

Julieanne Is there a workflow? I've never thought of it as a workflow. A workflow implies work, and the tablet doesn't really make me work, it's kind of the anti-work. The tablet is what makes it effortless to make composites, to isolate objects and then blend them seemlessly into another scene.

Ric Now that's nice. I'd like to use that. [laughs]

Julieanne Yeah, it's indispensable. I think one of the problems that most people have with Photoshop and with computers in general is just that they're struggling with the technology, and the Wacom tablet is one of the few things I don't struggle with. I mean, it's very intuitive. It's going back to drawing again, and it's more intuitive than anything I ever did in the darkroom, that's for sure. You had to cut out little pieces of paper to dodge and burn that way using Photoshop with a Wacom pen, it's so much more precise. A mouse just isn't interactive at all and the tablet really is. I think the only time I ever use a mouse is to do email or whatever, and then obviously I'll switch over to the mouse because I don't want to type with the pen in my hand. It's just easier to type with the keyboard and mouse but once I'm in Photoshop, there's really no reason. I have the Cintiq 21UX at home and I love it. It's great, you just work right on it, and at first you know it was kind of odd because your hand seems to get in the way but then I started thinking about it – "Wait a minute, I drew for years and my hand never got in the way and I'm not smudging anything. Like how fantastic is that, I can drag my hand over the artwork that I've just done and nothing is smearing.

Ric I used to have a special piece of paper and little tricks to prevent that from happening but now there is no need.

Julieanne Yeah, all those things are gone.

creative innovator
:Julieanne Kost

Ric I remember airbrushing and splattering white paint on my artwork at three o'clock in the morning and the project had to be ready the next day. That splodge of white paint ended up as a beautiful cloud. [laughs]

Julieanne Ah yes those little work-a-rounds.

Ric You mentioned about the intuitive connection between you and the computer when using your Wacom tablet. Did you know that 'Wa' in Japanese means harmony? Wacom is all about creating harmony between people and computers, and of course with the new brand direction for Wacom being 'Open Up, Sense More' so it's all about creating better human interface solutions and so a really interesting question I like to ask people is; what would you like to happen in the future around making technology better and easier? Maybe for you it's with Photoshop? Is there's some special thing that Wacom could innovate that would make your life better or easier or more creative?

Julieanne I mentioned the integration with the keyboard, just because I would like to use my left hand for the keyboard and still have the majority of the screen area to paint on so that I don't have to sit there and fumble reaching over to the keyboard.

Ric So you would like a software touch type keyboard actually on the screen?

Julieanne Yeah, I think that would be great. Anything interactive that I could pull up with my pinky and a keyboard appears and I just grab what I need temporarily and let go of it and have it disappear.

Ric Yes I think we'll have something like that for you. It's coming but will require some software integration from Adobe.

Julieanne Okay. That's what I want then.

Ric The touch and point technology is definitely on its way. There are already some Tablet PCs that use our tablet technology and also have touch screens built in.

Julieanne Yeah, I tried one of those. I think it was an IBM which reverses out and then you can just write on it, it was quite nice.

Ric We licence Wacom pen technology to many major laptop manufacturers.

Julieanne Yes, and this was definitely Wacom technology. I love my little Intuos3 tablet you know. If I travel with it, then it has to speak for how much I love it because I try to travel very light. I have to travel so much for Adobe that I am very tired of carrying everything around.

Ric Well thanks Julieanne, this has been fabulous.

Julieanne Thank you, Ric!

Ric Thank you for your time and I'm sure everyone will take great pleasure in looking at your images in this book.

Julieanne I certainly hope that they do, and thank you Ric for enabling me to participate and share what I believe to be one of the most essential tools for working with digital - regardless of it it's my Cintiqu or my tablet, I can't imagine the process of making art without it. .

Ric Thank you for participating in the Art of Making Marks.

"A workflow implies work, and the tablet doesn't really make me work, it's kind of the anti-work."

creative innovator

creative innovator
:Dr. Phillip George

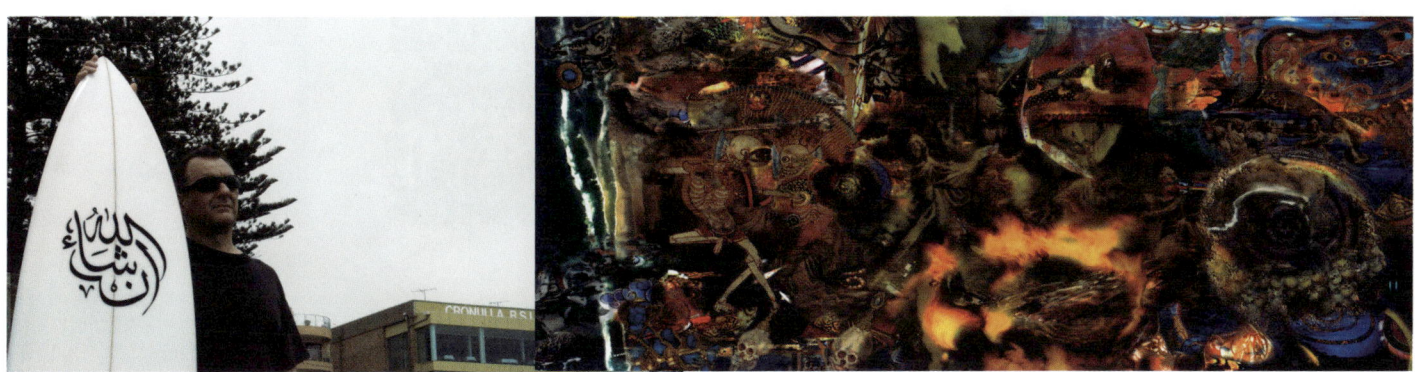

SEE EXTRA CONTENT ON www.artofwa.com

DR. PHILLIP GEORGE
Digital Media / University of New South Wales

Ric Welcome Dr Phillip George to The Art of Making Marks. Please introduce yourself and tell us a little bit about who you are and what you do.

Dr Phillip Well I've been, Originally I trained as an artist in, painting, drawing and photography, print making, all those sorts of things at art school and then got into digital image making in about 1989/90 and started working with digital pixel based practice, so photograph and painting on a computer. So my work I suppose has evolved into what they call digital imaging these days but I see it more as an evolution of painting and so I use hand marks, I use photographic work and I make these very large scale mural works. I use Painter, Live Picture and Photoshop generally. I just finished my Doctorate, so it's now Dr Phillip George, University of New South Wales College of Fine Art. I work in the digital media area and lecture in digital imaging. We have undergraduate programs, masters programs, honours programs and going up to PHD level so it's right across the board and I lecture in all those areas and was head of the School of Media Arts until about two years ago. So I established the digital media degree at the College of Fine Arts. Got it up and running and then jumped ship and I still teach there and do my own research plus digital and photographic base work.

Ric So you're one of those guys who really knows what's going on?

Dr Phillip Well maybe we're about to work that out. [Laughs]

Ric In the work that you've been doing over the years, how long have you been using Wacom tablets?

Dr Phillip Well I actually started off using a Summagraphics tablets in about 1990 so it's from the very first computer I ever bought I was using tablets and then from when I got rid of the Window machine, getting onto Mac I started using Wacoms from very early on. I've always used a tablet from 1990 up until present. I've never been without it. In fact I even use it for word processing. Everything I do on the computer I tend to use a tablet for.

Ric You actually just reminded me of my Summagraphics tablet although it was never very useful on my Mac plus! I too had migrated to Wacom by the time I had my Mac II, but sorry I digress and so what sort of tablet do you use now?

Dr Phillip I've got a Wacom, the Intuos3 which is probably the best tablet I've actually ever used. The pen's really ergonomically very, very good and I recommend it to all my students. I think I get the student in first year on their second week and I tell them, 'here's a Wacom tablet, use it or get RSI.' And that's part of our occupational health and safety speech and the only two things I ever ask my students to go and buy pretty quickly, is a portable hard drive and a Wacom tablet.

Art of Making Marks   103

creative innovator
:Dr. Phillip George

Ric Very pleased to hear that and you know I'm not just saying that because I work for Wacom.

Dr Phillip Well, it's critical. I mean it's just not for making marks on a computer, but actually using a Wacom is an occupational health and safety solution. I think because people who use a mouse to make work just end up with RSI in a week, you know, it's just stupid. So, the amount of time digital people work on a computer, you've got to have a Wacom. It's just an essential thing.

Ric So now Phil, could you tell us, about your work displayed in this book, how you go about doing them, and the software tools that you use?

Dr Phillip From probably 1993/94 on, I've been using essentially Live Picture and I still use Live Picture on an older machine with a tablet and my work is generally very large scale. I've got images installed in the Deutsche Bank building. There's one image there that's eight metres long and three metres high. So all the work I do is relatively large scale.

Ric What size file would that be?

Dr Phillip A several gigabyte file. Yes, several gigs and because I use Live Picture I can, I generally still shoot film, medium format film, scan six by seven film at three or four thousand BPI and I'll composite hundreds of transparencies and digital shots together so there could be several gigabytes of data in one image and some of the images I'm going to supply to the book of the older work, it's very complex work, called momonic notation which is sort of a series on memory and there's many, many images that are overlaid and overlaid and overlaid.

So you might have 20 or 30 transparencies or digital files overlaid each other and then constructed using Live Picture essentially. Then I use a little bit of Photoshop to do some cleaning up here and there but I still essentially do most of the big works in, in Live Picture and, and some cleaning up and maybe some works in, in Photoshop and Painter. So, yeah still very big fan of Live Picture.

Some of the works I've done are large scale four and a half metre long images of Little Bay and that's just photographs of Australian coastline but they've been inlaid with iconography from the Middle East and from Greece and it looks like almost people landing there and then doing their mark making and graffiti almost and then moving on into the country. And moving into stuff I'm doing today, within the Middle East. I'm doing large scale works on the border lands of various countries. I've done a series called the border lands of empires so there's very large scale works of archaeological sites and you might see falling debris of burning embers and burning bits of manuscripts. I was looking at the destruction of culture in the Middle East in particular.

So it all has a relationship, the work you can see over a period of time, it has a sort of connection to the memory and then going from personal memory to public memory. When you go to public memory, we call that history, so it's looking at the historic and the geopolitical and the cultural. So, it crosses all of those areas, and also the work on Border Land is photographic, it's painterly and it's digital. It's all of those things.

Some of the work I used to do, I'd put onto canvas and paint over it as well. So some of the work went from literally doing painting on a computer to a canvas that I'd then paint over again and represent that as a painting. These days I'm doing a bit more output onto just photographic based material but still coming from that mark making and painting background.

Ric Fantastic and so where do you feel that the Wacom tablet best helps you to innovate in your work?

Dr Phillip I come from the painting tradition, I use brushes. That's how I think. So without a Wacom I can't work. It's as simple as that. It just is so critical, it's so fundamental.

Ric It is the actual innovation?

Dr Phillip Everything. It's just not possible to use something like a mouse as an interface. I've never had a computer without some sort of graphic tablet interface so for the last 17 years I've been using a pen as an interface and it's an impossibility to even conceive working without one. It is just not possible. It's like having a camera without a lens.

creative innovator
:Dr. Phillip George

"Using a Wacom is an occupational health and safety solution. I think because people who use a mouse to make work just end up with RSI in a week."

Ric If you had the opportunity to look into the future of technology, and have some innovation from Wacom now, something that you feel maybe lacking for you at this point in time, what might that be?

Dr Phillip A tablet that you can move around with you. So it's a wireless tablet. I'm not sure if you've got them already.

Ric Yes, we do have a wireless Bluetooth tablet.

Dr Phillip Yeah, Bluetooth! I haven't used a Bluetooth but that's one thing that would be handy. But in terms of innovation, gees I'm pretty happy, pretty happy with the way it is. The levels of pressure sensitivity for me are very, very important, so the more sensitivity one can get. Because I use Live Picture, I'll zoom into the pixel level or even the film grain level and modify my work at the granular level. I actually have one file, it's a Live Picture file, but if I printed it, it would be 100 feet long and one metre high. It's a seven gigabyte file. So you can imagine how you can zoom in endlessly. It's a photograph which was taken from a boat at Sydney Heads and follows the cliffs right down to Bondi, so it's a six kilometre stretch of coastline. I think something like 37, 6x7 transparencies scanned at 3000 dpi, something ridiculous. And so I need to get into detail and actually modify things so when you look at it and you zoom back on it, the work that I do is invisible, it's seamless. So for me all the innovation from Wacom would be looking at improvements in sensitivity which is pretty good anyway, but that sort of area for me would be the most important thing and perhaps with software I suppose, getting software to keep up with the demands of being able to work seamlessly. If you pick up a pencil and you scribble on a wall, you want the tablet to respond as fast as you can think.

But I think it's doing a pretty good job of that. Where it may not necessarily be the tablets problem, it might be some software problem where you might have some brushes that are so memory hungry that it slows down your creativity. So it may not necessarily be Wacom, it actually may be the software manufactures that need to do better tricks with their memory management. So it's a bit hard to say. But those are sort of things I'd like plus sensitivity and the freedom to roam with a Wacom as well.

Ric Moores Law predicts the ongoing march of increased CPU processor power and so that response time you are talking about will just continue to get better. I had an interesting conversation with Russell Brown from Adobe around the time I was still using Live Picture and he said that Photoshop was going to stay committed to the technology they were based on and just allow the increase in processing power to solve any real competition from Live Picture they had at the time. So I guess he was right Live Picture is gone and forgotten for most people. Glad to see you're keeping Live Picture alive! Thank you for your insights on Art of Making Marks.

Dr Phillip Fantastic, love it, thank you.

Art of Making Marks

creative innovator
:Richard Luxton

SEE EXTRA CONTENT ON www.artofwa.com

RICHARD LUXTON
Fashion Photo Retoucher

Ric Welcome Richard to the Art of Making Marks please introduce yourself by telling us who you are and what it is that you do?

Richard My name is Richard Luxton. I am a freelance digital photo re-toucher. Primarily I do fashion retouching. But that probably takes up 85 per cent of my work. My other clients, other than fashion, are advertising clients and basically anyone who could use my skills.

Ric And so you use Wacom tablets in your work, how long have you been using Wacom tablets?

Richard [laughs] I only use one Wacom tablet at a time, but I've been using Wacom tablets every since digital imaging reared its head in Australia basically.

Ric [laughs] In the Jurassic period?

Richard Yes I go back to the Jurassic period. The first Wacom tablet I used was with the first computer I used, thinking back on it about 13 - 14 years ago, when Vision Graphics, the company I was working for, bought a computer made by Kodak called the Premier System, which was a closed loop system including a computer, a scanner and a film writer. It came with a Wacom tablet which was a bit fatter than this one I'm using now.

Ric Was it actually branded as Wacom or was it re-branded as Kodak?

Richard Oh yes. No, it was branded Wacom. That's the first one I'd ever seen.

Ric How much pressure sensitivity do you think it had?

Richard It was reasonably good. The pen wasn't quite so ergonomically designed as it is now, but there was a reasonable amount of pressure sensitivity way back then. I was never unfortunate enough to have to use a mouse. A mouse to me is a very foreign object! There are one or two things I use a mouse for, usually on the internet at my banking site or something. I use the pen for almost everything else I would say, because I mean how can you draw with a mouse?

Ric So you basically use your Wacom tablet for almost all your computer usage?

Richard Yes everything.

Ric So now Richard, you are a traditionally trained photo/film retoucher, so the introduction to using a computer the first time was using a Wacom tablet.
Is that correct?

Richard Yes.

Ric Right, so in fact your whole understanding of using a computer from day one is with a Wacom tablet?

creative innovator
:Richard Luxton

Richard Yes and it was a very smooth transition because right from the start it felt just like drawing. I'm a drawer and so I liked it. It seemed very quick to get used to it. For the first ten minutes or so it seems a bit odd as you're looking over at the screen and you're drawing down on the tablet, but very quickly it becomes just like drawing on a piece of paper. You just happen not to be looking at what your hand is doing and see your cursor moving instead.

Ric What type of tablet are you using now?

Richard I'm using an Intuos3 9x12 (A4) tablet which matches my Lacie monitor proportionately.

I've used much larger ones which could double as surfboards, but this one seems to be absolutely perfect for the size of the screen. If I was using a larger screen, I'd probably get a larger tablet.

Ric So you like to use a 'one to one' tablet to screen scale when working on a graphics tablet?

Richard Yes, I prefer that.

Ric And so, you can zoom into your image for closer detail.

Richard Oh God, yes.

Ric To have a lot of fine control.

Richard Oh amazingly fine control, and the sensitivity is amazing, you know, you can really touch so lightly and have a very light effect on the image, and vice versa, if you press hard, it happens very quickly and you can get very strong effects – it's really good.

Ric Do you customise your settings or just leave them at the default settings?

Richard Well not necessarily the default settings. I've used them in the same way for many years, and so I'm just used to it now. It's not quite at default, I'd most likely change a few things, but I've got into a way of working that suits my style.

Ric So would please tell us a bit about your work?

Richard Well most of it is fashion magazine work. Occasionally I'll do work for brochures and things like that, but mostly the fashion magazine work.

Ric I noticed some images that you were working on when I came in, and there seems to be a lot of work that you have to do on the model's skin.

Richard A lot of skin work, yes. [laughs] One of my main clients, a lady called Corrie, does a lot of beauty as well as straight fashion. The beauty work can be quite time consuming, because it's often close ups of faces and eyes that need a huge amount of work done. When you're looking close up on an eye, you think what can be done on an eye for God's sake? It's just two small things on either side of your face, but you go in close and you'll see there are all sorts of blood vessels and discolorations in the white of your eyes. All that's got to be fixed, and also all around the eyes usually has to be lightened, the eyelashes sometimes have to be separated because you know, they're clogged up and joined together. Some lashes go off at weird angles, and then you get a little higher up and you find the eyebrows and hairs growing off all over the place and so I neaten it all up.

Ric And so (it's) in some cases it's really re-illustrating the image. You actually draw back in the model's features?

Richard It's not so much drawing back in. I tend to think of it as subtractive than additive. Generally on first looking at the face of a female model's skin you would think "Wow, she's got fantastic skin". But when you go in close, it's just like looking at an alligator handbag. You have to work in close, and by the time you fix up all the little cracks and blemishes, you come back out again and it's all nice and smooth.

Ric There must be a fine line between beautiful and fake?

Richard Oh yeah, so many re-touchers go way too far – well I think they do anyway.

Ric So you've got to keep some sense of reality?

Richard Occasionally people want that absolute porcelain look, and it might suit the particular ad or the particular story the photographer is trying to convey, but generally, I don't like going too far. There are some magazines that I cringe at what they ask me to do, but I do it. I don't like it!

Art of Making Marks

creative innovator
:Richard Luxton

Ric Have you ever come up against a job where you really don't know how you're going to achieve what's been asked of you?

Richard Funnily enough, almost every job I look at and I go "Oh God, how am I going to do that?" But as soon as you get started, then oh yeah, it's starting to happen now and then yeah, that's working! For me it's just like doodling. I slowly work on little areas. It's a bit like painting or drawing, you just start and then it starts happening and you work and work and work and you know, it's like a drawing or a painting you just go over bits and over bits until they look right.

Ric What innovations in your work are due to using a Wacom tablet? I know that's probably a difficult question considering everything you do is done by using a Wacom tablet, but just in your words?

Richard I know what you mean. The thing that is so good about a Wacom tablet – or I should say 'Wah Com' tablet, is the fact that it is exactly like a pencil or a pen, or actually whatever you want it to be. You can adjust it. You can have big brushes or you can have little tight sharp brushes, you can have soft brushes or really fine in focus brushes. It takes a little bit of time to get used to setting them up, but depending on what you're drawing or what you're airbrushing or what you're doing, you can adjust this to be whatever you want it to be, and it's exactly like it always was with paper. [laughs] Me being nearly 100 now so I've been used to pencils and paintbrushes as well, and this is just like it, and so there's no big transition. Unfortunately or maybe fortunately I've never had to use one of those mouse things to draw. I've seen people using them, and think they are amazing – how can you draw with a brick? I can't do it.

Ric [laughs] It's usually my answer to those people as well.

Richard I've seen people do it and they're not bad, but I would hate to have had to learn to do it too.

Ric Some people are very proud of how clever they can be with a mouse, and I say "Well you know, I guess some people can paint with a paintbrush using their mouth to hold it, but it's kind of better using your hands".

Richard Exactly. So I've never had to use that. Right from the very start, as soon as I came out of the darkroom, I went straight to a Wacom tablet and there was no need for me to learn a new way of drawing, so the innovation all came from Wacom, not from me.

Ric What applications or combination of applications do you use?

Richard I virtually only use Photoshop. I used to have to use Quark occasionally, but I haven't since InDesign came along. I've always had InDesign and Illustrator there and some people will give me an Illustrator files to take something from. I know the basics of those programs which I can use.

Ric So how tightly integrated are Wacom tablets with Photoshop?

Richard It's seamless integration. I can't imagine anything else. I mean it's the only way I know of getting from this (Richard points to his head) to that (pointing to the computer screen).

Ric Can you talk about some of your current projects?

Richard This is what you might call a beauty shot. The next shot is the before.

Ric Oh yes she is very different.

Richard I mean you look at the skin, the eyes and the lips, and after it was retouched it went to that, so all the blemishes are gone, the eyes are all cleaned up, a lot of work has gone into the eyes, around the lips, highlights etc. She was very thin and slightly bony here (pointing to image)

Ric So of course reality isn't reality. Every image that we see most likely goes through a process similar to what you've just described?

Richard Not always. That was fairly drastic on that particular girl. I mean there's not so much done on this girl. See the before and after. See how the eyebrows have been fixed there, under the eyes – not too much. It's still got all the detail, but before it was a bit shadowy under there and all that stuff going on in the eyes. We just brightened it up a bit.

Ric Without giving away your trade secrets Richard to the Photoshop power users, I gather you've got some special tricks with channels and masks?

Richard I'm not telling you Ric! [laughs]

Ric Well good then, thank you.

Richard Oh Photoshop is amazing. You can fix anything really, and obviously channels are just one way to work on the image.

Ric Yes you can go into each individual colour to edit and retouch.

Richard Yeah, you can go into each individual colour and change things.

"For the first ten minutes or so it seems a bit odd as you're looking over at the screen and you're drawing down on the tablet, but very quickly it becomes just like drawing on a piece of paper. You just happen not to be looking at what your hand is doing and see your cursor moving instead."

creative innovator
:Richard Luxton

Ric Also with many channels and layers you can get very lost too…

Richard Yes, very lost. A good place for storing masks and things is in channels. There are so many places in Photoshop where you can do different things. It's not a mystery – I mean there aren't any real secrets to digital retouching. There were more in the old 'hand' retouching days where it was more about the chemical secrets to the dyes and bleaches we used. That knowledge was kept pretty tightly under a retoucher's belt because you know, you spent years figuring out how to do those things, and you weren't going to give it away lightly, well at least in the hey day of retouching when the retouchers were treated like gods. I only entered it right at the last minute because I was told "I wouldn't bother to learn that. It will take you ten years, and digital will take over in about ten years as well", but I still had that ten years experience of it. I thought I'm going to get to learn this anyway, and so I got the basics of hand retouching sorted out back then.

Ric Do you think Photoshop took on a lot of that knowledge through its early development, thinking of those early techniques you talk about somehow being encapsulated in the application or is it more about translating the traditional techniques into a new digital process?

Richard I think Photoshop came from the dark room originally, but it's been around for so long now that you can barely see the links. The very first software that came with that Kodak Premier Computer system was very simple and obviously made for someone who'd come from the 'dark room' environment. All increments were designed to be in terms of lenses, f stops, film stocks so everything had photographic terms and it was quite intuitive. It had to be because the day we got that computer system was also the same day that our masking dark rooms got knocked down, so we had no choice. We had a one week course with a woman who came out from Kodak in America to show us how to use the computer, and I had never used a computer before that. There were a lot of people around with PCs and Macs but they weren't up to high end retouching, at least not that I knew of anyway. And so we had a week to learn how to use it and at the end of that week there were jobs to do, we had to start and get them finished, and it was scary.

Ric Was the Kodak Premier System a multi-million dollar computer?

Richard I wouldn't say multi-million dollar. I think it was fairly close to a million dollars and it was very good, but nowhere near as sophisticated as Photoshop is today. Though we were working on 200 megabyte files all the time because that's what you need because everybody still wanted transparencies to look at as the benchmark. That's what had been used forever, so you had to do the retouching digitally and then output it to transparency film, and to output a 10x8 transparency, you need just over 200 megabytes, so the computer was designed to work on 200 megabyte files all the time.

Ric And so, it took a little while for the PC platform to catch up. So what happened in the gap in between?

Richard Well it was making money for the company I worked for, Vision Graphics, for probably eight or nine years before Mac based systems caught up. We actually bought a Mac when we first got the Premier as well, but hardly ever used it. We'd heard in America people were using Macs for odd things like, putting noise into skies or something, which we never did because we didn't know anything about Macs and how to use them. But about five years on, after getting that Premier, I think about around Photoshop version 4 it started to be quite useful. Then over the next four or five years, the power of Mac based systems started accelerating and after about eight or nine years of having the Premier, a Mac could do everything it could do.

Ric Yes PC's and Mac systems in general.

Richard Yeah.

Ric Though Mac obviously was the path back then.

Richard Mac was the tool that designers and photographers mainly preferred.

Ric And you're even still using a Mac?

Art of Making Marks

Richard Yes I'm still using a Mac. The new Macs now have got the Intel chip and so you can run PC software on them as well. There isn't anymore such a big gap between Mac and PC as there was over the last 10 to 15 years. Mac systems finally caught up with the cumbersome old Premier, and soon overtook it and they were so much cheaper.

Ric So now Richard if you could say something to the development guys at Wacom about what you might want in the way of future innovations, what might that be?

Richard Well I'm very happy with what they've got at the moment, but I tell you, there's that big fat pen that I keep seeing advertised, you know, sort of more for the airbrush users. I don't know who uses those? I've seen a pen with a huge great lump on the end. I've often wondered what that was.

Ric That's our airbrush pen.

Richard What is the difference with that pen to the standard pen?

Ric It's got a control wheel, so it gives you the feel of an airbrush, you pull back on the wheel the way traditionally a brush widens and closes its spray when you pull back on the trigger. Pulling back on the wheel gives you a similar feel to using a traditional airbrush.

Richard I must try one of those one day.

Ric So working with the Intuos tablet rather than working on the screen of a Cintiq is still your preferred method of working? Some people find the hand-eye coordination required is difficult for them.

Richard Really? Some people find that difficult?

Ric Yes, some people do! Mostly people who have never used a tablet before.

Richard Well initially, for the first hour or two maybe it's a little strange.

Ric That's right. It's just a bit like using a mouse for the first time, just getting the feel of it.

Richard Well I've used a mouse probably eight times and I've never got used to it.

Ric Did you know that Wacom pressure sensitive pen technology is in most Tablet PCs, our interactive pen displays and of course the Cintiq range?

Richard Yes, I've looked at those and I'd love to muck about with something like that. It looks great. I guess you're a little bit closer to the image I suppose. I've got used to this way of working though I can imagine for a person coming to a Wacom for the first time would find it even easier to get used to if you were actually drawing on the image on the screen as it were. For retouching photos I feel that your hand is kind of in the way.

Ric Well yes that is a common first reaction from seasoned tablet users. Photographic re-touchers tend to prefer to be able to see the whole screen uninterrupted, but then for a designer or an illustrator, being able to work with a tablet is like using a pen on paper. It allows for a more fluid and expressive hand motion.

Richard Yeah, I can't see that – having got used to this way of working, I don't need to change, but I can see how someone who is new to it might. Why bother to go here, (points to tablet) when you can just go straight there? (points to screen)

Ric Richard, thank you very much for your time today participating in the Art of Making Marks and showing us your very special brand of digital photographic retouching work.

Richard Thank you.

creative innovator
:Ted Blore

SEE EXTRA CONTENT ON www.artofwa.com

TED BLORE
PaintBox/Photoshop Artist + Advertising Retoucher

Ric Ted welcome to the Art of Making Marks. So firstly just to kick things off I'd like you to introduce yourself, tell us about who you are and what you do.

Ted I'm a traditionally trained graphic designer that basically fell on his feet with computers at an early stage. When the first Quantel Paintbox came to Australia I was lucky enough to be the first artist to work on it and to that end, I've been retouching on a digital level ever since.

Ric So please describe for us exactly what was a Quantel Graphic Paintbox?

Ted It was a British engineered device worth around a million dollars to purchase about 20 years ago. It was hardware based system instead of having software applications installed on it. The beauty of the hardware based system was that the airbrushing tool in particular could work in what's called real time which no PC based computers could do in those days. Even NASA was actually quite envious of the grunt in the thing back then. To look at it these days, if you quote the numbers compared to even a G5 or something like that, it's actually very funny. But in its day it was definitely the 'ants' pants' and we put conventional dark room film retouching out of business effectively over night.

Ric And it came with a Wacom pen tablet?

Ted It certainly did but pen/tablets have changed a lot over the years obviously. The pen in those days probably weighed the best part of four ounces, it had a cord hanging off it that we used to throw over our shoulder for convenience. You ended up basically with a bit of a 'Tennis Elbow' condition from working on it and using the interfaces 'flick on/off' method of changing menus. But having said that if the Wacom hadn't been available it would be safe to say that the Paintbox really wouldn't have existed the way it did. The reason the Paintbox was so successful was because it was as close to real time painting and image manipulating as was possible in those days.

Real time air brushing with pressure sensitivity as well, so with true pressure sensitivity actually allowed true fading of the air brush effect and didn't create any bad looking 'stepped' effects. The Paintbox actually had a dedicated hardware card for everything in it so upgrading was expensive. The air brush was a card, as was the screen refresh. Effectively the way it worked was that it had two screens, it had what we called a restore function where you could save a picture behind in the buffer space and actually use the airbrushes to pull pieces of that picture back through onto the working image. So it was very dexterous in that respect. The only problem being that it didn't actually have a command set in it for undo, so really you thought twice before hitting the save button, because once committed there was no going back. It was a steep learning curve from that point of view. We used to charge, in those days, (20 years ago) AU $500 per

creative innovator
:Ted Blore

hour and people were willing to pay it. We had people coming from literally all over the world, Japan, America, Singapore, etc because they were fairly scarce systems around the world and similarly too there wasn't a lot of people that could actually make them work to their full potential. Once again the Wacom was really the key integral human interface to it.

So yeah, I guess they were the good old days of digital image manipulation if you can say that. There were effectively two or three upgrades to the system over its six or seven year life span. Eventually Quantel bit the bullet and went software based and came up with a desktop PrintBox system which was basically backed up by a Macintosh. To that end it was sort of the death of Quantel prepress systems eventually, after that really Macintosh took over the prepress and print market. Towards the end of that era it actually got to the point where I worked on a Macintosh running Photoshop sitting beside the Paintbox, taking away more and more of its work. I was actually putting pictures that I'd made in Photoshop back onto the Paintbox because that's where people wanted to see them and as soon as they left I did all the corrections back on the Macintosh.

In that transition between using the Paintbox and the Macintosh we didn't have a Wacom tablet set up on the Mac and I was trying to re-touch without a pen/tablet. I ended up getting RSI in my wrist and needed a wrist brace. I had to get acupuncture and really I've had a click in my wrist every since. To that extent I could safely say that if it wasn't for Wacom I wouldn't have a career. I couldn't have done my job for the last 20 years without a pressure sensitive pen and the interface it allows.

Ric So basically you're saying with the amount of work that you've done and if you were only able to use a mouse then it would have ended your career?

Ted Oh very quickly, very quickly.

Ric But then by the same token you probably couldn't have been able to do the work that you did with a mouse anyway?

Ted No, it's physically impossible. The other day for Instance I was doing a job for an agency and the nature of the job was that there were very large files, 35 metre print posters. The deadlines were such that we were bouncing pictures on the internet backwards and forwards to the clients trying to get approval so it became necessary for me to actually go down to their studio and work on one of their Macs even though it was as slow as a 'wet week'. I was there for an hour before I just 'spat the dummy' and walked out. I drove back to my studio, grabbed my Wacom went back and plugged it in. It was ironic because later on that afternoon I had to go out and take a brief for another job. When I got back one of the designers had moved onto my computer and taken over my Wacom. I actually had trouble getting it back. It was the first time they'd ever used one. They were sold on it after only an hour I guess to adapt, after that there was no going back. I've often said, 'Once you've been spoilt by using a pen/tablet then there is no going back.' I just can't imagine using a mouse anymore.

Ric What tablet are you using now?

Ted 'If it isn't broken then why fix it' ..is what I like to say. Yes, it's a great big early Intuos tablet.

Ric You obviously like using big tablets?

Ted I'm actually quite happy now that Macintosh has come to the party and made their

creative innovator
Ted Blore

Cinema Display screens the same size as the Wacoms', it's about time! Well the trick I believe with Wacom tablets is it feels more natural to draw one to one than to try and teach your hand how to draw in ratio. My last employer tried to give me a little Wacom and I just couldn't use it. It was just impossible to get used to the idea of drawing small and everything being amplified on the screen. So the having a one to one ratio from tablet to screen is much more natural for me, it's almost like drawing normally once you get used to the eye to hand coordination. I mean so many people come in and look at me working and say 'how do you know what you're doing on the screen? I can't see anything happening on the Wacom'. And it's like 'well no you don't actually look at the Wacom you look at the screen'.

Ric Well Ted after all you have been using a large tablet and large screen together since the early days with the Paintbox so it is a case of not teaching old dogs new tricks don't you think?

Ted Yeah and that's why I'm good at the Playstation apart from anything else, it comes in quite handy.

Ric So then just getting back to telling us more about what you do, Firstly would you call yourself a retoucher, or a designer?

Ted I'd have to say I'm a retoucher first and foremost. I was trained as a graphic designer originally, that was back in the days of wax type, gumbo rubbers and doing things with scalpels. We got our first Mac Plus, we looked at it and thought won't it be great when somebody can actually print this out (and that was just black and white). Then Photoshop came out, I've seen the whole progression just as you have. I still do a bit of type setting and stuff when I have to, because you have to be a jack of all trades, but definitely first and foremost I'm a retoucher.

Ric But interestingly you're a retoucher who in a sense was trained digitally, so you haven't come from the darkroom days of dies and acid baths. You embraced the digital tools from day one.

Ted Correct. At Trannies, the second place I worked for with the second Paintbox in Australia, we actually had a bank of retouchers. At that stage when they first bought the Paintbox (and fair testament to them) it was a very brave move to spend a million dollars on effectively untried hardware. Especially when they were at that stage one of the best Pro Photographic Labs in the business at what they did as far as retouching goes. They had the best conventional retouchers; they had dark rooms coming out of their ears, but within six months really all the retouchers had to

"I had to go out and take a brief for another job and when I got back one of the designers had moved onto my computer and taken over my Wacom. I actually had trouble getting it back. It was the first time they'd ever used one. They were sold on it after only an hour I guess to adapt, after that there was no going back."

Art of Making Marks

creative innovator
:Ted Blore

do was retouch our outputs. In those days we actually recreated film transparencies where we had very expensive digital transparency writers. Because of the colour calibration and the nature of the film itself, there was always a bit of re-colouring to do, but that's all they did. The actual retouching was done on the Paintbox and they basically just colour balanced the outputs. Really that was the death of a craft for them. I actually tried to retrain a couple of those guys but I guess you're either digitally inclined or your not. They were obviously too used to their sable brushes, inks and dyes to be letting go of all that. So, some of them still working in the industry would be doing digital printing on digital enlargers and things, or have changed careers completely, who knows.

Ric Yes, the digital Pro Lab Vision Graphic that I used to be involved with has evolved into a digital display company last time I spoke to my ex business partner. So has the type of work that you are asked to do changed a lot for you?

Ted It's certainly harder these days because anyone with a Mac or PC with Photoshop and a Wacom tablet can call themselves a retoucher and to that end the industry will accept a lot lesser standard than they did when this technology first came out. When we were charging $500 an hour people expected $500 an hour of quality work! There's still a market for the top end of re-touching in that you get what you pay for. But having said that every time Photoshop comes out with a new version and trick set if you like, be it drop shadows or quick masks or whatever, it will take over one of the tricks that I spent 20 years perfecting.

Ric Smart Objects I felt was a big one.

Ted Yes that's a biggy! Part of the skill set you acquire over time is knowing what the client wants, being able to read between the lines, being able to second guess what they need. Some times you just have to say to them that, 'this is what you need not what you want.' And to that end obviously after 20 years I can second guess most clients as far as that goes and I'll ask those cutting questions when I get the brief, to avoid the usual problems later on.

The way I work is fundamental to the outcome in that you've got to allow for all the corrections and changes and a big part of the job is just that, being able to undo things very quickly and take steps back without having to start all over again.

Ric Yes and thank God for the concept of layers to arrive when it did.

Ted Exactly. I mean that changed my life as well. The Paintbox didn't have anything like vector paths. We used to virtually have to draw stencils by hand and draw around things whereas paths in Photoshop saved all that work.

Ric John Derry calls these things his 'safety net' which I totally agree; it's flying now with a net. Russell Brown also presents the concept of working with a 'no destructive' work flow.

Ted Yeah, well just having undos what a concept! As I said Paintbox didn't have any undo command so I often would have to say to clients 'I hope you like it that way because it's done now'.

Ric Could you just tell us a little about a typical job you would work on these days and what things to take into consideration.

Ted A typical job, well I tend to liaise a lot more with photographers these days and to that end you actually replace photographers a lot more these days. Oops sorry guys! The digital age is a wonderful thing but only for some of us. These days I can afford to work experimentally, I can literally change the light set up from one side to the other and still have all the images in register because they are digital from the beginning. It means that you can afford to cover myself and say right well I'll have one shot for the exposures for the darks and one for the highlights, I'll see what it looks like this way, and then that way. And very quickly you can change the whole feel of a shot.

Ric And of course they're shooting raw, and get a wider dynamic range.

Ted Yep and to that end I always insist on getting the raw files myself. Unfortunately, once again, any man with Photoshop and a Wacom considers himself a retoucher

114   Art of Making Marks

creative innovator
:Ted Blore

and photographers are probably the worst offenders of that, in that they do tend to do a bit of retouching themselves and therefore think they know everything about it. I've seen more photographers stuff a job before it was started because of the way that they've approached, or even opened the raw files. Because they've over-sharpened them, over exposed them or blown the highlights out just to get that contrast range in. I can't do anything with the image after that's happened. Once it's gone it's gone.

Ric If there's no image information to work with then that's that.

Ted That's right. It's dead. You put a hole in the picture it's now a hole in the picture. So I always insist 'okay if you want to do your bit sure give me your retouch pictures, I'll use that as a reference but I want the raw files'. And it gives me total control and I can take care of the sharpness. And as anyone knows who's done any serious retouching the last thing you want is un sharp masking on a picture whilst you're working on it, you can always do that later. But working on it with sharpening on it… you can see where you've been. It's like leaving footprints in the sand.

Ric So do you hand over the whole digital project, or what's your final result?

Ted I'll give people layered files to the point where it's manageable for them, if there's an element and they need to move around for different layouts, they can have that as a layer. But I don't hand over the working files for several reasons. I don't want to show too many people my tricks, I've spent 20 years of learning it, it's effectively intellectual property as far as I'm concerned. But the main problem is that if you give someone the layered file and they start playing with it they're going to break it, they're going to leave something off that should be on, they're going to turn a stencil off that's protecting something else… a bit like a game of chess, you know you have all your pieces set up and you move the wrong one at the wrong time and the whole place comes to pieces.

I actually had a client this afternoon ask me for a layered file and I had to quiz her on it and say 'well when you say layered file what do you mean?' and all she wanted was literally the shadow separate to the background separate to the picture in front. If I had I taken her on her word she would have got 110 layers.

Ric Thanks Ted for sharing those insights with us on the Art of Making Marks

116   Art of Making Marks

SEE EXTRA CONTENT ON www.artofwa.com

BRYN FARRELY
Digital Compositor and Editor

Ric Welcome to the Art of Making Marks. So Bryn, could you just introduce yourself and tell me a little bit about who you are and what you do?

Bryn My name is Bryn Farrelly and I'm a Digital Compositor and Editor.

Ric Extraordinaire!

Bryn [laughs] Extraordinaire, yeah, for editing and digitally compositing.

Ric So can you tell us how long have you been using Wacom tablets in your work?

Bryn I've been using Wacom probably since about 2000. I really got into it, when I started doing digital compositing.

Ric What sort of computer system would that have been on?

Bryn That was on Shake, when working on Ghost Ship up at Photon VFX in Queensland. I also always used tablets on Quantel products, and so that's why I sort of have the big tablet now, because I'm used to it.

Ric So what type of tablet have you got there?

Bryn Oh, my beautiful Intuos3. I think it is a 9x12.

Ric Yes, very good.

Bryn The bigger the better.

Ric And how long have you been using that tablet?

Bryn This one I bought two years ago as soon as they released the Intuos3.

Ric and you bought it?

Bryn Yes, bought it, yes it's mine. It travels around with me from place and job to job because usually I turn up and they don't have one so I whip home and grab it.

Ric What advantages does using the tablet give you in the user interface?

Bryn Well depending on if I'm using dual screens or one, I can always custom shape the palette for how much sort of desktop and how much movement I want to use. It's just easy to get around, easy to customise from place to place, download the driver, away you go. They're usually installed anyway on the machines I have to work on because somebody's usually had a tablet connected before I get there.

Ric And what software are you using there?

Bryn Well I'm working on Final Cut Pro doing a commercial which comes out next week. 100 years of scouts.

Ric Well I hope we will be able to see a little bit of that. So just tell us a little bit more about your work; what really does a compositor do?

Bryn A compositor composites pictures together.

" When I'm getting started into the paint work - painting with the mouse, if anybody's ever tried it, is impossible. It's good for doing stick figures, which is one of my specialties, stick figures, but when you go into the touch up work like rigs, ropes and wire removal and things like that, you actually have to start painting frame by frame, that's when a Wacom is indispensable."

Art of Making Marks 117

creative innovator
:Bryn Farrely

Ric Moving pictures?

Bryn Moving pictures, yes, as I've always said, anybody can make a billboard, the trick is making it move which is the hard part. Compositing and cleaning up anything from images to supers to graphics to special effects, anything that moves and that somebody wants to put together; making the unreal look real. That's what I do. Last one was Catch a Fire, by Phillip Noyce – is it Phillip Noyce? Better check that. He did Rabbit Proof Fence. His latest movie, Catch a Fire, nice little doco on the end of apartheid in South Africa, which involved a lot of factory explosions where we blew up an oil factory or parts of an oil factory, yeah, which was quite amusing for a few months down in Melbourne – very cold place.

Ric So there are times where you get all this material and you have no idea how it's going to go together is that right?

Bryn Nobody really knew what a big oil fire looked like, but they shot some very nice plates for us from the real oil factory that the story revolves around, because it's a true story. Nice aerials, and they had some great pyrotechnics, they blew up things and made big, big, big explosions – very big, the biggest I've ever seen for a movie. [laughs] Makes the Americans look like girl guides!

Ric So with things like fire, how do you isolate or should I say 'key' it out of the background and composite into your shot?

Bryn Well unfortunately sky is the worst thing to key off.

Ric But It's blue?

Bryn Yeah, it doesn't work that way. It never does. A lot of techniques, you start off keying and you get the best result you can and then it's down to rotoscoping, painting out frame by frame. Ah …such an enjoyable sport, rotoscoping!

Ric And this is where painting with the Wacom tablet becomes important?

Bryn Yes where it really comes into its own because you can get around your rotoscope lines and your paint work and touch up your mats very quickly and easily and so much better than using a mouse it's not worth thinking about.

Ric When was the last time you used a mouse for this type of work?

Bryn I still use a mouse, but not as much. Depends on what the job is. If there's paintwork and stuff like that involved, I definitely use the pen, because it's just better and you get sick of hearing the click, click, click.

Ric So you've got them both plugged in to your computer so that in any situation you can use the mouse or the pen at any point depending on what's required?

Bryn Yeah, and away I go. But it's usually the pen, especially for using Apple's Final Cut Pro and Shake applications, it's easier just to grab things – especially with Shake, it's usually a two handed operation.

Ric Can you describe for us what you are working on right now?

Bryn OK on this film job, you get artefacts off the actual film as in scratches, which usually people don't like and they want to get rid of. So down here we've got a nice big scratch which was induced by the camera and seemed to appear at the beginning of each roll. There must have been something inside the camera that's scratched the film but the director wants to use this take. So basically I have to remove the scratch at the end of the day and so I have to do a lot of roto splining, repositioning, junk matting. Here I've got what's called a travelling matt but it's very rough because I just started it. That's the section that I'm going to replace so I basically take some image and move it over a bit using a roto shape to cut just the section that I want, and then re composite it back over the original image with a travelling mat using a bit of a blur to make it nice. My usual trick is doing the easiest things first so you can get them out of the way so when you get down to the tricky stuff, then you don't have to worry about any of those silly little things. Doing the tricky stuff takes as long as, well how long is a piece of string?

Ric Just like in fashion photographic retouching, many people don't realise that these days just about every single frame that you see on TV or at the Movies (on average there are 25 frames to every second) has had some sort of digital manipulation or alteration done to it. Has the advent of these digital tools been the sole cause for this phenomenal increase in compositing?

Bryn In my experience going back to the days of actual film edit suites, as soon as we went digital and we could do this work, we did. Mainly because it was just one last extra finishing touch you could do to the work at the end of the day. You could remove all the artefacts, scratches, neg. dirt, just anything that sort of caught your eye and instead of spending hours and hours and hours sending it off to a lab with a video Paintbox system where they would suck in each frame at a time at a very high cost, we can now get in there and within half an hour retouch a whole commercial, just as a finishing touch for the client to make sure they are happy. So these days as soon as I've finished editing a job, I'll just go through it frame by frame, and if there is any neg. dirt or scratches or anything like that, I'll just touch them up without the client's knowledge so as soon as they see their finished product, they're amazed at the wonderful quality that they have achieved due to some brilliance that hasn't been seen by anybody.

Ric So back to using the Wacom pen/tablet, what part of your digital process is essential to using pen/tablets?

Bryn When you are getting started into the paint work, painting with the mouse, and if anybody's ever tried it, is impossible. It's good for doing stick figures, which is one of my specialties, stick figures, but when you go into touch up work, rigs, ropes and wire removal and things like that, you actually have to start painting frame by frame, that's when a Wacom is indispensable. Like when I was working on House of Flying Daggers, or was it Seven Swords?

Ric [laughs] Now you're starting to name drop.

Bryn Yeah, I can name drop! There's a scene in Seven Swords where there's a little village being attacked, and this guy escapes from the village, and he's running out through an arch way and he's got this humongous red lantern that he's attacking the baddies with, and it was attached by ropes, not wires – ropes are a bit thicker than wires, and so there was lots of ropes and lots of stunts going on. It was a 199 frame sequence and they needed all the ropes removed, and it had wonderful things in there like dust, smoke, cloth, you name it.

Ropes were overlapping everything, it looked like an Italian spaghetti fest, so I did a rough calculation at the end of the job, after about three weeks of painting it on and off, because you know, you could paint for a while and then you get sick of it and so you go and move on to another shot, then move back to it and get into it again. I think I did about 80,000 paint strokes over 119 frames at 2K digital film resolution.

Ric That's a lot of pounding on that tablet.

Bryn Yeah, you get a bit of a hand motion going. I tried every trick that there is to get rid of wires using plug-ins, matting, roto shaping, all the tricks I could come up with and at the end of the day I'd get 80 percent there and then just start doing the hard yards painting frame by frame. Moving pixels from one side of the screen to the other to cover something, but it seemed to work and it got approved. It made it into the final cut and into the cinema, and I've seen it, it looked cool.

Ric You didn't see ropes?

Bryn No, but I knew where the ropes were, you just know.

Ric It must be hard for you watching any sort of film without pulling it apart that way?

Bryn Well I usually sit there watching and say, there's one, there's one, oh look at that dodgy one! I saw a movie one day and it's a big blockbuster out of the US, and the guy flew across the road and you could see the crash mat that he landed on, and like it wasn't just off shot; it was in the middle of the shot and he lands on this crash mat and then jumps up amazingly unhurt. It was like – wow how did they miss that! In most blockbusters there is a lot of rigour removal, especially in the Asian action movies where people are doing triple back flips.

Ric So if you had the opportunity to have a wish come true from Wacom as far as providing you with some new tool or feature for the future, what might that be?

Bryn Oh this is something I've wanted for years ever since I started getting into the retouching stuff, I want a spinning tablet. People have laughed at me about this one in the past, but basically, when you're doing a touch up job, you know, it doesn't matter what it is, you sort of get in to a rhythm and you've usually got a paint stroke that works the best, so when you get to a situation where you've got to reverse the paint stroke, it's a bit annoying. So what I'd like to see from Wacom is the spinning tablet, so you spin the tablet, and as you spin the tablet, your picture revolves at the same way. So whatever my tablet does, my picture does to. If I wanted to go and touch up, say some guy's ear, I could spin the tablet around and he just span around on screen, and then I could touch it up at any angle really quickly. Because I'm doing touch up work so much, it

creative innovator
:Bryn Farrely

doesn't matter what I'm looking at, I just want to get rid of something, so instead of doing a reverse hand movement, I could just get in there and then away I would go.

Also here's one for those Wacom software engineers who might find a solution - I was working with some guys last year at a studio where we were cramming away on a film project. One of the guys on the night shift was left handed, and one of the guys on the day shift was right handed. Every time one of them sat down in front of the computer and pen/tablet after the other one had gone home, had to change all the settings and presets in the Wacom tablet driver menu. He had hot keys and all kinds of stuff going, and because the other guy had set it up completely differently, even the buttons on the pen were different, there was always five minutes of swearing from them as they went through the process of changing all the presets and settings back .

Ric He could have re booted the machine with a different profile setting but maybe the IT manager didn't want to do that or something.

Bryn I usually don't have a problem because when I'm on a job I'm dedicated to the one machine and nobody touches it so I have free reign there. Also usually nobody has time to touch it because I'm stuck in the room for 24 hours a day 7 days a week!

Ric Well Bryn it's a crazy life but I bet very rewarding also. Thank you for sharing your insights with us and opening your darkened studio room door of digital compositing.

creative innovator
:Craig Calhoun

SEE EXTRA CONTENT ON www.artofwa.com

CRAIG CALHOUN
Audio Engineer / Composer

Ric Welcome Craig to the Art of Making Marks. So please tell us a little about what you do as you are an artist but not in the style of most of my previous interviews, instead you are from the field of music so to kick things off please introduce yourself.

Craig I'm Craig Calhoun. I'm a composer, performer and multi instrumentalist.

Ric Fantastic. And I notice you've got a few Wacom tablets in your studio.

Craig Hmm. Yes I do.

Ric So have you been using tablets for a while?

Craig Since about 1998 was my first encounter with a Wacom tablet.

Ric So you're a musician but you dabble in the visual arts and other fields?

Craig Yes, back at that stage I did. I dabbled a bit.

Ric Now your really using tablets for a different purpose you're really using the tablet as a mouse replacement is that right?

Craig Exactly, because the majority of the stuff I do is with music software and I spend a lot of time doing clicks and moving around and after some time I discovered, you know, pains and just realised that there was another alternative to just break up the amount of time that I was spending with a mouse in my hand. Some recording and mixing sessions I'd be working for maybe eight to ten hours straight.

Ric And I notice you've got a Graphire Bluetooth over there. That obviously gives you some mobility around your studio?

Craig A lot of mobility but the beautiful feature of it was the fact that because it is wireless, and in my environment you know, if I'm tracking guitars or vocals or bass or whatever, I'm not restricted to being at the computer screen, operating from that one point.

Ric This is a tight little home studio with ergonomic issues since it wasn't purpose built so instead of having your back to the musicians while you're recording you can actually move around and interact with them.

Craig Either other musicians or if I'm working by myself I might be singing for example and I actually need to position the microphone in a spot where it's not getting fan noises from hard drives or computers, or it could be the acoustic treatment that I actually need the microphone in a different place. So I can physically take the tablet with me, sing from that position, view the screen and operate at the same time.

Ric Fantastic.

Craig So that was a really big advantage, which I think was a real innovation, especially in my field in the recording studio because I hadn't seen anybody doing that before.

Ric Well I guess there's some very big purpose - built studios, if you like, that have all the ergonomics built in. Being able to put people in the right place and be able to see them performing but in these days where many recording artists have a studio right in their own home, it's almost like giving you the ability to create your own ergonomics in a more dynamic way on the fly.

Craig Yes, that's right. There is really the biggest advantage because you know there are a lot of small private studios because the technology makes it a viable thing so you have to think creatively. You've got to utilise the best space and the best ergonomics because you are working for long periods of time and some of the problems that I've been able to overcome by having just that wireless connectivity have allowed me to get a lot more done in a smaller amount of time and with fewer restrictions.

Ric Is there software that allows you to use the pressure sensitivity in the pen, or is it really just as we were talking about, a mouse replacement?

Craig More of a mouse replacement for the music applications.

Ric I have seen software from Adobe where you can actually paint out parts of a track to clean up sound track and background noise

Craig Yes that's right plus there's also using the pen for music notation, that's another really valuable asset as a tool.

Ric So now I notice a very new Wacom product in front of you. You've been trialling the Cintiq 12WX in your studio so can you tell us honestly what you think?

Craig Oh, man. I'm in love. I am so in love with that thing because it just took the convenience and flexibility of the Bluetooth tablet another step further. Not only can I be away from this static position here in front of my screens, but I can also take the screen in the tablet right with me and so I'm not restricted to being in view of my main screen, and make sure I'm in the right spot for what I'm about to sing. I can literally just have it right in front of me wherever I'm about to play.

Ric I guess you've got your hands free to play your instruments?

Craig I can go back, record, drop-in, do all of that, right there just with the pen in one hand and the other hand on the music keyboard. When I am doing vocals for example,

creative innovator
:Craig Calhoun

I don't necessarily want reflective surfaces from these screens, so I'll place the microphone back over in another area where it's a different acoustic space to get the best sound of me singing and so I can take the screen with me.

Ric Tell us a little about the software you're running here and what set up you've got.

Craig I'm running Audio Logic from Apple, well the latest version of Logic, which is Logic Studio Version 8, and that's the main program that I run. The other thing that I do a lot is not only compose music but I also do sound design for Film and TV as well. So having the screen just that close to me, at an angle that's really comfortable as I'm working right allows me to see the vision running along the timeline and, drop-in, drop-out, and still be in sight of the instrument I'm playing as opposed to doing this and looking over there and moving a mouse around awkwardly.

Ric So in a sense this is a little bit of a revelation for music professionals?

Craig Oh man, in a big way. A big way, it's a revelation.

Ric So at this point I'd like you to tell us little bit more about your work and your career, different influences on your life, whatever you like?

Craig Oh right. Well. My father was in the military, so I travelled a lot as a kid. Moved to Germany when I was eleven. So I kind of grew up there. Originally from the US. Moved back to the US when I was sixteen and so had seen a lot of the world and realised that there's a lot more happening. Since I turned 21, moved back to Germany and ended up touring with The Supremes' European tour and when I'd finished went to Switzerland but just love performing and live music is what I've been doing over time. Was starting to delve into recording, when I came to Australia in 1985 on a tour with Don Burrows, the jazz legend, and I just kind of fell in love with the place.

I think about 1987 that I actually crossed that border into the technology so recording music with computers. Sequencing, and from there, you know, it was like a whole new world opened up that I could create music on a computer as well as with live instruments. My musical career path has gone from performing live to composing for film, television and also producing other artists as well, and just more recently teaching digital recording and composition for the screen.

Ric So you embraced the early days of the PC desktop revolution from a music/ audio standpoint and then have ridden that wave ever since.

Craig That's right I guess.

Ric And so, that journey has brought many new skills to your musical repertoire?

122   Art of Making Marks

creative innovator
:Craig Calhoun

"Not only can I be away from this static position here in front of my screens, but I can also take the screen in the tablet right with me and so I'm not restricted to being in view of my main screen, and make sure I'm in the right spot for what I'm about to sing. I can literally just have it right in front of me wherever I'm about to play."

Craig Oh, yes. A lot of new skills and I just love it. I absolutely love it. That's why something like this to me is like another great wave that's just come in. Yeah I was really taken by surprise with this Cintiq. That's forward thinking, I think.

Ric [laughs] So this is an innovation, a revolution, an evolution. I think we're all trying to come up with the right marketing spin for this product but I just like it too.

Craig Evolution really, yeah.

Ric I liked evolution let's use that. But moving further forward, are there innovations that you would like to see from Wacom that would help you in your work?

Craig Well, you know, all these little buttons here. I could see more functionality with the programming of those, maybe some a little display to give you some information because I mean nowadays with a lot of synthesisers that we are all using, they're all virtual synths. All synths these days are plug-ins. And the amount of manipulation that you can do within those programs is done with controller keyboards that are available, they're just knobs and faders, you know.

Ric So possibly if you had touch sensitivity as well as the dexterity of the pen, you could just touch a knob, or slider/fader, whatever the software interface provided.

Craig Oh yes exactly. I mean, I could compose something, go back and do a sweep of automation and use the Cintiq for manipulating the filters, everything without all the other interface devices I need. That would be so great.

Ric [laughs] That wish might just come true. We have just announced our RRFC™ touch technology, which works in combination with our EMR® pen input technology which means what you have just described, can now happen.

Craig Just the ability to slide my finger up and down and actually have that control of the fader. Now we're talking. I can see some real incredible uses for that. I had a look at the Cintiq 21UX when it first came out that's when it really dawned on me where this could go but it was physically too big to move around for better usability and but now here it is a smaller lighter Cintiq 12WX.

Ric It's smaller and lighter and unencumbered with a big stand Yes we're very excited about this product.

Craig You ought to be. Had Wacom actually considered how this would benefit musicians?

Ric We've been showing it to all sorts of people but it's wonderful to talk to you from the musical and audio point of view, where just purely the ergonomics of this device might be the key benefit. Thank you for sharing your world with us today on Art of Making Marks.

Craig Cool. Thank you, that's a rap.

creative innovator
:Steve Rosewell

creative innovator
:Steve Rosewell

SEE EXTRA CONTENT ON www.artofwa.com

STEVE ROSEWELL
Studio Kite - 3d props and sets

Ric Welcome to the Art of Making Marks. So Steve tell us a little about your studio's fascinating background.

Steve Studio Kite started about 20 years ago doing theatre shows, circus rings, that sort of thing all around the world. Then we moved to Sydney and set up a 'prop shop'. For years we were building sets and props, moved into the TV commercial world doing special effects and then makeup right through to large rigs and Animatronics as well as simple model making. At one stage there was a big threat to us with the introduction of a Computer Graphics component into film and TV productions. That came about 12 years ago. This at first seemed like a big threat and then it turned around that all the art directors' ideas were let loose. Because they thought that anything was possible with 'digital' it worked out that it was easier to do many special effects for real in-camera than to do it the new 'computer' way.

Then as the years went by a lot of the best work, and especially the large budgets, did start moving into the CG (Computer Graphics) world. We became very disappointed when we found that a lot of clients were calling up when they had absolutely no money and thought it was going to be cheaper to do it 'in-camera' than to use CG. We found that the really low budget jobs were heading towards the model makers like us. I heard about the AU $300,000 budgets that went into very mundane special effects and could have been done so brilliantly as in-camera effects. So we started moving towards computers quite some time ago and then realised there was just no way we wanted to sit there and stare at a screen all day. A lot of our guys just love the hands on work so we put the computer away, that was way back when 3D Studio Max first came out. The deflating hardware and software value was a big put off. Basically you had to get a job done to pay for a software or hardware purchase within a couple of months or you'd lost your money as newer technology came along.

Ric Yes I the equipment costs were high and you just had to keep rolling it all through or you would get caught with high overheads and redundant technology.

Steve Yes that was it and that was really visible. A piece of hardware would be AU $80,000 and two months later it would be AU $20,000 and then a few months later it would be useless.

Ric It's what gives you the edge in this business though so you have to keep doing it.

Steve Yes, that's exactly right. There was certain companies that were given technology and sponsored by companies like Silicon Graphics, and with out being sponsored there was just no way they could have survived.

creative innovator
:Steve Rosewell

But then what we've discovered is as the years went by we started designing and working out concepts in the computer, because it was a quick way, a good way of getting client approval before you started the job. Then I saw the first 3D printer that was on the market. I went to a manufacturing trade show and I thought this thing is the 'bee's knees,' this thing's amazing. It was a pretty big investment for us but I convinced my partner to just say let's go for it! We did and because of that as soon as we had the printer we needed the software to drive it. We tried Rhino and a few other applications which didn't sort us out and then finally went with Solid Works. I had a guy working for us that knew Solid Works so we went down that route and really got into some beautiful design work. Designing for the real world rather than designing for animation or the CG world.

It just kept expanded from there. Before we had a lot of problems getting some of the older software to work properly, we just couldn't get the polygons to do what we wanted them to do for the real world environment. Things would print with holes in them and it became so time consuming to fix. Over the years we have worked out techniques that worked and the software has come a long way to actually be able to achieve a good result quickly. After buying the 3D printer that lead to us to buying a big industrial robot arm for milling out large polystyrene shapes. We got a much more accurate seaming machine for doing fine detailed work fast. We also have a wax printer that does infinite detail for things like jewelry clasps or fine sculpture work. So using those four different machines, we can pretty much cover any size of medium as such, the medium being in the 'real' world of mediums, not just in CG. So then it was a matter of producing the sculptures. Now Solid Works is not good for sculpture work at all or any sort of organic 3D work.

Ric Yes it is really for industrial design, product design and engineering.

Steve That's right and it's great if you want something square and a particular size with lettering embossed. For things like that, it's perfect because they come out of the printer solid; there are no holes in the objects. We played around with Maya for quite a while, we still use an old version of Maya which is good for just blocking out some polygon things. It's becoming less and less useful for us now because we don't need the rendering and animation side of it, we only need one very small part of it which is the modelling.

But then we discovered ZBrush, which for the sculptural work is fantastic, we just loved it. I was very frustrating with the first version because it just didn't work, they said it worked and it just didn't. However later versions they got right. We've tried a couple of other programs like Mudbox which we used a little bit but I found that it's harder to see the object in the version we looked at.

Ric Now that Autodesk own the product I would suspect they have addressed that issue and I believe that it's possibly an easier learning curve than ZBrush, but of course ZBrush has already become well integrated into CG pipelines. I guess it is really just about which one you start with and get used to first.

Steve Yeah, that's right and once I got used to ZBrush I could literally sculpt, paint and rotate the objects as I went, which was ideal. The final rendering for us is just for a quick impression, because we're going to recreate the thing as a real world object. We have done a few jobs, simple photo 'stills' jobs where we've spent a lot of time in Photoshop and rendering stuff, like rendering 3D 'stills' out as images but that's not our speciality so we try to concentrate on what we're good at.

Ric Do people bring 3D files to you or do you just create everything in-house?

Steve There's a little bit of bringing the 3D to us. It may even be a real object that we scan and then fix it up to increase the size for output.

Ric So you have 3D scanners?

Steve We work with a company called Wysiwyg that does a lot of scanning for us and they've actually got a full body scanner. They were in here yesterday scanning a model for a new 'up and coming' film. So we've got a good relationship with them. We can send stuff out and we get it back straight away. Scanning technology is kind of limited in a way because it gives you a great amount of measurements of an object

Art of Making Marks

> "...once I got used to ZBrush I could literally sculpt, paint and rotate the objects as I went, which was ideal. The final rendering for us is just for a quick impression, because we're going to recreate the thing as a real world object."

but sometimes if we want to mess around with the object and play with it's geometry, it gets very messy. You want a really nice mesh to work with so then that's when you're better off starting from scratch and just use the scan data as a really good reference.

So there's a trade off, it really depends on the project. If it's a quick thing that you want to do then just scan and send down to the machines that's fine and it can be done. Obviously reducing something in size is great in the scanning process but a lot of the time they want to blow it up which means your detail is lost. You lose your detail as it goes up in size and the geometric shapes are all rounded off. For instance if you have some sharp lettering that is embossed then all of those sharp vectors are gone when you enlarge. You end up with muted surfaces, which is fine with organic shapes. It's actually really good with organic shapes because it's already muted anyway like a body scan or a small sculpture.

When extruding the scan data we realised that we needed the right interface tool to get the sculpting done. We looked at quite a few different things. 'Farrow Arm' pen devices that you can sculpt in space on screen. We tried using this type of pen; it's like a mechanical arm and there's a few different versions of this around. It's a pen on a small mechanical arm and you literally sculpt looking at the screen, sculpting in space. You can get 'feedback' through the pen. We had a little play with it at an early stage, you know I'm sure they've come along way by now, but we decided it's not the way to go'.

Ric I've seen those types of interface devices used in medicine for training to do surgical procedures and things like that.

Steve Yes and it's the same sort of technology for driving industrial robots.

Ric The feedback you get through the pen helps you know if you are about to poke a hole through someone's lung or something.

Steve You feel the pressure of the lung when you touch it, that's right, or if it's a blob of clay you can kind of feel it. That's maybe something to explore in the future maybe. I believe there are all sorts of technologies with virtual gloves and these sorts of things that are coming out for sculptors.

Ric Now at this stage I'd like to ask you how long you've been using Wacom tablets in your production process. I see we've got a lovely big Wacom Cintiq 21UX here on your desk. Please tell us a little about how that's working for you.

creative innovator
:Steve Rosewell

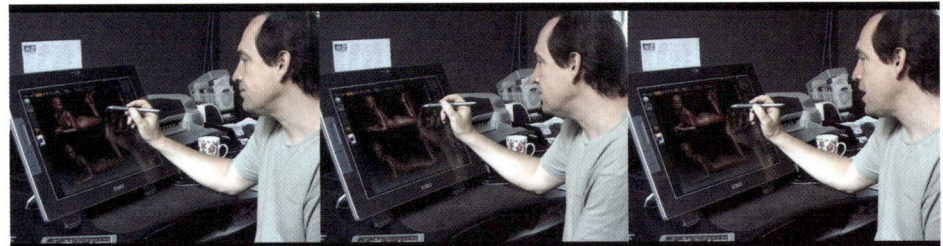

Steve We got our first Wacom tablets years ago when they first came out. I think the early Intuos type tablets the guys were using but I was the sort of person that could never get into that. You know, your hand over here and your eyes over there, sort of thing! Even though I used a mouse I just couldn't get used to it. Then finally I saw this screen tablet thing. I'm not exactly sure where I saw it, I think it might have been in one of those trade magazines you advertised in.

Ric You didn't actually get to try one out first at a trade show?

Steve No I never actually saw it for real until it actually arrived on my desk. I'd never even touched it or tried it. I just saw it, read about it, got on the internet and read a few reviews and I just thought, 'Oh I just want this thing!'

Ric So from without actually ever trying out a Cintiq to having it actually arrive on your desk ,how do you feel about it?

Steve It was actually better than what I had anticipated. The fact that you can pull it off its stand and put it on your lap, yes it's heavy but great in the winter because it puts out a bit of heat and keeps your lap warm. Being able to orient it however you want becomes really comfortable. The fact that you can just lay it down is great. Actually if you're doing a lot of fine line work or something, you can really get comfortable, it's like your working on a piece of paper and you can use rulers on it, straight edges or curves. You can trace over a drawing, put a photo on there and you can trace over it and all that sort of stuff. Your results are being seen so you only have to look in the one spot, whereas with the pen/tablets you'd be tracing something and your eye would be flashing backwards and forwards to the screen.

Ric So in a sense the Cintiq finally brought together the right work style in a device that worked for me.

Steve Probably one of the other really important things is the old RSI issue (Repetitive Strain Injury) with the mouse. The pen eliminates that. You can see here that I'm trying all sorts off different devices.

Ric Yes I couldn't help to noticing your mouse and strange human interface device collection.

Steve Yeah I have tried lots of alternatives. This is my 'rat' which I was using for a while. I've heated the foam around it and put my hand onto it to make it more ergonomic for me. I've realised that it's the orientation of my arm and I've heard that from quite a few people that having your arm up like that is much more natural.

Ric From the research that we've done, the repetitiveness of scrolling as apposed to the one to one pen interaction on the screen just tends to cut down on the number of repetitive movements that can usually occur when working normally.

Steve Yes, that's just it. Especially being able to change your rotation of the screen is great. If you were having to work in the one plane then your arm would be very sore after a while from holding it up. The fact that you can start to rest on the screen and it's a nice durable surface. The Cintiq is the perfect interface for my 3D sculpting solution.

Ric Thank you Steve for allowing us to come into your Studio and sharing with us your in sights on the Art of Making Marks.

128   Art of Making Marks

creative innovator
:Julian Tylney Taylor

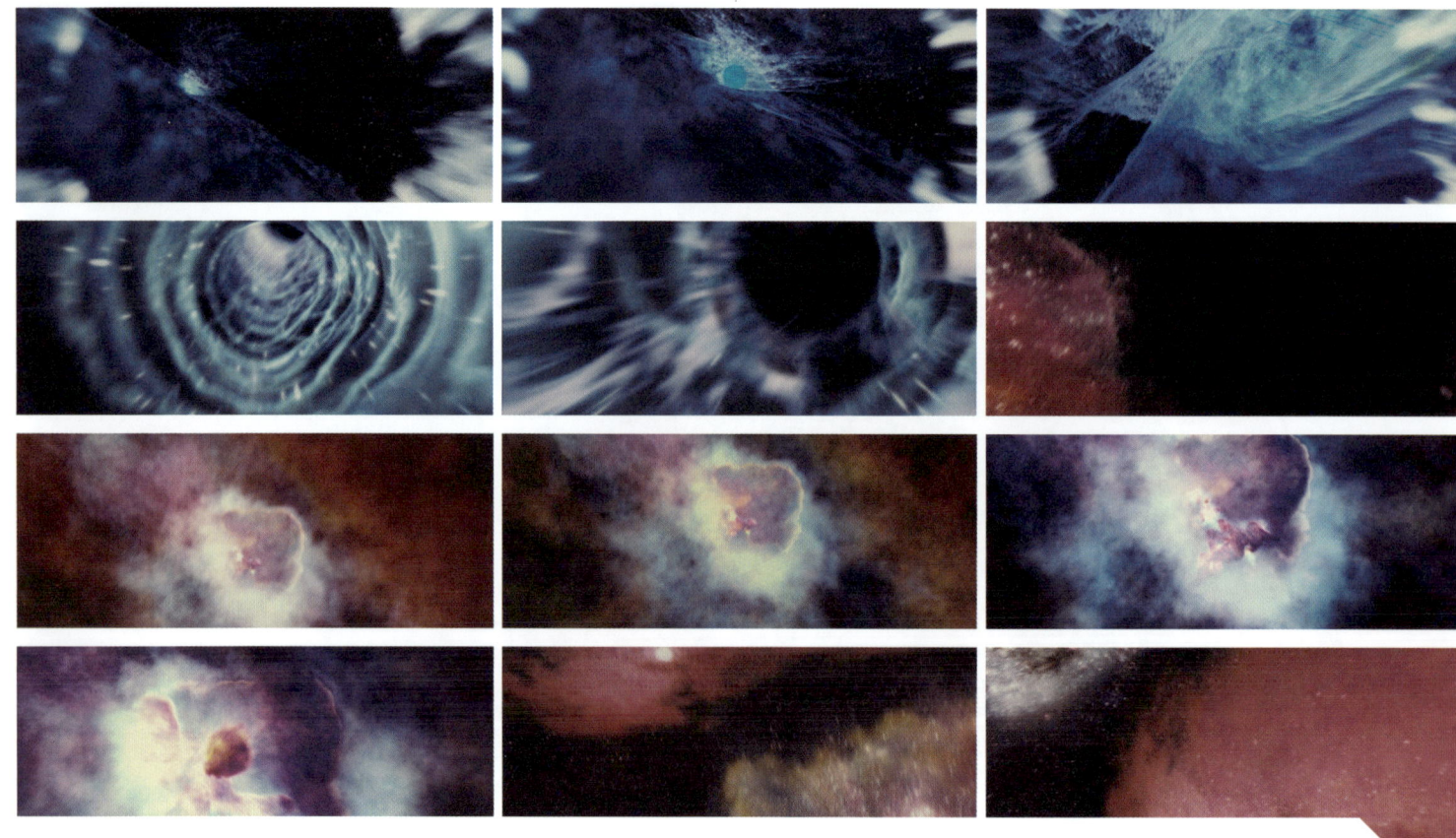

SEE EXTRA CONTENT ON www.artofwa.com

JULIAN TYLNEY TAYLOR
VFX / Technical Director

Ric Welcome Julian to the Art of Making Marks. Please introduce yourself and tell us a little bit about who you are and what you do.

Julian Okay my name is Julian Tylney Taylor and I do freelance animation, visual effects and have been moving more into technical directing and supervising, that's basically what I do most of the time and a little bit of engineering work from time to time when required.

Ric In your production process do you use Wacom tablets?

Julian Yep! I use Wacom tablets pretty much everyday and I own two of them.

Ric Excellent.

Julian I have one permanently in front of my workstation and I have another one which I move from which ever laptop I use, whether it's a PC or a Mac and I'll plug them in and out in order to get my Photoshop work done and to sign contracts and all that kind of stuff, so yeah, I use Wacoms.

Ric So you use pen/tablets with Maya?

Julian I use a pen/tablet with Maya actually a lot. I use it a lot for painting an object, that's the obvious part but actually I find that it saves me around 50% of my time for 'poly pushing,' selecting components, being able to very quickly pinpoint components and move them around for sculpting and modelling. It's incredible! Even if I'm just manipulating individual objects on the screen.

Ric So it's become almost a mouse replacement from that point of view?

Julian Oh certain things I can't do with the mouse anymore. I get RSI (Repetitive Strain Injury) with the mouse. If you're sitting there for six to eight hours doing polygon manipulation where you're picking individual points and doing that with a mouse you will definitely get RSI. I did, and I wake up with a numbness in my little finger, on both arms. When I use the Wacom it doesn't happen and so I use the Wacom for that reason all the time.

Ric So how do you deal with the many mouse settings in Maya that people often ask me about. How do you set up your pen?

Julian I have a Wacom Intuos3 and the first thing I found with the Intuos3, because in 3D or in Maya certainly there's one hand that's always on the keyboard. This means somehow some other part of my anatomy is on the board, which means I have to switch off all the extra buttons (ExpressKeys). So I know in Photoshop they're great to use but because I need a lot more access to the keyboard I switch those off first thing. I have the left mouse button as the actual pen tip. Basically just the normal pen setting. Then the tilt switch

130 Art of Making Marks

on the top of the pen is set so front click is the middle mouse and the back click is the right mouse button. I can either use it with my thumb or with my index finger. That's how I use the pen and it works perfectly.

Ric So how long have you actually been using pen/tablets in your work flow?

Julian I can't remember not using one. I think the first time… I started doing 3D in around 1997/1998 and that's when I started using them. I think it was an Intuos 1 at the time.

Ric A big pen/tablet?

Julian No it was, well bigger than some of the ones now, when you consider the big one, and when the small ones came out I continued using them. It's, for me, just a natural interface into the computer.

Ric So tell us a little bit more about the types of work that you're doing and have done and maybe explain some of the beautiful images that you've included.

Tylney Initially I started off being really a 3D animator and working through all the different skills but I concentrated more and more on the technical aspects and making the impossible possible, the difficult projects possible. And so the

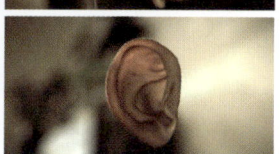

projects that I've grown into are more and more supervising/technical directing and looking after tricky bits in a pipeline or being picked by a supervisor who would say 'here you go Julian, here's the intro-sequence to a feature film we want you to do this and figure out how to get it done'. I recently did the opening sequence to an Australian production called Gabriel. That was a 1,475 frame, full HD production.

Ric You know every frame?

Julian I know every single frame by the pixel and it had multiple layers of fluids that we used in the compositing tricks, geometry, everything. Every trick in the book I used to get that one happening. And I rendered it actually in Renderman running in the background with a lot of Photoshop matt painting work being done again using the Wacom. That was 10 weeks of non-stop working on one box and rendering on the same computer. There was nothing else rendered from anything else. It was all done on the one machine. I've also been doing a lot of concept art recently which I cannot include. That's for a project, a larger project we're working on. And otherwise just different 3D work for different people like Channel 7 and NAB adds, general kind of 3D stuff.

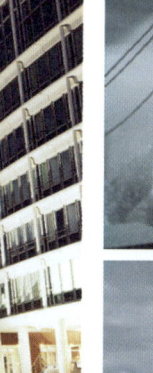

creative innovator
:Julian Tylney Taylor

If you're sitting there for six to eight hours doing polygon manipulation, where you're picking individual points with a mouse you will definitely get RSI. I did, I used to wake up with numbness in my little finger, on both arms. When I use the Wacom it doesn't happen and so I use the Wacom for that reason all the time.

Ric Beautiful work, beautiful work! What innovations or advantages do you find by using a pen/tablet?

Julian For a lot of manipulation I do in 3D I find it more intuitive to actually work with the pen. The mouse is always a reference point where actually I need to re-reference where the mouse pointer is in order to move my hand and kind of push the mouse around. Whereas with the pen, I use a direct relationship or a direct ratio on the Wacom and I know exactly where I put my hand, that's where the pen's going to be. So I have a direct relationship between my hand and where I am on the screen, so that saves me a lot of time. It also saves me about 30-40% of time on any manipulation of components drawing and painting. I mean with the mouse forget it. It's just no way… it's really made our work not just easy but really in a way actually possible.

Ric From concept art to the crunch rendering stage the pen/tablet is there right through your workflow.

Julian Pretty much and I've seen it used in many ways. I was working as the Technical Director on a production at one of Australia's largest animation labs and designing the 3D pipeline. Working pretty much with all artists directly in helping them create better outcomes. They were using Wacoms in many different ways. Some of them were using it like a mouse, in mouse mode. Other people were using it in the direct access mode. A few people that had never used a tablet before, we just said 'use it for two or three days and you'll never use a mouse again,' which is exactly what happened. People just started using it and they become completely familiar with it, they would just pick it up and they were in there, it's a direct interface. It's nearly like mind control of where the mouse is suppose to go. You move your eyes to where it is and your hand just moves in directly the same position. It's very, very nice working with a pen/tablet.

Ric If you could have a present from Wacom, a future vision or innovation that would enhance how you currently work, what would it be?

Julian Well I think you already have brought it out, the direct pen/tablet/screen, what do they call it again…

Ric The Cintiq 12WX?

Julian The Cintiq 12WX! The Cintiqs up until now for 3D work have been a little bit strange for me because you really want to see everything that's underneath and it's different to drawing with a pen/tablet. It's also been rather large and normally 3D workstation space is limited and very intense for long periods of time. So we haven't tended to use the Cintiq 21UX in this situation, they haven't really worked for us. But I think being able to draw on the smaller one which is coming out now and having that as a direct input that you can switch on and off is, well that's magic. That's pretty much what I've been looking for. Everything else, well I know how to manipulate around a computer, I don't really need a 3D manipulation tool or something… they've sort of come and gone whereas this seems to have just stuck around because it's a natural interface.

Ric Fantastic, well hopefully next time we meet you can show me how your Cintiq 12WX has helped take 3D production pipelines to the next level.

Julian I look forward to it.

Ric Julian Tylney Taylor, I thank you for being a part of the Art of Making Marks and we look forward to seeing you again in the future and looking at your fabulous work on the big screen.

SEE EXTRA CONTENT ON www.artofwa.com

NIGEL ALLEN
Cinema 4D evangelist

"...applications like BodyPaint, you're actually able to just pick up a paintbrush, go to your object and just paint directly onto it in 3D space as well as manipulate the 3D geometry."

Ric Thank you for joining us on the Art of Making Marks. Please introduce yourself and tell us a little bit about who you are and what you do?

Nigel I look after Cinema 4D in Australia. It's a 3D application for rendering, animation and general 3D production. I am an operator and I also a certain amount a technician so I can go out and help people. I teach, I produce a certain amount of content myself, and over the years I've held many different jobs in various aspects of the entertainment industry. I started out as a sound engineer. I first bought my Wacom tablet in, I think it was 1996. I became a trainer for the sound engineering company I worked for. I had to create content for them which was a computer-based training scheme, and part of that content was to go around and photograph all of their pieces of equipment and then go back and, in Photoshop, extract the backgrounds from the photographs and put them onto plain backgrounds. So in order to do that, without getting 'horrendous' RSI (Repetitive Strain Injury), I decided to go out and buy myself a Wacom pen/tablet. Back then it was on a Macintosh using the ADB port, rather than USB as we are now. From there on, I never really stopped using it once I got into Photoshop. After that I actually left sound engineering and I became a freelance digital designer, if that's what you'd call it I guess. I was working in 3D, I was teaching myself Cinema 4D at the time, and working with Photoshop and learning Adobe After Effects.

I was very glad of having my Wacom pen/tablet while doing my next large project this time for Toyota. We had to photograph five different cars on a turntable being rotated. They were eventually going to be used in a virtual reality booth at the motor show, where you walk up to the screen and touch it and choose whichever car you wanted. They also wanted to be able to rotate the car and change the colours on the car. They also wanted to be able to change accessories on the car, so we had a lot of photography to do. We had a fixed camera and we'd rotate each car ten degrees, thirty-six shots per rotation. Then I went home with probably about four and a half thousand photographs and using an iMac at the time I spent three months working in Photoshop and Adobe After Effects 'deep etching' each car. I had to create transparency matts (channels) on all the windows and the overall shape of the car, so when the images came into Adobe After Effects I could use these channels to produce different coloured cars with different accessories on them, mix and match the accessories of the cars, and wheels and all sorts of things like that. It was only possible to endure sitting infront of my computer drawing

creative innovator
:Nigel Allen

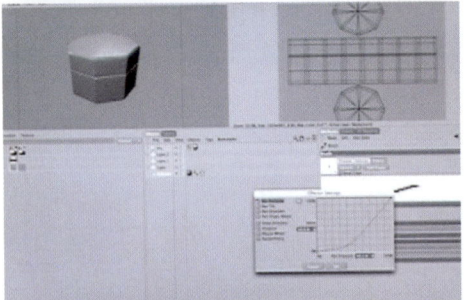

parts in Photoshop for three months because I was using a Wacom pen/tablet.

Ric   What was the key benefit for you by using a Wacom pen/tablet?

Nigel   I'd say that the main reason for using the pen/tablet was merely because I couldn't get the level of control with a mouse. I needed the pen/tablet to be able to intuitively push points around whilst I'm playing with Bezier Curves (paths) in Photoshop. And it was essentially to save my right hand, because sitting there clamped up on the mouse for three months, I certainly wouldn't have been able to survive it. Just by holding a pen in your hand it's certainly a lot more ergonomic and more comfortable.

Ric   So, Nigel it's obvious what the benefits are by using a Wacom pen/tablet in 2D applications like Adobe Photoshop and Adobe After Effects but tell us some of the benefits for using one in a 3D application like Cinema 4D?

Nigel   A rather large part of Cinema 4D is actually an application called BodyPaint, which gives you the ability to paint directly onto 3D models. Previously when you're working in 3D, you've either had to just create a generic texture entirely separate to your 3D object, and not really have any control about the detail, or you had to go into Photoshop, create textures, map them onto your objects and hope that they fit. If they didn't, you'd go back to Photoshop, edit your texture and remap and re do it until it worked. Now with the advent of applications like BodyPaint, you're actually able to just pick up a paintbrush, go to your object and just paint directly onto it in the 3D space as well as manipulate the 3D geometry.

Ric   That actually looks like a lot of fun, being able to manipulate the 3D object with the pen.

Nigel   There's various applications that allow you to paint pixels but actually painting physical geometry onto an object is quite an interesting and different way to work.

Ric   Would you like to just tell us about some of your more recent projects?

Nigel   Sure. The majority of what I've worked on in the last four years has been animated. I don't do an awful lot of still work any more. I've done some jobs for Gloria Jean's Coffee. They had a convention last year in Hawaii, and they came to me on relatively short notice because they needed an opening video for their coffee convention in Hawaii. I was able to use the new Geographic landscape module in Cinema 4D which I hadn't used previously to come up with something showing them where all their different Gloria Jean's Coffee branches were around the planet and also a shot of earth in the universe and various other things like that. I've done lots of different shots for TV commercials and some things for feature films and then I produce lot's of training videos for Cinema 4D showing how to do stuff like photorealistic rendering, etc.

Ric   Fantastic. So what new products of innovations would you like from Wacom?

Nigel   The number of times I find myself reaching for this tablet with my finger, because I'm used to using it with a laptop computer. So I'm sitting there working on my laptop computer and I've got my finger on the touch pad and then I'll go "oh, I need to use the pen" and I just move my finger over here and expect it to work. So if they could ever add touch capability as well that would be great.

Ric   So you would like touch and point capabilities from your Wacom pen/tablet. Very interesting and so all I can say is watch this space! Thanks Nigel for being part of the Art of Making Marks.

creative innovator
:Mattt Taylor

■ SEE EXTRA CONTENT ON www.artofwa.com

MATT TAYLOR
Sixty40 - Animation Director

Ric Welcome to the Art of Making Marks.

Matt Thank you very much.

Ric Could you just introduce yourself to us and tell us a little bit about what you do?

Matt Sure thing. I am Matt Taylor animation Director here at Sixty40, which is an animation and design company in Darlinghurst, Sydney. I run a company with Mark Simpson sitting over there, the Design Director.

Mark Hello there (Mark Simpson)

Matt We do broadcast design and animation television mostly, we do a lot of work for MTV and Nickelodeon, TV commercials, titles, combinations of broadcast design and 2D animation and 3D animation and putting them all together in wonderful new ways.

Ric Great, fantastic, so have you been using Wacom tablets in your work for very long?

Matt Six years now, I used to use a mouse for everything and then I started to get RSI and it was just slow and laborious. Once you get past that first little phase of adjusting to the parallax, I was away.

Ric So what kind of tablet are you using at the moment?

Matt I think it is the Intuos3. It comes with a fancy new pen; it's got different attachments which I haven't actually used yet.

Ric Tell us about your work.

Matt It involves bringing characters and design together. I do a lot of the story boarding and character design, which then get composited by Mark or built into 3D and so I draw a lot. I find that a lot of things that I start with as sketches often then grow into the final product, so I really enjoyed working on the screen and I work in Flash all the time, so things that start as a doodles can then be Flashed up into a finished illustration or character design and get animated or made into an illustration.

Art of Making Marks 135

creative innovator
:Matt Taylor

Ric So in your workflow, I can see here that you are doing your story boarding in Toon Boom.

Matt Yes, that's right, it's really great for that.

Ric So, what other applications would you be using in your workflow?

Matt I use Flash heaps, and Photoshop are probably the main programmes I use all the time.

Ric Do you like to design directly into Flash using the Wacom pen/tablet or do you build your imagery up first on paper?

Matt I start just drawing on paper, I think it's still the start of everything for me but then basically just do the roughing out on paper, because I could then get a light box and trace it, and trace it and trace it, but I prefer doing all that stuff on screen. Then just build it up and clean it up and add stuff, this is really good for making animatics and taking a drawing a bit further than you could otherwise.

One of our recent jobs which were the titles for music jungle which is a show on Channel 9 that screens every week, we did the titles for it and cartoon Edger Gander Panda Show. This is probably one of the best examples of taking a doodle and then making into a variety of other things, in that we made a central character it was M.J the Monkey and then this got made into as a cardboard cut out style version of the character and then a Muppet version of the character and then a 3D version of the character and then a 2D version of the character. I guess in a way this method of just building and building on the same original concept drawing really came through because I did the rough drawings, they weren't that rough but the drawings which got made into sort of fake cardboard cut outs here which were stuff I did in flash and then got put into Maya and mapped onto cardboard elements.

I designed a Muppet which we got sewn into a physical representation. All the drawings for the Muppet were based on the original drawing. Those plans for the Muppet puppet then became the basis for the model when it got made in 3D Studio Max and the model was also then used for animating it in Flash as a final to the animation as well. This has been one of the best things we've done this year and our Panda.

Panda is the Edger Gander Panda Show, a cartoon we've been working on for quite a long time and Panda's become a bit of a mascot for Sixty40 and the fact that we can now put Panda on Channel 9 every week is fantastic. I think the way we work with Flash and Wacom's would have been impossible to achieve these results otherwise.
We tried to make it look like an old vintage science cartoon that never got made, or never got screened. But basically the way we work now today made it impossible to turn around a weekly cartoon like this, in the old days, and the ability to draw in screen, send small files to someone in another city to animate and sent back to me, really brings together the whole promise and wonder of technology helping the animation go forwards into the next century.

creative innovator
:Mattt Taylor

Ric It's an amazing time isn't it?

Matt Yeah, we're up to episode 15 of Panda now and we are going to be making a longer series the Edger Gander Panda Show which chronicles what happens to Panda after each episode going out engaging in the world, the life of the cartoon character, his feelings, and his emotions. Back to the bar afterwards with Mouse, it's really quite special and exciting.

Ric Fantastic.

Matt Other things we are doing are turning around a weekly cartoon for Creature Features which is the highest ranking kids' show in Australia, currently. I'd like to think the world! This has been great because we love using puppets basically, but we're using photo collage and Photoshop-ed images, textures and Adobe After Effects and Flash. The bodies are all animated in Flash and the heads put into Photoshop. It's been very exciting and right now turning around work on a weekly basis is great because it also gives us the opportunity to really grow as a studio and develop.

Ric If you had the opportunity to tell Wacom about what you'd like in future innovations, new tools does anything spring to mind?

Matt Maybe more paper texture surfaces on Wacom pen/tablets. That's all I need.

Ric OK that's great I'll get onto that one for you. Thank you Matt for participating in the Art of Making Marks, we love seeing your work and so until next time…cheers mate.

Matt Thanks for having me it's been a pleasure to offer my humble opinions.

Art of Making Marks

creative innovator
:Cindy Bower

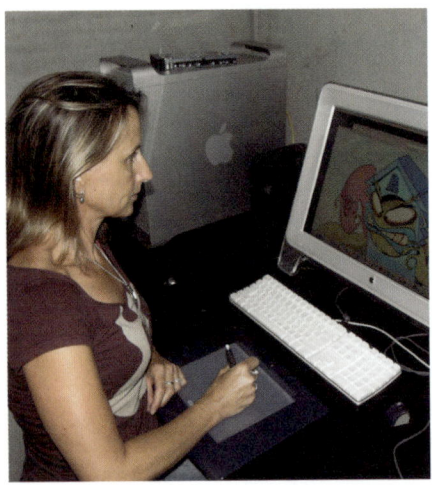

"A lot of things that are animated in Flash look like they're animated in Flash because they look very shape driven and built. But this was lovely, free-flowing and experimental, I was glued to the Wacom."

SEE EXTRA CONTENT ON www.artofwa.com

CINDY BOWER
Traditional cell animator using Flash and Toon Boom

Ric Hi Cindy, welcome to the Art of Making Marks. Please introduce yourself and tell us about who you are and what you do.

Cindy My name's Cindy Bower and I've been working in animation all my working life really, which is now probably 22 years. Animation has gone through a lot of changes since then. I work for a production studio at the moment and I also teach animation at a computer graphics college.

Ric How long have you been using Wacom tablets in your workflow?

Cindy I would think it would be now probably is about six years. As I said 2D frame by frame or 'cell' animation has changed a lot in the last ten years. I used to do a lot of pencil on paper and we still do, but a lot of the stages of animation are cut out now so it's really handy to just work straight into the computer.

Ric So when you first started using pen/tablets was it a period where you would work semi-traditionally?

Cindy Yep. Scanning in and then cleaning up lots of frames. Not so long ago we were still scanning in drawings that were already cleaned up on paper as well but it wasn't as good as some of the drawing programs today.

Ric So now it's a completely digital process, drawing directly in the software.

Cindy Just about, yeah.

Ric And what applications are you using go directly in.

Cindy The main one that I use at the moment is Flash but we've also started to use Toon Boom for log format animation. Flash is a fantastic drawing program I find and not just for animation but just for actually drawing. It's got drawing tools like the pen tool which you can get exact drawings as well as it's got a wonderful freehand brush tool with brushes.

Ric And they're all pressure sensitive?

Cindy Yes. I really enjoy using it as a drawing program. And so therefore, with things like cleaning up characters for animation, it's a good program to use with a Wacom pen/tablet.

Ric Please tell us more about your work?

Cindy I gave my Wacom a great workout at the end of last year, I was employed to do a pilot in Flash for Nickelodeon which was a three minute pilot. There's a lot of different ways to draw in Flash, but the style that I had to do was very loose. So that's where I got very familiar with Flash as a drawing program and so the Nickelodeon pilot that we did ended up having a lovely half traditional animation look. A lot of things that are animated in Flash look like they're animated in Flash because they look very shape driven and built. But this was a lovely, free-flowing and experimental; I was glued to the Wacom. At first we didn't know if we could do it quite like that, but I found it a really good approach which linked to the way I would do it traditionally. One of the other ways that I use the Wacom is with the Painter program and you feel like you're really holding the utensil, like the brush or the pencil or pen or whatever it is, the tool that you're using in the program, and I've been experimenting a lot and doing a lot of illustrations.

Ric Fantastic.

Cindy Which is completely different from my animation.

Ric If you could ask for anything from Wacom, some new feature or some area that you felt specifically that you'd like, have you got any thoughts on that

Cindy Well I haven't had an opportunity to use the one where you're drawing straight on the screen so I think that would be interesting. I'm used to how it is where you look up at the screen and not look down at your hands on the tablet. I'm so used to that I can't imagine what else I might need.

Ric Well it looks like you're all very busy here today, so I don't want to get in the way of a deadline. Your work is wonderful and it's been such a pleasure to have you on the Art of Making Marks.

Cindy Thank you.

Art of Making Marks

Wacom
SHOWCASE

this page + next 2 pages:

Man Qin
//Guangzhou /China
c_bird77@126.com

* view more information and content from this artist on www.artofwa.com

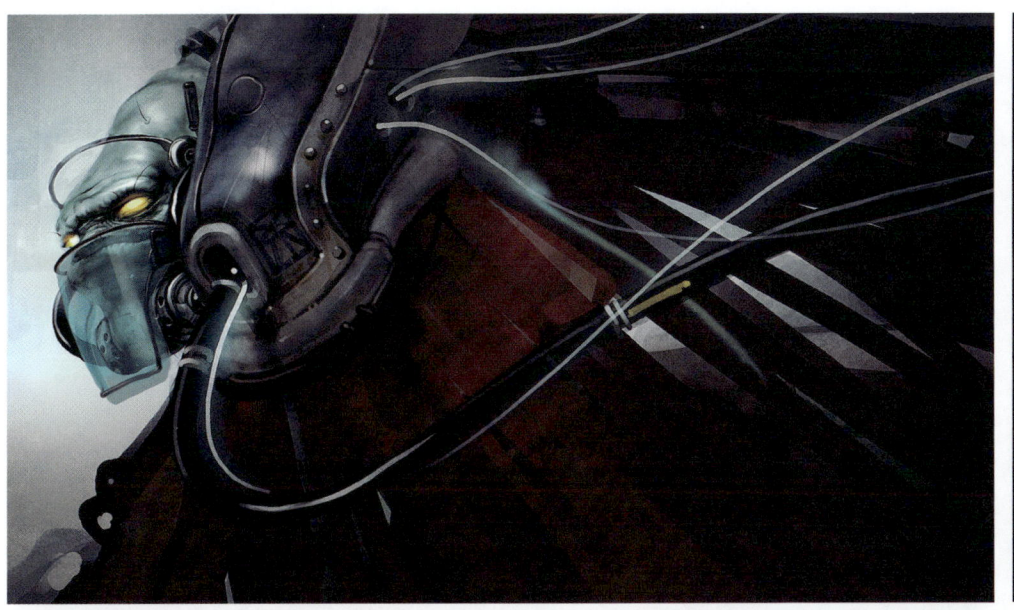

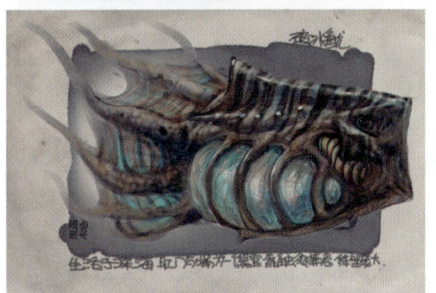

this page:

Antonis Kotzias
//Athens /Greece
http://www.vattica.com

* view more information and content from this artist on www.artofwa.com

this page:
Davide Bianca / Saizen Media Studios
//Milan /Italy
http://www.saizenmedia.com/

* view more information and content from this artist on www.artofwa.com

this page + next page:

David Davidson
//UK
http://www.max3d.org

* view more information and content from this artist on www.artofwa.com

this page + next 2 pages:

Fernanda Cohen
//Brooklyn /USA
www.fernandacohen.com

* view more information and content from this artist on www.artofwa.com

this page + opposite:

Jeff Wong
//New York /USA
www.jeffwong.com

*view more information and content from this artist on www.artofwa.com

this page + next 2 pages:

Lawrence Callender //Ottawa /Canada
http://www.robotfollow.com/artists/
lawrence-callender/

★ view more information and content from this artist on www.artofwa.com

this page + next page:

Evan Shipard
//Sydney /Australia
www.ecsdesignvfx.com

* view more information and content from this artist on www.artofwa.com

this page + next 2 pages:

Hui Tian
//Beijing /China
http://www.huitianart.com

* view more information and content from this artist on www.artofwa.com

this page + next 3 pages:

Lok Jansen
//Tokyo /Japan
http://www.lokjansen.com

* view more information and content from this artist on www.artofwa.com

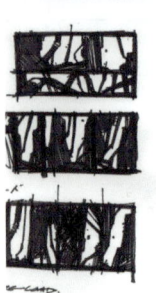
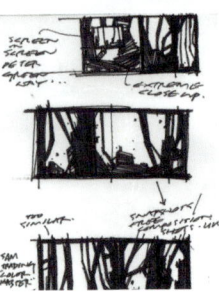

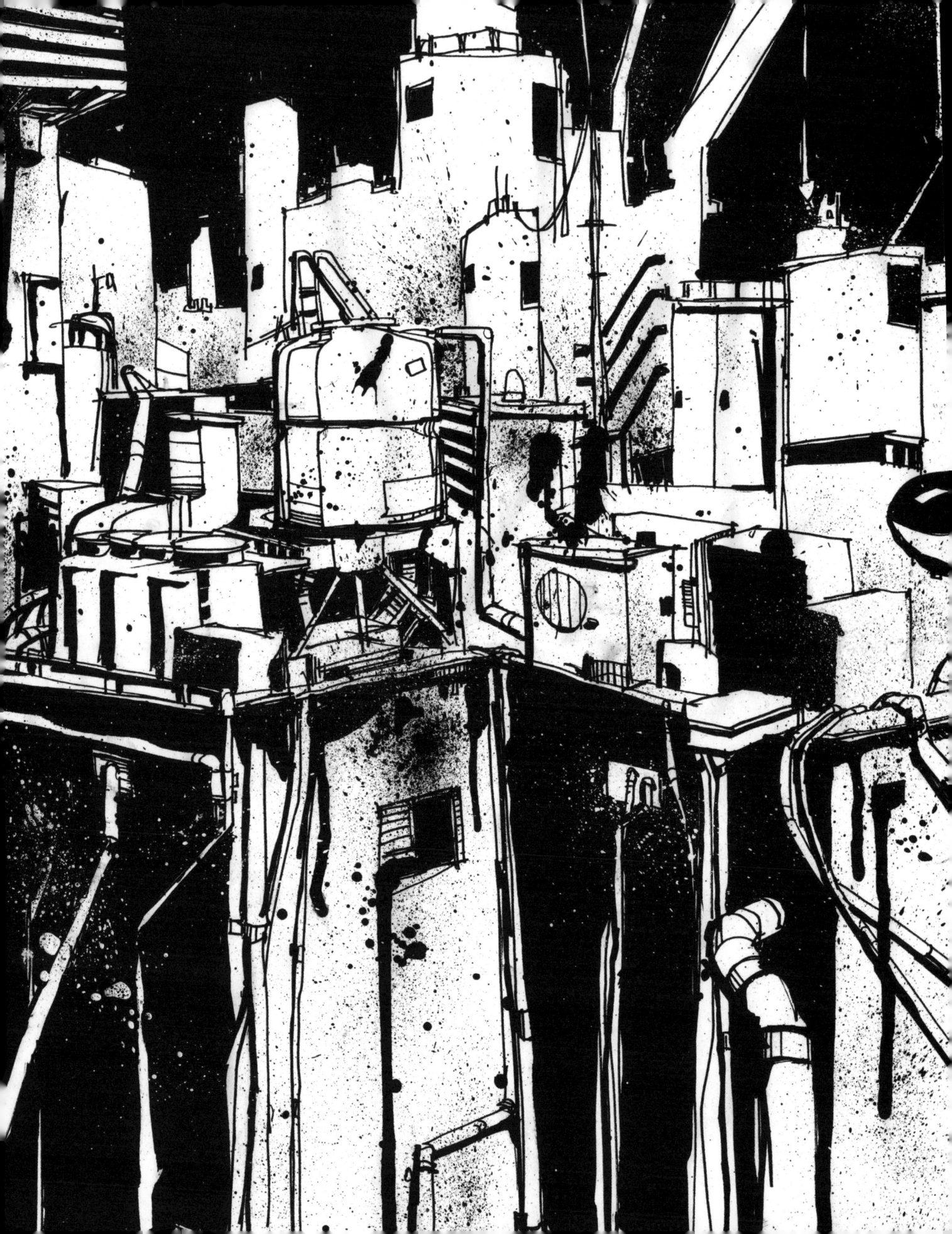

this page + opposite:

Raziman Baharudin
//Singapore
razb07@hotmail.com

*view more information and content from this artist on www.artofwa.com

this page:

Martin Nebelong Henningsen
http://www.martinity.com

★ view more information and content from this artist on www.artofwa.com

this page:

Robin Preston
//London / UK
http://www.nw-5.com

* view more information and content from this artist on www.artofwa.com

this page:

Noor Muhammad
//Malaysia
http://www.vectorbros.com

*view more information and content from this artist on www.artofwa.com

this page + next page:

Saul Zanolari
//Switzerland
http://www.saulzanolari.com/

* view more information and content from this artist on www.artofwa.com

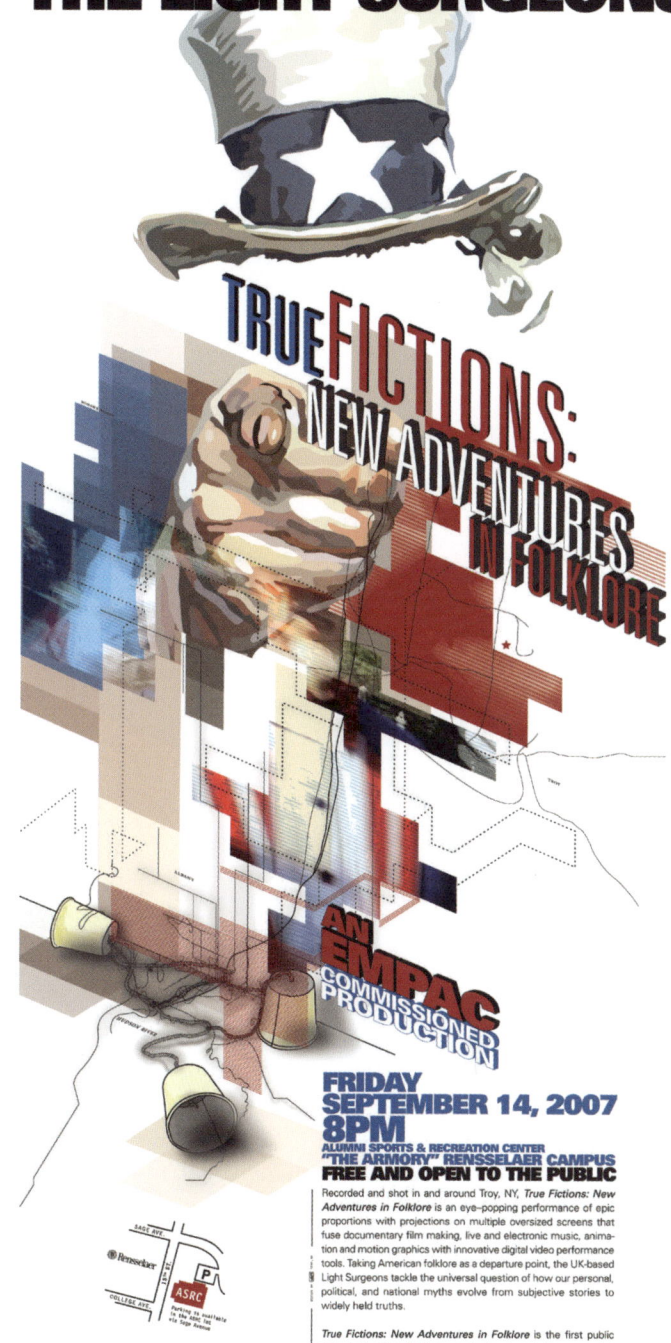

this page:

Bryan Kahrs
//New York /USA
http://www.id29.com/

* view more information and content from this artist on www.artofwa.com

this page:
**Yongkiat Karnchanapayap &
Onuma Chintanasathit** //Bangkok
http://www.pictoverse.com

* view more information and content from this artist on www.artofwa.com

// INDEX

Ric Holland
www.artofwa.com

Masahiko Yamada
www.wacom.com/info.html

Keshen Teo
www.pa-jama.com

Jeremy Sutton
www.jeremysutton.com

John Derry
www.pixlart.com

Russell Brown
www.russellbrown.com

Douglas Olson
www.microsoft.com/expression

Bill Buxton
www.billbuxton.com

Duncan Brinsmead
http://area.autodesk.com/index.php/blogs_duncan/tag_list/welcome/

Ron Cobb
www.roncobbdesigns.com

Nick Pill / Rising Sun Pictures
www.rsp.com.au

Marco Nero
www.pbase.com/nero_design

Jake Hempson
www.jake-hempson.com

Steve Stamatiadis
www.kromestudios.com

Ken Lambert / Ink Project
www.inkproject.com

Gerry Haggerty
www.linkedin.com/pub/1/3b4/230

Allan Macdonald
www.designertechniques.com/designers/allanmacdonald1.htm

Tin&Ed
www.tinanded.com.au

Julieanne Kost
www.jkost.com

Dr. Phillip George
http://phillipgeorge.net/new/

Richard Luxton
r2n2@iprimus.com.au

Ted Blore
www.linkedin.com/pub/1/457/7a4

Bryn Farrely
www.imdb.com/name/nm1619345

Craig Calhoun
www.musicdomain.com.au

Steven Rosewell
www.studiokite.com

Julian Tylney Taylor
www.bold-vfx.com

Nigel Allen
http://nigela.cgsociety.org/gallery/

Matt Taylor
www.sixty40.com

Cindy Bower
www.designstrokes.com.au

Man Qin
c_bird77@126.com

Antonis Kotzias
www.vattica.com

Davide Bianca / Saizen Media Studios
www.saizenmedia.com

David Davidson
www.max3d.org

Fernanda Cohen
www.fernandacohen.com

Jeff Wong
www.jeffwong.com

Lawrence Callender
www.robotfollow.com/artists/lawrence-callender

Evan Shipard
www.ecsdesignvfx.com

Hui Tian
www.huitianart.com

Lok Jansen
www.lokjansen.com

Raziman Baharudin
razb07@hotmail.com

Martin Nebelong Henningsen
www.martinity.com

Robin Preston
www.nw-5.com

Noor Muhammad
www.vectorbros.com

Saul Zanolari
www.saulzanolari.com

Bryan Kahrs
www.id29.com

Simon So
www.vectorbros.com

Yongkiat Karnchanapayap & Onuma Chintanasathit
www.pictoverse.com